BROADCASTING
THE OZARKS

Ozarks Studies
EDITED BY BROOKS BLEVINS

Other Titles in this Series

Men of No Reputation: Robert Boatright, the Buckfoot Gang, and the Fleecing of Middle America

Newspaperwoman of the Ozarks: The Life and Times of Lucile Morris Upton

Twenty Acres: A Seventies Childhood in the Woods

Hipbillies: Deep Revolution in the Arkansas Ozarks

The Literature of the Ozarks: An Anthology

Down on Mahans Creek: A History of an Ozarks Neighborhood

BROADCASTING THE OZARKS

SI SIMAN AND COUNTRY MUSIC AT THE CROSSROADS

KITTY LEDBETTER AND SCOTT FOSTER SIMAN

THE UNIVERSITY OF ARKANSAS PRESS
FAYETTEVILLE ✶ 2024

Copyright © 2024 by The University of Arkansas Press. All rights reserved. No part of this book should be used or reproduced in any manner without prior permission in writing from The University of Arkansas Press or as expressly permitted by law.

978-1-68226-250-4 (cloth)
978-1-68226-251-1 (paperback)
978-1-61075-819-2 (e-book)

28 27 26 25 24   5 4 3 2 1

Manufactured in the United States of America

Designed by William Clift

Cover photo credits, clockwise from center: Si Siman (circa 1963), courtesy of Siman Family Papers; Wanda Jackson, courtesy of John Richardson; Porter Wagoner, courtesy of Siman Family Papers; Brenda Lee, courtesy of Missouri State University Digital Collection; and Chet Atkins, courtesy of Siman Family Papers.

LIBRARY OF CONGRESS CATALOGING-IN-PUBLICATION DATA

Names: Ledbetter, Kitty, 1952- author. | Siman, Scott Foster, 1954- author.
Title: Broadcasting the Ozarks : Si Siman and country music at the crossroads / Kitty Ledbetter and Scott Foster Siman.
Description: Fayetteville : The University of Arkansas Press, 2024. | Series: Ozarks studies Includes bibliographical references and index. | Summary: "Broadcasting the Ozarks explores the vibrant country music scene that emerged in Springfield, Missouri, in the 1930s and thrived for half a century. Central to this history is the 'Ozark Jubilee' (1955-60), the first regularly broadcast live country music show on network television. Dubbed the 'king of the televised barn dances,' the show introduced the Ozarks region to viewers across America and put Springfield in the running with Nashville for dominance of the country music industry—with the Jubilee's producer, Si Siman, at the helm."— Provided by publisher.
Identifiers: LCCN 2023036709 (print) | LCCN 2023036710 (ebook)
    ISBN 9781682262504 (cloth) | ISBN 9781682262511 (paperback)
    ISBN 9781610758192 (ebook)
Subjects: LCSH: Country music—Missouri—Springfield—History and criticism. | Siman, Si, 1921-1994. | Ozark Jubilee (Television program) | KWTO (Radio station : Springfield, Mo.)
Classification: LCC ML3524 .L36 2024 (print) | LCC ML3524 (ebook)
    DDC 781.64209778/78—dc23/eng/20220824
LC record available at https://lccn.loc.gov/2023036709
LC ebook record available at https://lccn.loc.gov/2023036710

CONTENTS

ACKNOWLEDGMENTS   vii

INTRODUCTION   3

CHAPTER ONE
FAR FROM NORMAL: YOUNG SI   5

CHAPTER TWO
KWTO AND THE GOLDEN AGE OF HILLBILLY RADIO   33

CHAPTER THREE
THE *OZARK JUBILEE*:
THE CROSSROADS OF COUNTRY MUSIC   63

CHAPTER FOUR
THE *OZARK JUBILEE*:
PRODUCING A NETWORK TELEVISION SHOW   105

CHAPTER FIVE
AWARD-WINNING MUSIC PUBLISHER   129

CONCLUSION   161

APPENDIX: SI SIMAN PUBLISHING DISCOGRAPHY   167

NOTES   171

BIBLIOGRAPHY   209

INDEX   221

ACKNOWLEDGMENTS

IN 1980, SI SIMAN SENT me a note of thanks for interviewing songwriter Wayne Carson on my radio show at KTTS in Springfield, Missouri. I didn't know then that this note would become a keepsake of mine. I certainly didn't think that, after retiring from careers in country radio and academia, I would spend two years writing about Si Siman, but I can honestly say it's been the most rewarding experience I have had in either career.

At the top of my gratitude list is my erudite editor, Brooks Blevins at the University of Arkansas Press. He carries the history of the Ozarks to cities and towns throughout Missouri and Arkansas by writing foundational scholarly books while serving as the Noel Boyd Professor of Ozarks Studies in the Department of History at Missouri State University. I am deeply indebted to Dr. Blevins for his astute guidance and tenacious pursuit of a better manuscript. I would like to thank the anonymous reviewers whose copious suggestions for revisions were honest, thorough, and spot-on. I never doubted their wisdom or devotion to scholarly purpose. Thanks to Janet Foxman, Managing Editor at the University of Arkansas Press, and to my razor-sharp copy editor, Emily Bowles, for further shaping a wandering narrative. I am also grateful to Tom Peters, Dean of Library Services at Missouri State University. He unselfishly shared his extensive research on the *Ozark Jubilee*, and we spent many mornings at the Dancing Mule coffee shop talking about everybody who ever performed on that show. I am deeply indebted to Wayne Glenn, the king of priceless local artifacts and Ozarkiana. His book *The Ozarks' Greatest Hits: A Photo History of Music in the Ozarks* is a treasure trove. Wayne does research for the fun of knowing, and then he freely shares it with anyone who is interested.

I especially want to thank Jayne Siman Chowning for generously sharing her family memories and archives with me and for being my part-time research assistant. She is a consummate listener, supportive critic, diligent helper, and now my good friend. She allowed me to pursue her father's history with the unflinchingly balanced perspective required for scholarly study. Her husband, Randle Chowning, was a fun source of Springfield music history. He guided me through his early days of rock and roll and shared his firsthand experiences as a founder of the Ozark Mountain Daredevils.

ACKNOWLEDGMENTS

A large support group of friends kept me sane and persistent throughout this project. I am grateful to the following people for their support: Bo Brown, Virginia "Curly" Clark, Michael Cochran, Kathy Green, Susan Croce Kelly, Katie McCroskey, Melinda Mullins, Peggy Mullins, Mike O'Brien, Dan O'Day, John Richardson, Elliott Rogers, Celeste Skidmore, Janice Ryals-Rogers, and Greg Turpen.

I am also grateful to those who responded to my queries about music history: Curt Hargis, Pat Jackson, Bill Jones, Larry Lee, Bill Malone, Bobbie Malone, Dan O'Day, Mike Odell, Mark Ringenberg, Nick Sibley, Don Stiernberg, Leroy Van Dyke, and Craig White. I wish to thank my former colleagues on the board of Music Monday of the Ozarks for teaching me more about the Springfield music scene: Chris Albert, Stormy Cox, Curt Hargis, Robin Luke, Bob McCroskey, Mike Maples, John Sellars, Mike Smith, and Miles Sweeney.

Archivists at many institutions contributed to this research. I wish to thank Kathleen Campbell, Senior Archivist, Reference and Print Collection, Country Music Hall of Fame and Museum; Haley Frizzle-Green, State Historical Society of Missouri; Brian Grubbs, Local History and Genealogy Manager, Springfield-Greene County Library District; Annette Sain and Tom Debo, Ralph Foster Museum, College of the Ozarks; John Sellars, former Executive Director, History Museum on the Square; and Alan Stoker, Curator of Recorded Sound Collections, Country Music Hall of Fame and Museum.

My coauthor, Scott Foster Siman, deserves a hearty thanks for his participation in this project. His knowledge of baseball and the music business was thoroughly interesting and essential to the success of our narrative. He and his wife Teresa graciously opened their Nashville home for me to explore the invaluable Siman family archives.

Much gratitude goes to the only intellectual at my house, my banjo-playing husband and author Alan Munde. He was a steady companion who fed Ruthie the dog, watched all the *Ozark Jubilee* television shows, shared his substantial knowledge about country music, and sparked my creativity. He patiently listened as I read aloud every word of every draft of this manuscript at least once, sometimes twice, even thrice.

KITTY LEDBETTER

ACKNOWLEDGMENTS

THIS BOOK WOULD NOT HAVE been possible without the fearlessness of my father Si Siman and his belief that he could make a significant contribution to country music from the hills of the Ozarks. He had the perfect partner in my mother Rosie, as she provided support in so many ways personally and professionally. She also preserved and organized many of the family records relating to Si's work in radio, television, and music publishing, which were vital in bringing this book to life.

No less important to the project was Ralph Foster, my father's mentor who I am named after. None of Si Siman's story would have happened without Mr. Foster's willingness to give Si an opportunity to bring his vision of making Springfield, Missouri, a force in country music to life.

I am especially grateful to lead author Kitty Ledbetter, who provided such wonderful assistance creatively and technically. She was undoubtedly my professor in the process of researching, writing, and rewriting. Thank you!

Special thanks go to my sister Jaynie Chowning, who was a driving force in bringing this story to life. She never gave up on the idea of making the story of the *Ozark Jubilee*, the role of Springfield, Missouri, and our father's part in making country music known to the world, and she contributed to the research on the book as well. Other family members who helped and inspired me in the pursuit of this story include my sister Susan Winn and my wife Teresa. I also want to acknowledge my grandparents, Lillian and Ely Siman Sr., who helped maintain family records around Si's baseball endeavors, especially preserving the priceless letters that Charley Barrett sent to Si.

Others who deserve a big thanks are my brother-in-law Randle Chowning; his fellow Ozark Mountain Daredevil, Larry Lee; Wayne Carson's wife of many years, Wyndi Carson; and Si's childhood friend Jack Hamlin. All of them graciously made time for interviews.

Finally, thank you to the University of Arkansas Press and Brooks Blevins for their belief in the value of this book.

SCOTT FOSTER SIMAN

BROADCASTING THE OZARKS

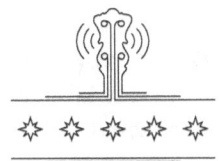

INTRODUCTION

A BIOGRAPHICAL REVIEW OF THE MEMBERS of the Country Music Hall of Fame confirms the influence of two musical institutions that enabled many of them to rise to prominence during the 1940s, '50s, and '60s: the *Grand Ole Opry* in Nashville and the *Ozark Jubilee* in Springfield, Missouri.[1] Despite this, the eight-part documentary series *Country Music*, directed by Ken Burns in 2019, ignores the *Ozark Jubilee*. The absence of the *Jubilee* in this series, marketed as a comprehensive history of country music, was a glaring omission.

By the early 1950s, Springfield was a worthy competitor with Nashville as the home of country music, and "several other cities, including Chicago and Cincinnati, were equally well placed at the end of World War II to become Music City USA."[2] Atlanta, Dallas, Lubbock, and Shreveport might also be added to the list of cities building a reputation for country music. But Springfield, Missouri, had the first continuously running live country music show on network television, ABC's *Ozark Jubilee* (1955–1960), and one of the first in color, the *Five Star Jubilee* (1961). These shows made all the difference.

Performers, promoters, advertisers, talent managers, booking agents, and tourists from every part of the country followed the music trail to the Ozarks for the *Jubilee*. Springfield was close to the center of the United States, and at the crossroads of major roads in the National Highway System. Route 66, running right through the middle of Springfield on St. Louis Street, a half block from the *Ozark Jubilee*, was most the famous of these. A motorist could head northeast for about five hundred miles and be in Chicago, or travel west and be looking at the Pacific Ocean from a California beach in just two or three days.[3]

In 1956, only a year after the *Ozark Jubilee*'s first broadcast, the *St. Louis Post Dispatch* designated Springfield as "the recognized center of the country music world": "It's generally agreed in television, recording, and radio circles, that Springfield, now a city of 90,000, has shaken Nashville, Tenn., home of the *Grand Ole Opry*, and longtime mecca of hillbilly musicians, to its very foundations."[4] Dubbed the "king of the televised barn dances," the *Jubilee* introduced country music and the Ozarks region to viewers in the farthest corners of the United States during a time of rapid transition in the music industry. The show became the vehicle that would put Springfield in the running for dominance of the country music industry, with its producer Si Siman at the helm.[5]

Siman's life story is almost as remarkable as the country music television show he produced. Though he once had his sights set on a baseball career—and even traveled the country as the teenage driver and secretary for a legendary St. Louis Cardinals scout—Siman's true talent lay in the field of entertainment entrepreneurship. He was booking Tommy Dorsey, Ella Fitzgerald, and Glenn Miller during the mid-1930s while still a high school student in Springfield.

After serving in the navy in World War II, Siman came back home to Springfield and played an essential role in the city's rise to prominence as a center of country music performance and recording, including in the creation of a nationally broadcast barn-dance radio show at KWTO. In the late 1940s, television's formative years, he partnered with Springfield's greatest media talents to create and produce the *Ozark Jubilee*, broadcast nationally on ABC television from 1955 to 1960, and NBC's *Five Star Jubilee*, which aired in 1961. He helped to shape and expand the country music industry as a charter member of nascent landmark organizations such as the Country Music Association and turned Springfield into a launching pad for the careers of many future Country Music Hall of Fame artists including Porter Wagoner, the Browns, and Brenda Lee.

After the *Jubilee*, Siman became an award-winning music publisher responsible for some of the greatest hits in twentieth-century music. He influenced other talented Ozarkers to make their mark in the music business. Because of his efforts, Siman became an icon in Springfield music history, and he did it all from his hometown. Yet until now, his full story has remained unexplored. Told largely through the life story of producer, promoter, and publisher Si Siman, *Broadcasting the Ozarks* takes us back to a time when Springfield, Missouri, sat at the crossroads of country music.

CHAPTER ONE

FAR FROM NORMAL: YOUNG SI

A BOY'S LOVE OF BASEBALL AND entertainment is not unusual, unless he tries to make a career out of them at the age of ten, as Ely Earl "Si" Siman Jr. did. Siman's parents could not anticipate the creative energy that would take their son from batboy to Grammy winner, but they did their best to teach him respect and decency. He took care of the rest.

Siman was born on January 17, 1921, in the living room of a modest, two-bedroom house on East Normal Street in Springfield, Missouri. Later in life, Si jokingly claimed to be the "only abnormal thing that came out of Normal Street."[1] People rarely called him Ely when he was young, and never Earl. He was "Junior," "June," "Junebug," "Muggies," and sometimes the more formal "E. E. Siman Jr." It was later, when he went into the navy in 1942, that he started going by "Si."

Siman's family history is complicated—full of conflicting stories and dates that might derail even a persistent genealogist. His grandfather, James Siman, came to the United States from Ireland with his parents during the potato famine of the 1840s.[2] The Simans settled in Louisville, Kentucky. As a young man, James set up a business as a carriage maker. He served in the Union army during the Civil War. When he returned from the war, he began shoeing horses and "had fitted shoes on many of Kentucky's greatest racing thoroughbreds."[3] James married a woman from Alabama named Sarah, and they moved to Springfield, Missouri, in 1876. He opened a blacksmith shop on a farm located at 1515 St. Louis Street.

Although he was married to Sarah, James apparently had another "wife" who was twenty-five years his junior. Records indicate that James, Sarah, and their two surviving children shared their house with Clementine Allen and her five children.[4] There is no record of James's divorce from Sarah, but we know that Clementine and her children took the Siman name in 1910 and that Sarah Siman went elsewhere.[5] By age sixty-five, James Siman had nineteen children—Si Siman's father, Ely Earl Siman Sr. (1897–1969), was among them.[6]

By the 1920s, James Siman was in his eighties and "reputed to be the oldest blacksmith in Missouri who was still able to work."[7] Family members generally agree that James was a bad seed. A great-granddaughter, Jayne Siman Chowning, said she never heard anything good about James, who evidently once beat his son Charles so badly that the boy had to miss two days of school because of his bruises.[8] James Siman died in October 1928, apparently due to being kicked by a horse.[9] Clementine outlived her husband and was a much-revered grandmother in her very large family before she passed at the age of eighty-one.

Ely escaped the chaos of his large family household by enlisting in the army during World War I at age twenty-one. He was assigned to a new military training post called Camp Pike in Little Rock, Arkansas, and later served as a supply sergeant at Camp Bowie in Fort Worth, Texas.[10] After the war, Ely married Lillian Saxton, a divorced woman with two daughters from a previous marriage to an abusive husband. In spite of having had an abusive father, Ely was a good husband and a kind, if stern, father to his two stepdaughters, five-year-old Maxine and three-year-old Virginia. When Lillian's ex-husband returned to harass her, Ely threatened to kill him if he ever came back. He later adopted Maxine and Virginia, who took his last name. When the girls displayed signs of depression at a young age, a doctor advised Lillian not to have more children because of the risk of genetic mental illness. Ely wanted to have a child, but Lillian hesitated at first because of this history. Ultimately, they had a baby boy they named Ely Earl Siman Jr. Fortunately, "Junior" Siman never suffered from mental illness or clinical depression.[11]

Ely Siman Sr. was able to afford an adequately comfortable living for the family of five through his work as an auto mechanic at Thompson Pontiac in Springfield.[12] Lillian was a busy housewife whose name often appeared in the Springfield newspaper as a member of pinochle and bridge clubs or as a party organizer for Junior's two half-sisters. The Simans were members of St. Paul Methodist Church, where Ely Sr. served as a greeter at the same door every Sunday.[13] He was also active in the American Legion, the Abou Ben Adhem Shriners, and the Blue Lodge of the Masons.

In the early 1930s, during the Great Depression's worst years, Lillian's parents had to move into the Simans' little house on Normal Street. Due to space constraints, Junior moved into a tent in the backyard, where he slept year-round. "That may sound terrible," he later recalled, "but I never did have a cold. I always felt great."[14] In fact, Junior found that his tent made him quite popular with the neighborhood kids, who were eager to camp out in his backyard. He had an open and friendly nature, a quick creative drive, and boundless energy. He liked to fish, hunt, and swim like the other boys, but he had two great loves beyond his family: baseball and entertainment.

BATBOY AND CARDINALS SCOUT DRIVER

When playing baseball, Junior Siman was a small and scrappy underdog against bigger, stronger, and older kids, but his love of the sport fueled his competitive nature. He was a good team member, both in ball games at school and in pick-up games with his friends in sandlot fields all over town. His father shared his love of baseball and actively participated as a coach. In the early 1930s, Fox Theatres sponsored Little League teams for boys under the age of sixteen in an effort to advertise their business while also helping the community. Springfield's Gillioz Theatre and Electric Theatre worked within the larger Theatre League to set up local baseball teams in Springfield, Carthage, Sedalia, and Pittsburg, Kansas.[15]

In March 1933, Ely Siman Sr. helped organize the Br'er Fox baseball club in Springfield to represent the Gillioz Theatre. Junior- and senior-division players signed contracts with regulations such as: "The player must keep himself in first class physical condition and must at all time[s] conform his conduct to standards of good citizenship and good sportsmanship."[16] George Thompson, the owner of Thompson Pontiac and Ely Sr.'s boss, agreed to sponsor the Br'er Fox club, and his son, George Jr., joined the team. Gillioz Theatre manager Gene McMahon was the team's first coach. He was assisted by team captain Junior Siman, who began developing his sales and promotion skills; he found merchants to help pay for the Br'er Fox uniforms by promising them a prominent company imprint on them. As a result of Junior Siman's salesmanship, the Br'er Fox team was the only boys' club team with uniforms. They also had a bus, likely donated by Thompson and Ely Sr.'s colleagues in the automobile business.[17] When McMahon quit coaching the team after thirteen games to spend more time at the Gillioz, Ely Sr. stepped in to manage the club. The formidable pitching duo of Junior Siman and his buddy George Thompson Jr. helped the Br'er Fox team win the

ABOVE

The Br'er Fox baseball team, with Junior Siman (fourth from right, back row) wearing his St. Louis Cardinals uniform. *Courtesy of Siman Family Papers, private collection of Scott Foster Siman and Jayne Siman Chowning.*

LEFT

Junior Siman at bat. *Courtesy of Siman Family Papers, private collection of Scott Foster Siman and Jayne Siman Chowning.*

Theatre League championship in 1933—their first year—with a 29-9 record. Their club won the Theatre League title again the following year.

When Junior and George weren't playing baseball, they were watching baseball at Springfield's White City Park. The city's minor-league teams had done poorly in the 1920s, only winning a title in 1926.[18] In 1931, St. Louis Cardinals general manager Branch Rickey made a deal with Springfield executive Al Eckert to replace the town's money-losing Western Association League Midgets with a Springfield Cardinals team. To increase attendance and make the team profitable, Rickey invested in improvements to White City Park: installing bright lights, constructing a new outfield fence, and replacing the rocky infield grass. Cardinals scout Charley Barrett then brought competitive players to the team.

Charley Barrett was an accomplished professional baseball scout who had started out working for the St. Louis Browns in 1909. He was famous for his strong work ethic; he reportedly traveled more than a million miles in his search for baseball players over the course of his career. Among scouts who "beat the bushes" for talented new players, Barrett was called the "King of Weeds."[19] He joined Rickey and the Springfield Cardinals in 1919 and became "Rickey's right arm," helping develop the Cardinals' pioneering farm system and discovering many successful major-league players such as Baseball Hall of Fame member Jim "Sunny" Bottomley.[20] Barrett is known for signing sixty-six major-league players, a number second only to that of his colleague Pop Kelchner.[21] While Rickey was renovating White City Park, Barrett made recommendations for improving the playing field and increasing attendance to make the team profitable. He made frequent trips to Springfield to run the annual spring tryout camps and observe players during the regular season.

Within three years as a St. Louis Cardinals minor-league team, the Springfield Cardinals won three consecutive Western Association championships. Six Springfield Cardinals players went to the major leagues after the successful 1933 season, and the 1934 Springfield team featured five future major-league players, including "Fiddler" Bill McGhee, Lyle Judy, Oscar Judd, Emmett Mueller, and player-manager Mike Ryba.[22] For the first time, fans began turning out by the thousands for weeknight games. Advertised promotions provided discount tickets for people who otherwise couldn't afford to attend games.

Branch Rickey brought a "Knothole Gang" to the Springfield Cardinals. He got the idea, intended to help poor kids attend baseball games during the Great Depression, from St. Louis Cardinals' owner Sam Breadon. Instead of restricting kids to watching games through knotholes in a wooden fence behind the bleachers, Rickey built bleachers specifically for them along the third base line and gave them free admission to the games. These bleachers added "hundreds of screaming elementary, junior high, and high school aged students" to the crowd, including Junior Siman and his friends.[23] "On good nights, at least seven hundred children piled onto the 'gang's' bleacher section. By late in the decade the 'gang' had grown to over twelve hundred members."[24] An "Agreement of Membership" made the Knothole Gang promise to attend games with parental approval, demonstrate good moral behavior, and not skip school.[25] Membership would be forfeited upon breaking the agreement. Eleven-year-old Junior Siman was busy playing on the Br'er Fox and Pontiac teams when he landed a position as batboy for the minor-league Springfield Cardinals.[26] His job included handling bats during the game and gathering dirty uniforms afterwards. The work was challenging, according to Siman: "There's a lot more to being a batboy than you think. It's not just grabbing a bat and handing it to them. You've gotta be there at four in the afternoon and start getting ready and getting the bats out and get the balls all cleaned up. You gotta help clean the shoes of the players, you've gotta see that the uniforms are out."[27] Batboys received an official Springfield Cardinals team uniform, and Junior proudly wore his at Br'er Fox games to show off his connection with the Cardinals.

One of the privileges of being the mascot for the minor-league team included the occasional opportunity to serve as a batboy for the major league St. Louis Cardinals.[28] Junior Siman earned extra money with part-time jobs to help finance trips with his dad to Sportsman's Park in St. Louis to serve as batboy. Between 1930 and 1934, the Cardinals won three National League pennants and two World Series. The spectacular play of the team's legendary "Gashouse Gang" was what Branch Rickey and Charley Barrett had been building toward for years. The team featured an array of characters, and Junior got to know many of them, including Jay Hanna "Dizzy" Dean, famous for pitching thirty winning games in the same season; his brother, Paul "Daffy" Dean; Frankie Frisch; Johnny "Pepper" Martin; and Joe "Ducky" Medwick. For his contributions to the team, Junior Siman earned a 1934 World Series ring.

In 1935 Siman was still splitting time between his job as the Springfield Cardinals batboy and his position as star player for the Br'er Fox baseball club. At the same he was playing on the Pontiac Chiefs senior team, he organized the Pontiac Juniors and played second baseman or shortstop for three seasons.[29] Junior Siman and George Thompson Jr. led the juniors division again, with

Springfield Cardinals with batboy Junior Siman sitting cross-legged in front. *Courtesy of Siman Family Papers, private collection of Scott Foster Siman and Jayne Siman Chowning.*

Siman pitching nine games and Thompson six. Junior's best game that season saw him striking out fourteen and allowing just one hit in a 5-1 victory.

In addition to Junior's success as a Little League player, there was growing appreciation for his work as a Cardinals mascot and batboy. Childhood friend Jack Hamlin noted that "everyone with the Cardinals organization just loved Si." As Hamlin was from the north side of Springfield and Junior was a south-side boy, a friendly rivalry formed between the two when their baseball teams competed. According to Hamlin, Siman was a good ball player, but the Cardinals players and executives especially liked his "energy and personality."[30] Cardinals scout Charley Barrett was chief among his admirers. Barrett hired drivers to help him get to the smaller bush leagues around the country and scout for talented players. When his regular driver quit, Barrett hired sixteen-year-old Junior as his scouting driver, a job he kept for three summers from 1937 to 1939.

As the chief scout of the St. Louis Cardinals, the co-builder of the farm club system, and the man widely acknowledged as the number-one scout in

ABOVE
Photo of Charley Barrett autographed for Junior Siman. *Courtesy of Siman Family Papers, private collection of Scott Foster Siman and Jayne Siman Chowning.*

LEFT
When folks in the Midwest and Southeast saw this custom-made license-plate holder, which read "St Louis Cardinals Scout" and featured the team logo, everyone knew that Charley Barrett was in town. *Courtesy of Siman Family Papers, private collection of Scott Foster Siman and Jayne Siman Chowning.*

baseball, Barrett had many options for drivers, but Junior Siman's energy—both as a player and a batboy—mirrored Barrett's own work ethic. "I had learned to type and took shorthand, so I was kind of half secretary and half driver, and would do anything [Barrett] asked me to do," Si later recalled.[31] He spent his last two summers of high school traveling with Barrett to bush leagues across the United States, Canada, and Mexico in search of baseball players.

During the scouting off-season, Junior and Barrett corresponded by letter. Barrett was a "prodigious letter-writer and all of his correspondence was carried on in longhand," according to one observer.[32] "He scorned the use of a stenographer and would sit for hours at his desk in the winter, laboriously writing to all parts of the country and to all kinds of people who had lent him a helping hand in finding a ball player." His first letter to Junior, on April 24, 1937, was a short note asking him to call so they could make plans for their first summer trip. He instructed Junior to reverse the telephone charges, and closed his letter with "So long your pal Chas Barrett."[33] By June 5, Junior Siman was in St. Louis, where Barrett shared with him a list of forty-four cities, primarily in the Midwest and Southeast, that they would visit by car that summer.

Junior and Barrett began their 1937 summer trip in Asheville, North Carolina, likely because it was home to a Cardinals minor-league team. From there they ventured as far west as Jacksonville, Texas, as far north as Duluth, Minnesota, and as far northeast as Pittsburgh, Pennsylvania. In his letters to his parents, Junior clearly enjoyed describing what he and Barrett were doing, once noting self-importantly that he was "pretty busy as Charlie and I haft to map out our trip in advance."[34] Referring to a player for the St. Louis Cardinals he had met as a batboy, Junior added, "Say, Pop, did you know that Paul Dean has started working out he says his arm feels great he also wanted to know what I was doing up here. He remembered me without saying a word."[35] His excitement about having a routine conversation with Dean, one of the top pitchers in baseball, is sweetly understated. Junior was thrilled to be entrusted with work for the Cardinals and later proudly recalled, "I'd go to spring training, and, boy, you talk about being in the big leagues. There wasn't a star there that was any bigger than I was. You know, [it was] an answer to a kid's dream."[36]

Barrett's fatherly interest in Junior is evident in his letters, as Barrett wrote to him, "I want you to know I miss my old pal, Junior" and "[A]nd last, wishes to the best pal I have Junior Siman. The boy wonder."[37] In December 1937, after receiving a Christmas fruitcake made by Siman's mother, Barrett wrote to Junior, "Your to good a kid to be so generous to me but I think good of you and I want you to know that. All the boys at office often ask about you.

So you are not forgotten."[38] As they were winding down their first summer together as driver and scout, Barrett became aware of Junior's other love: music. He wrote to Junior's parents: "Junior is a good boy but doesn't know how to pick the hit parade."[39] Little did Barrett know that Junior's ability to recognize music talent was as good as his own for identifying baseball talent.

As Barrett's trust in Junior grew, he knew he could share with him confidential news about the team. In December 1937 he wrote to Junior: "Confidentially we will have our spring camp at Springfield 1938 ... You have a standing invitation to work with us any afternoon after school."[40] He gave Junior many such opportunities and privileges, but always on the condition that he complete high school. No doubt Barrett had seen many young players bypass school for big-league opportunities. Understandably, when the 1938 season rolled around, Barrett again emphasized the importance of education to Junior: "Whenever you get out of school come on to me any time later part of April or middle of May. What ever time you get out. I will be waiting for you but you must stay in school, until you see that [baseball] won't interfere with your education. I will wait for you what ever date it is."[41] These words must have had a profound impact on young Siman. While for a boy of his age baseball must have seemed like a possible career, Barrett had learned by watching the lawyerly skills of Branch Rickey that education should trump the ball field, and he never let Siman forget it.

Siman, writing to his parents from the Hotel Irvin Cobb in Paducah, Kentucky, mentioned Nixa, Missouri, native Arnold "Mickey" Owen, who was hitting a .322 average, and future hall-of-famer Enos Slaughter, the "Wild Hoss of the Osage," who "isn't doing so bad."[42] Owen was in Springfield for the 1936 season and hit .310 against Western Association pitching. He made his major-league debut with the Cardinals in 1937 after Barrett spotted him in Southern California.[43]

By the summer of 1938, Barrett and Junior were back on the road in search of the next big star. A special memory of this trip for Junior occurred when they were on the road in Louisiana and Mississippi and came upon a baseball game with two Black teams playing each other using torn baseballs. Barrett always had new baseballs in his car for him to autograph, so he told Junior to give the teams some balls. Siman went to the car trunk and threw boxes of balls out onto the field. Apparently afraid of this abrupt action from a white man in a car, the players scattered. Siman retrieved the balls and this time gently rolled them out onto the field.[44] The experience gave Junior an awareness of racial inequality and taught him a lesson about compassion, humility, and respect.

Junior Siman sitting on Charley Barrett's car bumper. *Courtesy of Siman Family Papers, private collection of Scott Foster Siman and Jayne Siman Chowning.*

Junior Siman was especially excited when he got to work out in St. Louis with the major-league Cardinals because it made him feel like part of the team. He wrote to his parents from the Hotel DeSoto in St. Louis: "From now on I am Mr. Charles F. Barrett's secretary but also a baseball player. Today I worked out and did do swell and the Cardinals sure shouldn't have lost that game."[45] The next day, Junior wrote another letter to them, this time on official St. Louis Cardinals stationary and using his new L. C. Smith & Corona typewriter, which he said cost $55 (over $1,000 today).[46] He boasted: "I pitched batting practice today and did swell and the players and every one up here treats me just grand."[47]

Following Siman's second summer as a scout driver, Barrett wrote to tell him what a good scout he had been: "I want you to know you were a dandy companion all summer . . . So save your money and be a good boy, from now on, and be good. Kindest regards and best wishes from the best friend you have out side of your parents."[48] Junior returned to high school in the fall, and Barrett wrote to him on November 28, 1938 from the Cardinal offices at Sportsman's Park: "I think a ball park is the most deserted place you ever saw in Winter time."[49] Soon after the holidays, Barrett's letters about the upcoming 1939 season indicated his eagerness to get back out on the road mining for talent: "I would like to talk to you first about our trips in 1939 . . . There is no one I would sooner have than Junior Siman, and that's from my heart you know. I never go back on a good friend."[50]

Barrett sent Junior a check for five dollars as a high school graduation present and asked him to join him on the road as soon as school was out. On May 26, 1939, Barrett wrote: "Well Junior they all ask about you. I miss my old pal, but when ever you are ready, let me know, and I will tell you where to meet me if its possible—unless I am in St Louis boy the cards look great . . . I will be waiting for you. If you need a salary check let me know and I will send it to you."[51] Soon after, the two headed out on their third scouting tour, with Junior, who could type and take shorthand, serving Barrett as a secretary as well as being a driver.

On the night of July 4, 1939, the day after he dropped Junior off at his parents' house following their tour, Charley Barrett, the dean of baseball scouts, died of a heart attack at age sixty-eight. At his funeral, Branch Rickey "stood before Barrett's casket, tears rolling down his face, and sobbed: 'Charley, old man, you can't run out on me like this' . . . Then the Cardinals' general manager almost collapsed, unable to go on as one of the pallbearers."[52] Barrett had a history of helping young men, of giving them a hand up, as noted in the *St. Louis Star and Times*: "One of Barrett's hobbies was to make the path of life somewhat easier for unfortunate youngsters. He was known to have assisted many young boys and their families in a financial way."[53] Barrett was a father figure who had taught Junior Siman to aim to be the best he could be.

The loss of his pal and mentor left Junior at a crossroads. Now out of high school, he applied for a job in the St. Louis Cardinals' office. He worked the switchboard, pitched at batting practice, and traveled a bit with Branch Rickey. He became acquainted with many Cardinals players while in St. Louis, and his roommate at the Fairgrounds Hotel was Sam Breadon's nephew, Bill Walsingham Jr.[54] Siman thought this connection might come in handy sometime: "Had I stayed in baseball, I have reason to think that I would have gone into business with him and for him. All the scouting experience that I had made me worth a little more than just anybody you would hire to work in baseball. I had that experience [both] in playing, [and] going out and looking for ball players."[55]

While not quite ready for a big-league executive job, Siman thought he might be considered as Barrett's replacement. He drafted a letter to Branch Rickey, and shared it with his friend, Art Fetzner, Rickey's assistant, who quickly replied: "I would suggest you write this letter on plain white bond paper; not Cardinal stationery. I think it would have a better effect." Fetzner closed with a PS: "Mr. Rickey will be here for two or three days, I believe, so get your letter in right away."[56] Siman made the changes Fetzner suggested and fired it off to Rickey on July 12, 1939. In the letter he summed up his qualifications: "I have been connected with the Cardinal[s] Organization for the past eight years. I was batboy and club house boy for the Springfield Cardinals for five years before taking the position with Mr. Barrett." He closed with words of praise for his mentor: "Someday I hope to carry on the work [that] Mr. Barrett was doing ... However, I know there will never be another Charley Barrett and there will never be another scout as good and with such sound judgment."[57] No record of a reply from Rickey exists, but Siman liked to tell people that Rickey said something to the effect of "we don't hire eighteen-year-olds as scouts for the St. Louis Cardinals."[58]

Siman still had ambitions to play baseball and thought that perhaps his relationship with Charley Barrett would give him an advantage, so he went to tryout camp. In 1940, Siman was sent to play second base with a summer league team in Junction City, Kansas. His roommate there was a pitcher from Springfield named Duff McCoy. "They called us 'Mutt and Jeff' because he was about six-foot-five and I was about five-foot-six," Siman recalled. Junction City players earned rewards instead of money for their success. A double play earned twenty-five cents of laundry service, and a winning run at home earned a free milk shake at the local drug store.

Siman's dream of being a major-league baseball player ended abruptly when he was farmed out to a team in Beloit, Kansas. There he battled an injury and faced stiff competition from bigger, more talented players. One night, after a loss in which Siman struck out four times, the team's bus turned over: "The manager kind of blamed me ... he said the bus driver couldn't get any air to breathe because 'that damn Siman pulled all the air out of the park.'" Siman didn't make it through the summer as a player: "I wasn't big enough. I wasn't good enough," he recalled.[59] A local columnist reported his unfortunate return to Springfield: "June Siman is back in town with today's best tale. The Kansas baseball team on which he was playing farmed him out to a club that paid three bucks a week, plus feed and flop. He quit, of course, with only twenty pennies in his pocket. He swears he hitchhiked home, never missed a meal—and without separating himself from a cent."[60] Siman was officially ready to give up his pipe dream of being a professional baseball player.

BOY SALESMAN

Back in 1931, when Si Siman was ten years old and happily living in a backyard tent at 616 E. Normal Street, the world seemed full of opportunity. "It was quite an adventure . . . I realized [the neighborhood boys] were interested in entertainment. So, I was the great impresario on Normal Street. Little did I realize it was really the beginning of what was going to follow for me." Siman had a natural ability to make something out of nothing, not in the mechanical way that his father could, but in his own way—as an entrepreneur. His father came from a long line of carpenters and mechanics who could fix or build just about anything but who did not understand how the entertainment business could pay the bills. Siman once quipped that his father worried about his son's future because "he didn't know that I was going to have one."[61]

At age ten, Siman made a movie theater in the family's garage by fashioning a control booth out of a large junk refrigerator shell donated by a local refrigerator company, mounting it, and borrowing a movie projector. Soon he was showing feature movies to the neighborhood kids on a garage wall and charging a small fee.[62] "If you couldn't pay you could bring something to eat. We had a ticket taker and regular performances on Fridays and Saturdays." As business grew, Siman sold refreshments and encouraged friends to spread the word about his new theater enterprise on Normal Street. He was a natural salesman and began to love the entertainment business. "I thought I might be a performer at one point. I wasn't, but I liked to dream." Following a dream would become one of Si Siman's favorite pursuits, but at the age of ten his main motivation was to make enough money to go to St. Louis for Cardinals baseball games with his father.

His garage movie theater was only one of Siman's childhood fundraising enterprises. In 1933 he put wheels on an orange crate, filled it with dry ice, and hit the streets of Springfield to sell Popsicles and roasted peanuts. Garage mechanics like his dad were his first customers. As cash was sparse, twelve-year-old Siman learned about credit by collecting his quarters on Saturday's payday. When he could avoid eating the product, which was a challenge, his business averaged a thirty-three-percent profit. The possibility of increased sales lured Siman into selling at the municipal court, until a legal hitch threatened to halt his Popsicle business altogether. During a heavy-business day at the court, a policeman approached Siman and said, "I hate to tell you this, but you're out of place selling in here. The judge is complaining that the people are eating Popsicles. They are not paying attention to me, and . . . you don't have a

Ralph Foster at his desk at KWTO radio station. *Courtesy of Ralph Foster Museum.*

peddler's license, do you? Cause I want to see it." A peddler's license cost three or four dollars, and Siman would still have to pay for his product. He decided to abandon the city government "account" and move on.

When Siman rolled his cart through downtown Springfield the following summer, he saw an opportunity in the new KWTO radio station. He met station manager Ralph Foster and explained that he wanted to sell some Popsicles. Foster replied, "Well, lay your pitch on me." The pitch convinced Foster to purchase enough for everyone working in the building—a sellout performance on Siman's part. The audience members at the radio broadcast underway upstairs were undoubtedly pleased to get a free Popsicle. As Siman left, Foster said, "Wait a minute. I didn't mean *everybody in the building*. I meant all the people who *work* here." Siman replied, "That wasn't the way you explained it to me." Nevertheless, Foster offered him a part-time job emptying trash bins and doing odd jobs around the station until he was in high school.[63]

PROMOTIONAL PRODIGY

Siman's early interest in entertainment is not unique to a boy his age, but he was far ahead of most in two regards: his ambitious desire to make money and his successful bonding with influential mentors in the business of planning and promoting events. In 1936, when Siman was in high school, he met Walter Hickman, who owned a popular dance hall called Half-a-Hill on a dirt road about five miles southeast of Springfield in Galloway, Missouri.[64] The ten-acre property was not just a dance hall; it included the Hickman family home, as well as a restaurant that had started as a barbeque shack. Almost any Springfieldian born before 1960 will remember a dance, concert, special occasion, party, or dinner at Half-a-Hill. It had a large dance pavilion for Saturday night events, and big-band groups such as Ernie Fields from Tulsa and Butch Jennings from Springfield often played there. Siman credited Hickman for teaching him how to promote events by sending him out to put up posters, sell tickets, and find businesses to serve as ticket outlets.

Siman put the training he received from Hickman to work earning a little extra cash for himself by sponsoring Half-a-Hill events for his high school sorority and fraternity friends at Springfield High School.[65] When he was fifteen, Siman promoted a "skirt skript" dance for Alpha Tau Phi girls, described by Siman as "a sorority subsidized thing [that] became a winner during winter."[66] A "winner" for Siman meant an event that made money for him when baseball was out of season. He also promoted fraternity "sunrise dances," which he described as "come-as-you-are, four-o'clock-in-the-morning parties" held in the wee hours of Saturday or Sunday.[67] The established go-to guy for successful parties, Siman was president of the high-school fraternity Chi Sigma Chi during the school year 1938–39.

In 1936, Half-a-Hill's Walter Hickman decided to start booking big-name dance bands at Springfield's Abou Ben Adhem Shrine Mosque, and Siman was eager to help. The Shrine Mosque was a 3,200-seat auditorium built in 1923 to host events for a new local Shriners organization. A lower-level area held an additional 1,300 attendees. At the time of its dedication, the Shriners claimed that the Shrine Mosque was the largest auditorium west of the Mississippi, with a stage that was second in size only to that at the New York Metropolitan Opera. For the next sixty years, the auditorium hosted all the major entertainment events in Springfield. Siman "muzzled in on" the lucrative concessions at the Shrine Mosque and kept the contract until he joined the navy in 1942.[68]

Chi Sigma Chi high school fraternity, with Siman seated in front row, third from left. *Courtesy of Siman Family Papers, private collection of Scott Foster Siman and Jayne Siman Chowning.*

Hickman's first big-band show at the Shrine Mosque, publicized with Siman's help, may have been Fats Waller on July 7, 1936. Daily newspaper ads appearing a week before the show promoted advance tickets for $1.11, including tax. The Shrine was noted as being "air cooled" and having an abundance of tables, lots of refreshments, and a newly refinished dance floor for dancing from nine to two.[69] A much bigger show sponsored by Hickman was Duke Ellington and his orchestra on October 28, 1936. Local businesses such as Jarman Shoes at 310 St. Louis Street capitalized on the event by selling tickets and advertising themselves as the "ticket headquarters for Duke Ellington."[70] A local columnist promised that the show would prove that Ellington was "one of the greatest dance orchestras this country has ever produced," and offered a short course in Ellington so readers wouldn't be embarrassed at a dinner party or a favorite bar when Ellington's name came up.[71] Among other big-band acts booked by Hickman were Fletcher Henderson (March 31, 1938) and Deacon

Moore and His Syncopated Swingsters (April 21, 1938). At the age of seventeen, Siman was still too young to sign contracts, but he was becoming known around town as a promoter of shows at the Shrine Mosque and Half-a-Hill.[72]

A few months after Siman graduated from Springfield High School in 1939, Hickman booked Ella Fitzgerald at the Mosque for November 17. A newspaper ad announced Fitzgerald as "The Queen of Swing" and "The Original 'A Tisket-A-Tasket' Girl!" in reference to the recent hit that had catapulted her into the spotlight.[73] Advance tickets to see Fitzgerald with Chick Webb's band, marketed as the "Hottest Swing Band in the U.S.A. Today!," were only eighty-five cents.[74] While contemplating his future, Siman started taking classes at Southwest Missouri State Teacher's College, where he booked bands and other events for college fraternities and sororities.[75] By December 1939, a columnist reported that "June [Junior] Siman, ex-batboy for the Cards, is doing the promoting for the promoter who's bringing the big bands to the Mosque."[76] Although the city did not allow "theatrical advertising" on the Springfield square, "some enterprising person connected with the appearance of Ella Fitzgerald . . . plastered a car with placards" and parked it on the square where everyone could see it.[77] This description suggests Junior Siman was the "enterprising person."

Siman had a promising career ahead of him, but he still had a lot to learn about being a promoter. His experiences with Hickman taught him that a town the size of Springfield couldn't support big acts more than once a month.[78] He began to watch *Billboard* magazine for band tours so he could bargain for open dates along a tour route. For that industrious plan he would need a lot more money than Hickman had, and KWTO manager Ralph Foster stepped in to guarantee financial backing in case an event failed. Siman booked the bands, promoted their events, and handled all the business. With Foster behind him, Siman could charge forward and book all the big bands he loved.

When he brought the Tommy Dorsey Band into the Shrine Mosque on January 29, 1940, Dorsey's performance shook the town with jitterbug mania.[79] Wry columnist Allen Oliver commented on the show: "Estimates on the size of the crowd ran all the way from 10,000 to around a million and a half. The last estimate was ours. It was arrived at when we finally abandoned the dance floor walking on our ankles, one hip out of joint, and carrying various portions of our anatomy in a basket which we carried for the purpose of picking them up as they were wrenched loose and tossed carelessly about by the other dancers."[80] Oliver reported that a man wanting Dorsey's autograph for his wife begged him to forge one because the mob around Dorsey was too thick to penetrate. He described the crowd as a "tidal wave," a "surging mass of humanity" that swept him in and out of the dance area as a fight broke out somewhere. The surge threatened to trample a small guy "who had climbed us like a telephone pole and was riding on our back like the Old Man of the Sea."[81]

After the show, Siman went home and woke his parents by turning on the light and throwing boxes of money into the air. Siman recalled: "My daddy said, 'Where have you been? What have you been doing?' He couldn't believe this because you know I'm the guy that [he thought] was going to starve to death." Siman's mother demanded he store the money with the next-door neighbor until the banks opened the next morning in case a robber had followed him home. Siman later used part of the money to buy himself a bright green Pontiac with yellow wheels. When the car salesman became hesitant about selling such a fancy car to a young man barely out of high school, Siman "just peeled off $925" and bought the new car. "I thought, boy things couldn't be any better!"[82]

Siman booked Woody Herman and his orchestra at the Shrine Mosque on April 29, 1941, but his show with Glenn Miller on July 7 was more successful with the jitterbug crowd than either Woody Herman or Tommy Dorsey. A post-concert article in the *Springfield Leader and Press* included a photo of Miller backstage with a group of Siman's Sigma Nu fraternity brothers cooling off "between numbers for a steaming mob of dancers." According to the article, a record 3,100 dancers packed the arena and basement of the Mosque, "700 perspiring people more than heard Tommy Dorsey."[83] Siman continued his winning streak by booking Artie Shaw's orchestra at the Shrine on October 22, 1941. The band leader drew only 1,700 dancers for his show, "most of them boys and girls of high school and college age."[84] However, advance tickets brought in $1,200, according to the *Springfield Daily News*.

Booking bands for jitterbug mobs was not Siman's only success during and after high school. By his twentieth birthday he had explored a full range of business opportunities including event promotions, advertising sales, baseball, a motel business, and a refreshment franchise. In his *Springfield Leader and Press* column The Benchwarmer, Perry Smith took note of Siman's extraordinary achievements: "Just to look at the little guy with the kinky hair and the swanky, multi-colored wardrobe, you'd swear he was playing hookey [sic] from a college campus, but a few minutes conversation with verbose Ely Earl Siman Jr., is enough to convince the most skeptical that he's a promotional prodigy."[85] The Benchwarmer provided a stunning list of Siman's current commitments, to which he added that he "owns 100 card tables and stacks of bowls and spoons, which are necessary to his concession business. These he frequently leases. He operates a cottage court, café, and filling station on North Glenstone."[86]

Siman's "cottage court, café, and filling station" ownership adventure lasted about a year before it turned sour when he realized it was a seven-days-a-week job. "Business was good, but you had to serve breakfast, dinner, and supper," Siman recalled. He also had to find skilled people to work in the filling station or do it himself. One day, Siman drained the transmission fluid out of a customer's car instead of the oil: "I thought that's the dirtiest oil I've ever seen. I had to call my dad to come and bail me out. This is when he told me if I ever touched anything mechanical again he'd kill me." Two things Siman learned from his experiences were that being the boss is more profitable than being an employee, and if he could get people to work for him, he would have time to go fishing.[87]

At the same time Siman was booking big bands at the Shrine Mosque, its wrestling franchise came up for sale. In June 1941 he bought the wrestling ring and the franchise from J. Oliver Gideon, who had been the Shrine wrestling promoter since the mid-1930s. The Benchwarmer noted that the franchise purchase added "another venture to a growing string of promotions that must have begun just after he quit swaddling clothing."[88] Siman promoted Tuesday night wrestling matches at the Shrine Mosque every week. He drove the wrestlers into town in the same car, but he had to arrange their arrival at the Mosque in separate cars so it would look like they were mad at each other. "We'd plan the strategy of how the matches were going to go. So, I really wasn't unhappy to get out of that business." The Tuesday night mats went well until the Japanese bombed Pearl Harbor on December 7, 1941. As it happened, Siman had booked a Japanese American wrestler, Sugy Hayamaka, for the Tuesday, December 9 schedule. Although Hayamaka was born in Texas, the Missouri governor would not let him cross the state line because his name was Japanese. The next day the newspaper simply reported Hayamaka as a no-show.[89] According to Siman, "Me, the wrestlers, and the concession stand outweighed the dang customers. So, I lost my tail."[90] He suspended all Tuesday night wrestling matches until January 1942 and sold the franchise to Miles Walker just before going into the navy in June.

Perhaps the most sensational event Siman promoted during 1941 was an appearance of notorious fan dancer and bubble-dance inventor Sally Rand at the annual Ozark Empire District Fair.[91] Although Rand sometimes danced with skin-colored undergarments, she was arrested many times in her long career for perceived nudity, including four times in a single day at the 1933 Chicago World's Fair.[92] News came out on May 18 that Sally Rand would be one of the stage show events at the fair in September. Letters to the editor of

Sally Rand. *Courtesy of Kitty Ledbetter.*

the *Springfield Leader and Press* about her threat to decency soon followed: "We as a nation have lost our morals and our morale . . . and today we read that the clean little city of Springfield will have Sally Rand to demonstrate her fan and bubble dance at your fair this fall, although under the laws of Missouri such exhibitions are in violation of the law. Just a little indication our country is crumbling."[93] The extended controversy fueled excitement about the show.

The week before the fair, a large newspaper advertisement promoted the "Stars over America" grandstand show featuring Sally Rand, big-band performances by the Bernie Cummins Orchestra and stars from his radio shows, "7 Big Time Vaudeville Acts," and a "Gorgeous Group of Glamorous Girls." It was going to be a "High Class Musical Show," according to the ad.[94] Si Siman had likely booked them all.

A separate newspaper article announced the addition of a special bubble dance to Rand's act on Mondays and Wednesdays. Siman constructed a new open-air pavilion specifically for the bubble-dance shows. With a 5,000-square-foot dance floor, cabaret tables, and Chinese paper lanterns replicating an outdoor night club, it involved extensive preparation and expense. But there were problems: "About the third night of the fair it rained, and I mean really rained. I had a rented piano. The drummer in their band took the tarp off my piano when it started raining and put it on his drums. I got out there the next morning, and I could flip the ivory keys off the piano. I called the man I had rented it from and said, 'Guess what's happened to your piano.' He came out and looked and said, 'Guess what's happened to YOUR piano!'"[95] Siman had used rented lumber for the floor, which had to be returned, but the wet paper lanterns had dyed the boards bright red, green, and blue, meaning he had to pay extra for the damage.

In addition to dealing with the rain damage, Siman worried about theft. Because he had a van full of refreshment equipment and Pepsi, he decided to stay overnight at the fair the last night to guard his investment: "I had a chair, and my mother brought me an afghan and put it over my legs so I wouldn't freeze to death. I took a nap and woke up and the afghan was gone. All the pop was gone. It went to the next town, I'm sure, with the carnival."[96]

Rain would normally threaten fair attendance, but when the fair manager saw the overflow crowd for Sally Rand, he exclaimed "Why, they even put chairs out in the mud for them."[97] After the fair was over, organizers credited Sally Rand for setting a new record for fair attendance at 175,000 visitors. They said income from the fair not only paid all new expenses, but it cleaned up old deficit.[98] The fair board cited two reasons: big-name acts and Sally Rand.

NAVY MAN

After the attack on Pearl Harbor, Siman's options for the future narrowed as the United States prepared for total war. He was still booking shows at the Shrine Mosque, but found the wrestling business no longer appealing. He obtained a student flying license and joined the Springfield Flying Club, hoping he could work on civil air defense patrols. Siman and his father were first in line to register for the third selective service registration on February 14, 1942.[99] A photograph of the smiling father and son appeared in the *Springfield Leader and Press* with a caption quoting Ely Siman Sr. as saying he would be "glad to serve in any way I can" in this war as he had the previous. At forty-four years old, Ely Sr. was just four months under the upper age limit for registration. Siman, still known as "Junior," told the paper he was interested in aviation and wanted to join the air corps: "We've got a job to do, and I hope I can help to do it."[100] Neither Siman nor his father were drafted. Ely Siman Sr. turned his mechanical talent to working on airplanes, while Junior Siman joined the navy in June 1942 on the buddy system with his two best friends, Dwight Shultz and Jim Shirk, and went to boot camp together in Great Lakes, Illinois.

Going into the navy as a big-time promoter, Siman thought he would be the smartest man there: "I wanted to tell them how to do everything. And after I'd been there for a while I was with some guys that were a helluva lot smarter than I was . . . I hate to admit it, but I think I was just a little below normal." It was here that Ely Earl Siman Jr. became "Si," as he explained: "In the navy they shorten everything. So instead of [saying my] regular name they just shortened it to 'Si' and it stuck."[101] He was okay with the nickname because it would be good for show business. Hard work and long hours in boot camp changed Siman's perspective about more than a few things. He wrote to his parents on August 3, 1942: "I never knew there was so much to do when you became a navy man. Both of my arms are so sore from shots I can't hardly move them. Get up at 5:30 to bed at 9:30. I have guard duty tonight from 12 p.m. until 4 a.m."[102]

The buddy system didn't quite work out the way Siman had planned. After graduating from boot camp, Schultz was shipped to another base and became an aviation mechanic, Shirk went to yet another part of the country as a yeoman, and Siman went to learn weather forecasting in aerology school at the Naval Air Station in Charleston, South Carolina. There, reality set in and Siman's confidence was busted for the first time. His girlfriend in Springfield, Mary Lou Scott, had stopped writing him letters, his buddies Schultz and Shirk were in different parts of the country, and he was in a strange city in the Deep South, far away from the Ozarks and with no money or friends. Siman later recalled: "Up there [they] would throw you the crying towel and say, 'You want me to go get the preacher and tell your story to him?' They knew how to handle it. [They'd say,] 'Are you a man or a mouse?'"[103] He began to plot an escape, but instead hung on. It took a strong man to endure the experiences Siman had in the navy.

Siman's job as a weather forecaster took him many places—some interesting, some dangerous, and some unforgettably tragic. His first job as petty officer was with an anti-submarine air patrol unit that monitored the East Coast from Charleston up to Cape Hatteras, North Carolina, and back down to the Banana River in Jacksonville, Florida. German U-boats had been a concern since June 1942, when German saboteurs landed submarines at Amagansett, New York, and Ponte Vedra Beach, Florida. One of the German commanders, George John Dasch, turned himself in to the FBI in June 1942. His crew was arrested and sent as prisoners to Charleston Naval Air Station. Their mission had been to sabotage specific East Coast power facilities and factories. Siman's job was to make sure the US air patrols had accurate weather forecasts for their mission to protect citizens from such threats.

In May 1943, Siman received orders to report to Norfolk, Virginia, where he departed on the USS *Schuylkill*, a fuel tanker. Siman's job was to forecast weather for refueling ships at sea. In a letter dated May 17, 1943, Siman enthusiastically assured his parents that he was not worried or anxious about going to sea: "I don't know where we are bound for and to me it doesn't make much difference just as long as we go where we can do the most good for the US and the most harm for the enemy."[104] The tanker left Norfolk on May 20, went through the Panama Canal on June 1, and headed to Pearl Harbor to join the campaign for Pacific invasions led by Admiral Chester W. Nimitz, commander in chief of the US Pacific fleet.[105]

On the way, the tanker was detoured by secret orders to go north to the western end of the Aleutian Islands to reclaim Kiska Island from the Japanese. They pulled into Aleutian waters on July 5, but the Japanese had temporarily left to regroup. They stopped long enough for Siman to take the entrance exam to become an officer before leaving to fuel ships preparing for an attack on the Gilbert Islands. The *Schuylkill* eventually joined Admiral Nimitz in what Siman called a "monstrous convoy" that left Pearl Harbor for the Gilbert Islands on November 15.[106] As the convoy continued toward Tarawa atoll in the Gilberts, they had to travel a zigzag route to avoid being torpedoed. "We were carrying 118,000 barrels of aviation gas with 130-octane gasoline and the rest of it was fuel oil," Siman recalled. "The captain used to tell us, 'Don't worry about getting torpedoed and sinking because if we ever do get torpedoed, we'll be halfway to heaven.' "[107] On November 24, a Japanese submarine torpedoed a converted aircraft carrier that was running beside the *Schuylkill*, the USS *Liscome Bay*. The carrier sank within twenty-three minutes of the explosion and 644 men died.[108]

The *Schuylkill* was always at risk of being hit by enemy fire. "When [a] tanker is loaded," noted Siman, "the main deck is a wash. It's underwater. It makes a beautiful target for a submarine."[109] While the weight of the loaded oil tanker brought the main deck to water level, when it was empty it had to be weighed down with ballasts to keep it from looking like a three-story building on the surface. Once, Siman was on the *Schuylkill*'s deck when the ship fired on a submarine. An eight-inch gun went off just above Siman's head, bursting his eardrum and knocking him to the deck. As a result, Siman had hearing

ABOVE
Ely "Si" Siman Jr. (US Navy), Lillian Siman, and Ely Siman Sr. (US Army). *Courtesy of Siman Family Papers, private collection of Scott Foster Siman and Jayne Siman Chowning.*

RIGHT
Si Siman's official US Navy portrait. *Courtesy of Siman Family Papers, private collection of Scott Foster Siman and Jayne Siman Chowning.*

problems for the rest of his life, especially during his later years. On another occasion, a Japanese airplane shot the ship's anemometer and pieces of it cut Siman's forehead. He thought he had been shot.

On the same day as the sinking of the *Liscome Bay*, Siman witnessed the US Marine invasion of Tarawa: "Our poor Marines on those landing barges . . . couldn't get to the [sand because of low tide]. They let the bow down, and [soldiers] jumped in the water and a lot of them carrying 25- and 30-pound packs drowned. They never even got to the beach at all." Later in life, Siman admitted that "a lot of things happened [in the navy] that I don't really ever talk about and you never forget. But God bless 'em, [the soldiers] did their job, even if they were going to be lost, they were trying . . . It's a cheap price for living in America."[110] These experiences lingered in his memory long after coming home with three battle stars for participation in the invasions of Tarawa and the Gilbert Islands.

Following these missions, Siman's tanker went to the Ellice Islands, where the sailors spent Christmas 1943 diving off the ship and swimming in the equatorial waters. A break in radio silence congratulated them for Admiral Nimitz's victory and gave Siman the good news that he had been accepted in the V-12 Navy College Training Program designed to train specialists, increase the navy's supply of commissioned officers, and improve student enrollments at small, private colleges. Participants enrolled for classes and earned completion degrees. Although most recruits returned to active duty after the program, it was not required.[111] Siman was relieved: "I was really fortunate, indeed, because I'd been in the invasion of the Gilberts, and I'd really had all the sea duty that I'd care to see, and how much, really, hell war was, and I had no ambitions at all to stay out there."[112] His preferences for schools were Massachusetts Institute of Technology in Cambridge, University of Southern California in Los Angeles, and Westminster College in Fulton, Missouri, but he was assigned to Berea College in Berea, Kentucky. Siman had never heard of it.

Founded by abolitionist John Gregg Fee in 1855, Berea College was the first racially integrated coeducational college in the South. At the Christian liberal arts school, Berea students work their way through a college degree in lieu of tuition.[113] The Springfield newspaper heard that Siman was in a "sailor's paradise—there are only 1,200 girls and 400 sailors. Only one drawback, according to Siman, and that is the fact that the V-12 program calls for the boys to be in their rooms at 7:30 p.m. Too bad, huh?"[114] His sixteen-month assignment to Berea for officer training school was fortuitous because it was the hometown of his future *Ozark Jubilee* host, Red Foley. He met Foley's family and became a regular visitor to the Renfro Valley Barn Dance founded in the 1930s by John Lair, Red Foley, and Whitey Ford.

Every stop in the navy that didn't involve being on a ship offered opportunities for Siman to get involved in sports and take courses at nearby universities. He loved college and thought he might like to study law, but decided he wouldn't make a good attorney: "By nature I'm a pretty positive-thinking person, and that's a negative world if you want to get into it. I feel sorry for them at times, but it's awful hard to feel sorry for a rich man."[115] When he was in aerology school in Charleston, Siman took courses at The Citadel and played basketball for a navy cage team that placed second in the navy league. At Berea College he managed a softball team while taking college courses for a few semesters. After sixteen months in Berea, Siman had the option of either going to Columbia University and return to the fleet or going into the Naval Reserve Officer Training Corps 3C at Duke University in Durham, North Carolina, where he could continue working toward a college degree leading to a commission as a navy officer. Siman was not interested in being a commissioned officer, but he took the opportunity to attend Duke University in the summer of 1945.

When the war ended, Siman had two choices: stay in the navy or go home to the Ozarks. According to Siman, the navy's thinking was that he should remain in the navy to pay for the college education they had given him, but his thinking was that having "been in [the] invasions of the Gilbert Islands and Aleutian Islands . . . I had paid for my college education in advance. So, I elected to come home."[116] When he came out of the navy in January 1946, Siman started taking night classes at Drury College in Springfield to finish his degree, while also playing basketball for the college team. After six years and attending five colleges, he finally graduated at the age of twenty-six on June 2, 1947. Siman appreciated the opportunity offered by the navy programs and understood why people choose military careers, but he felt that always having a superior would stunt his creativity. He liked being his own boss and hoped that Ralph Foster would give him free rein to create his own destiny while investing in his dreams.

CHAPTER TWO

KWTO AND THE GOLDEN AGE OF HILLBILLY RADIO

IN 1932, WHEN RALPH FOSTER and his brother-in-law, C. Arthur Johnson, partnered with Lester E. Cox to bring the first commercial radio station to Springfield, Missouri, they dreamed of building a station that would feature local artists performing live the music familiar to listeners in the Ozarks. Foster saw music of the Ozarks as "hillbilly music," widely defined as country, western, gospel, and traditional string band music. The process of getting Springfield's first radio station on the air demonstrates the aggressive self-motivation of Foster and Cox, who worked their way toward success at a time when money was sparse but opportunity was as big as they could make it.

Foster was born in 1893 in St. Joseph, Missouri, to a father who was a pioneer in weather forecasting. When Foster was a young man, he opened a tire store with Jerry Hall in St. Joseph. Foster was a "natural showman" and had occasionally performed in a vaudeville act with Hall as "The Rubber Twins."[1] In 1926, Foster and Hall decided to set up an amateur radio station in a forty-square-foot room in the back of the tire store. They acquired a license with the call letters KGBX, and used a microphone, a home-built panel, and a few watts of power to broadcast radio shows. According to a 1949 article in the *KWTO Dial*, "Foster and Hall were the announcers and entertainers and anyone who came in the store and could sing, whistle, or act, served as talent. Programs were frequently interrupted and the air left dead as the announcers stepped outside to patch an inner-tube."[2] Just to see if anybody was listening, Foster offered free ashtrays to the first hundred visitors to the station—a demonstration of his talent for radio promotion. The Rubber Twins became so popular on the radio that Firestone Tire and Rubber Company and Lucky Strike cigarettes used their images in newspaper ads, billboards, and posters.[3] In 1930, Foster and Hall upgraded the KGBX license from amateur to commercial, and two years later Foster's brother-in-law C. Arthur Johnson bought out Hall's portion of the station.

Springfield businessman Lester E. Cox sold radios at his Ozark Motor & Supply Company, and he was anxious to expand his business by bringing a station to fulfill his product needs. He had been approaching stations in northern Missouri about moving to the Ozarks when he persuaded Foster and Johnson to bring their license down to southwest Missouri. The Columbia Broadcasting System (CBS) was available in the Ozarks, but there were no radio stations in Springfield. When Foster and Johnson agreed to relocate, Cox went to Washington, DC, at his own expense and appeared before the Federal Radio Commission to get permission to move KGBX to Springfield.[4] In 1932, KGBX began broadcasting from a building located at the southeast corner of Kimbrough and St. Louis.

Cox was a phenomenally creative marketeer who saw opportunities everywhere and figured out how to make them profitable, as well as useful, for his community. He learned about hard work when he was a boy on a 160-acre family farm in Republic, Missouri. At the age of twelve he was earning $2 a week at a local hardware store, enough money to buy a new bicycle for $28. In high school he worked as a janitor, and after graduation he taught at nearby Prairie View School for $40 a month. He attended Drury College in Springfield, where he convinced the school newspaper to let him sell advertising. He was a salesman for a grain company until World War I, when he left Springfield to serve in the Army Air Corps.[5]

For the rest of his life, Cox expanded his investments and philanthropic interests, including a regional hospital system—today CoxHealth—in Springfield. He was quick to offer motivational mottoes for self-improvement and salesmanship, such as "Find something the people need and meet that need"; "If you are not made to work when you are young, you will never enjoy the thrill of accomplishment that comes from good, honest labor"; "You are as big as you are right; as little as you are wrong"; and "When you have provided yourself with the necessities of life, there are only two worthwhile ways you can use your money: To give others the opportunity to succeed; to make other people happy."[6] He served as a model for younger men including Foster and Siman, who applied many of Cox's mottoes to their own lives.

On December 25, 1933, at the end of one of the worst years of the Great Depression, Cox and Foster purchased a 100-watt radio station license in Worth County, on the Missouri-Iowa state line, for a second station in Springfield. Its call letters were KWTO, creatively tagged "Keep Watching the Ozarks" to reflect its focus on regional programming. Cox "envisioned it as a potentially powerful radio station, with coverage sufficient to blanket the Springfield trade area, indeed, the whole Missouri-Arkansas Ozarks area."[7] Foster acquired the lower AM frequency of 560 for KWTO because it would transmit farther into the Ozarks countryside than KGBX's 1260.

By 1936, KWTO was broadcasting at 5000 watts, and its signal reached beyond Independence, Kansas, to the northwest; Rogers, Berryville, and Harrison, Arkansas, to the southwest; northeast toward Rolla, Missouri; and west toward Oklahoma. KWTO and KGBX offered separate programming but shared the same building at the corner of Kimbrough and St. Louis streets for more than ten years. Neither station had any competition in Springfield, until 1942 when KTTS came on the air.

Many listeners lived in remote parts of the Ozarks and experienced hard times with few modern conveniences. A town ten miles away might as well be in another state. In some counties south of Springfield, electricity was not widely available until the 1950s. Battery-powered radios became a much-desired possession by the 1920s, but a basic radio might cost $35, the equivalent of $600 today.[8] Yet some people chose to do without a refrigerator rather than give up their radio.[9]

Foster had a good ear for country music and a good eye for opportunity. In 1933, hillbilly music was hitting full steam on the radio, according to *Billboard*: "Hill-billy acts have been getting the breaks lately, most of them leaving vaude[ville] for a much warmer welcome in the studios. Stations that did not have a single hill-billy program a few months ago now run them several times a week."[10] By the mid-1930s, more than 82 percent of homes had radios, and most stations were offering country music: "Between 1931 and 1939 the number of commercial stations more than tripled in America. And at one time or another, nearly all of them programmed some kind of country music."[11] Before television became common in the Ozarks during the 1950s, families were bonded by the music they heard on their radio or played together in the home.

KGBX featured a wide selection of music programming on its NBC Red Network radio feed, such as gospel quartets, polka music, selections from the NBC Symphony Orchestra, the US Army Band, marching bands, and big bands.[12] In contrast, KWTO's main fare was live, local hillbilly and western-swing types of country music, as well as daily news reports, weather, religious services, farm news, and topical programming related to the Ozarks. Musical artists came from all corners of the listening area to perform on KWTO during the 1930s and 1940s. Among the most popular of these was Christian County native Clyde "Slim Pickens" Wilson, acclaimed by Wayne Glenn as the "first homegrown Ozarks radio superstar."[13] Wilson was from a talented family of six singing sisters in Nixa, Missouri. He sold bluing (a laundry product) door-to-door to buy his first violin and learned to play hillbilly songs on it. He and his sisters entertained the neighbors on the family's telephone party line and at music parties on the lawn during summer nights in Nixa. In 1933, Wilson went to St. Louis looking for opportunities in music before heading to Kansas City to join a vaudeville troupe called Uncle Wash and his Stumpjumpers.[14] The group performed on WHB, but Wilson was back in the Ozarks by 1934.

Wilson was a versatile, talented showman who played fiddle left-handed, because he "just picked it up that way" when he was eight years old, and played guitar and bass right-handed.[15] He was working on a farm north of Bolivar, Missouri, when he started hitchhiking to Springfield to perform at KGBX/KWTO radio. By 1937, Wilson was performing at least four shows a day on KGBX/KWTO radio with various groups, as well as his family band, the Goodwill Family. Wilson was "Uncle Slim," and his sister Vancie was "Aunt Martha." Her son, Herschel ("Junior" or "Speedy") Haworth, started performing with the Goodwill Family in 1932 when he was ten years old. He was a central force in various KWTO bands for the next twenty years before moving to Nashville. Wilson was in several musical groups through the years, including the Prairie Playboys and the Tall Timber Boys, with Nixa, Missouri, fiddler Zed Tennis and western-swing artist Shorty Thompson (Henry Head, father of songwriter Wayne Carson). He also occasionally performed in a hillbilly comedy duo called Flash and Whistler with Floyd "Goo Goo" Rutledge.

Local talent on KWTO during the 1930s and '40s often came in the form of family groupings that evoked for listeners an intimate sense of close personal relationships. The Haden Family was a steady presence on live radio shows, as well as syndicated programs, at KWTO. Douglas County native and patriarch Carl Haden began performing on KGBX in 1933 and led his family of six children into musical performances that took them to several towns outside the Ozarks before settling in Springfield. Haden was known as "Uncle Carl," and his son Charlie became "Cowboy Charlie" before leaving in the 1950s to

The Tall Timber Boys: Shorty Thompson, Slim Wilson, and Zed Tennis. *Courtesy of Wayne Glenn.*

The Haden Family, 1943. *Courtesy of Wayne Glenn.*

become an internationally renowned jazz bass player, educator, and composer. Carl Haden's pawn shop on Commercial Street in Springfield specialized in musical instruments. He also owned the Seven Gables truck stop and restaurant on Route 66 near Springfield in the 1940s.

Through KWTO, Ralph Foster explored the full range of homegrown musical variety from the Ozarks during the 1930s. Women were increasingly seeking opportunities outside the home for additional family income during the Depression. If they had musical abilities, they often traveled to nearby cities where radio stations offered the chance to be a radio star. Sister duets on KWTO included Millie and Sue Bybee, Violet and Vesta Gamble, and Ann and Dora Schaffer. Sister acts became so popular that Springfieldians Boots and Bobbie Faye adopted stage names to appear related, although they were not sisters.[16]

When the Federal Communications Commission (FCC) handed down new rules against the ownership of multiple radio stations in 1944, Cox and Foster sold KGBX to the Springfield newspaper. KWTO continued to be the dominant radio station for local talent in the Ozarks region, but it could now offer national programs through its affiliation with NBC's Blue Network. During the evening hours until midnight, Springfield listeners could tune into musical programs featuring such notable popular and big-band artists as the Andrews Sisters, Bob Crosby and his Orchestra, Jimmy Dorsey, Tommy Dorsey, Woody Herman, Harry James, Spike Jones and His City Slickers, Guy Lombardo, Glenn Miller, Vaughn Monroe, and Dinah Shore.

After coming home from the navy in January 1946, Si Siman went to Ralph Foster for a job. Foster, who had hired Siman to do odd jobs around the station at age thirteen, was happy to see him and offered $70 a week to work at KWTO. With KWTO separated from KGBX, Foster promised a station expansion rich with opportunities for the ambitious war veteran. It was the continuation of a father-and-son-like relationship that lasted more than fifty years. When Siman became a full-time member of Foster's team, KWTO was the dominant country station in a region of rapidly expanding competition. He became Foster's man Friday, making arrangements for fishing and floating trips with advertising clients, meeting them at the railroad station or airport and carrying their bags. *KWTO Dial* editor Jean Kappell remembered him as a man with "boyish intensity and grown-up keenness."[17] Over the next ten years, Siman brought his energy to various jobs connected with KWTO radio. As he had during his boyhood, he apparently managed to do them all at the same time.

BREAKFAST IN HOLLYWOOD AND RADIOZARK

Siman's standout talent was in radio promotion and advertising sales.[18] He frequently served as anchorman for host George Earle Wilson ("George Earle") on KWTO's *Breakfast in Hollywood* shows, which were modeled after Tom Breneman's popular 1940s radio network series of the same name.[19] Siman made extra cash after hours by booking special evening programs of *Breakfast at Hollywood* for local organizations such as the local PTA, Lion's Club, and Rotary Club. He would travel with the show to any venue within two hundred miles of Springfield. It was a moneymaking project for the local organizations, as well as for Earle, Siman, and KWTO. Breneman also benefited by the extra attention and occasionally flew in orchids for presentation to the oldest woman in the audience. On one occasion, in March 1946, KWTO teamed up at the Shrine Mosque with Breneman's original live *Breakfast in Hollywood* as a fundraiser for the Springfield civic club the Co-Operettes. The *Springfield Leader and Press* reported 1,000 attendees, a number far surpassing club expectations. The oldest woman at the show was ninety-six. When she received her orchid from Breneman and her kiss from George Earle, she responded "This is not my first orchid nor my first kiss."[20] Such a busy broadcast required much coordination, and Ralph Foster noticed the travel and work Siman was doing for *Breakfast in Hollywood*.

One of the most varied KWTO enterprises Siman worked with during the 1940s and early '50s was RadiOzark transcription radio shows. Tape recorders and magnetic tape were available after World War II, but they were not in common use at radio stations until the mid-1950s. In the meantime, stations used electrical transcriptions—high-quality, low-noise recordings on sixteen-inch discs similar to long-playing records—to duplicate live radio programs.[21] Speed on the transcription disks was 33-1/3 revolutions per minute (rpm), instead of the standard 78 rpm then used on commercial record players. Machines recorded live radio shows by engraving blank discs with a recording lathe and cutting stylus. Fifteen minutes of material could typically be recorded on each side. Radio networks, record companies, and private enterprises also offered transcriptions of advertisements, jingles, programs, and other audio material for radio broadcasting. Patrons could pay to record anything from a song to a funeral.

In 1940, Ralph Foster and KWTO's commercial director Leslie Kennon began producing transcriptions for the Assemblies of God's thirty-minute religious program called *Sermons in Song*.[22] When the organization wanted to offer the programs to member churches and radio stations across the country, KWTO purchased new equipment to produce and syndicate *Sermons in Song* for nearly two hundred other stations.[23] In 1944, Foster formed RadiOzark with Cox's backing, partly to produce broadcast-quality commercial transcriptions of KWTO entertainers for sale to radio broadcasts across the country.[24] The first RadiOzark transcriptions were of gospel singers the Matthews Brothers Quartet and Shorty and Sue Thompson's Saddle Rockin' Rhythm western swing band.[25]

KWTO's first transcriptions with the Assemblies of God were "tailor-made," meaning they belonged to the source, with no outside commercials. However, most RadiOzark transcriptions were "open-end" programs, available for sale to radio stations with breaks inserted for local commercial breaks or announcements. Radio stations could tag on any sponsor who purchased the station's package for the show. RadiOzark charged subscribing stations according to market size, which was based on a city's population rather than metropolitan area population or broadcast coverage area, although 20 percent would be added for 50,000-watt stations below 1250 kilohertz. They sold program transcriptions to small market stations (in cities under 5,000 people) for as little as $2.50 per episode. The price increased incrementally according to population; stations in cities with a population of two million or more paid $50 per episode.[26] Stations would add the program cost to the sponsor rates, meaning the program wouldn't cost them anything.

Siman worked with John Mahaffey to sell, produce, and sometimes write RadiOzark programs, with later help from writers Bob Tubert and Don Richardson. Siman said: "We did a postmortem on every joke book you ever dreamed of and rewrote them and we found ourselves going around the barn lots of times because when you've got twenty shows to do and you've got five days to do them in, well..."[27] Recordings for radio shows were mostly done in the KWTO studios, according to Siman: "After they'd go off the air at midnight, I'd go to work, and we'd produce these shows [for RadiOzark] from midnight till four, and then they'd go [back] on the air at five."[28]

When RadiOzark contracted with Ford Tractor–Dearborn Farm Equipment dealers in 1949 to do transcriptions of the Dearborn Roundup radio program, it was RadiOzark's "largest order and its most heavily cast show to date."[29] The Dearborn shows consisted of performances by KWTO radio staff members Shorty and Sue Thompson, Penny Nichols, Zed Tennis, Doc Martin, Bob White, Bob Money, and the Matthews Brothers. To acquire the client, Siman and announcer Joe Slattery took the full cast to Detroit on January 19 for a

Si Siman, Lou Black, and Al Stone with transcription machines at KWTO. *Courtesy of Siman Family Papers, private collection of Scott Foster Siman and Jayne Siman Chowning.*

sales presentation. After two days of rehearsals, the crew presented a demonstration program to over two thousand company professionals at the Detroit Shrine Temple, and they later performed at a formal banquet and reception at the Statler Hotel. The *KWTO Dial* reported that the show was a "bigger hit than Babe Ruth in his prime."[30] One Ford-Dearborn official was later quoted as saying "It's a fine thing to meet entertainers who aren't show-offs, and who are so beautifully behaved."[31] The cast followed its Detroit success with Dearborn-sponsored trips to Indianapolis, Columbus, and Louisville.

George Morgan's *Robin Hood Flour Show* was a tailor-made transcription for International Milling Company from Greenville, South Carolina. Morgan was best known for his Columbia Records hit "Candy Kisses" which was number one on the *Billboard* folk chart for three weeks in 1949. When Morgan agreed to make the trip to Springfield once a month for cutting radio transcriptions, the *Grand Ole Opry* complained about Siman stealing their talent. However, the *Opry* didn't have a contract with Morgan. Siman told the *Opry* managers "We're all in the business, and the client expressed interest in Mr. Morgan." He reasoned that "this was a lot of money for George."[32] Backup bands on the show included Slim Wilson's Tall Timber Trio and other KWTO musicians.

A hefty mailbag full of letters from appreciative fans was a show's best ratings guide. Advertising agencies also created premium offers to test listener response to RadiOzark shows. Certificates, coffee cups, saucers, even kitchen utensils might be inserted into sacks of Robin Hood Flour to attract buyers to the product and get a sense of its success. Occasionally, Siman's crew got the star to help out by recording a tailor-made commercial for an open-end show. Local exposure to the artists on transcription shows was important, especially in areas needing help or merchandising. Siman believed it was "one of the greatest offers that country music's ever had ... you can't get the Sammy Davis Jr.'s and the Frank Sinatras to go out and do that sort of thing."[33]

When RadiOzark wanted to try for a larger investment in talent, Siman approached Red Foley in Nashville about doing an open-end transcription series, but Foley turned him down because he was having "complicated personal problems" at the time, and he was still doing the Prince Albert Show on the *Grand Ole Opry*.[34] Siman then went to Hollywood with John Mahaffey and director Bill Ring to approach Tennessee Ernie Ford's manager, Cliffie Stone, about producing a show for RadiOzark. Ford's recent history of two number-one hit records—"Mule Train" (1949) and "Anticipation Blues" (1950)—recommended him for the project.

In 1950, RadiOzark signed Ford to 260 open-end, quarter-hour shows produced in Hollywood by Siman, Mahaffey, Ring, and writer Don Richardson. It was an expensive production because of the travel involved and the high quality of guests signed for the shows. Siman went through Gardner Advertising in St. Louis to sell a regional arm of the *Tennessee Ernie Ford Show* package to Griesedieck Brothers Beer in St. Louis. The sale allowed RadiOzark to sell the show with two or three other sponsors, rather than being held up by an open-end arrangement without commercials. By the time they finished the transcriptions, they were out of debt, and the show was a winner.[35]

Top musicians signed up to back Ford, including Speedy West on guitar, Billy Liebert on accordion, Harold Hensley on fiddle, George Bruns on trombone, and Cliffie Stone on bass. Big-name guests also scheduled appearances on Ford's show, but they could only record transcriptions during the Christmas holiday because of touring commitments, which meant Siman and his colleagues missed a lot of holidays with their families. The RadiOzark crew would leave Springfield on Christmas day and spend the rest of the holiday season,

Si Siman and John Mahaffey raiding the pockets of Tennessee Ernie Ford. *Courtesy of Ralph Foster Museum.*

including New Year's Day, producing shows in Studio A of Sunset Studios in Hollywood. "We'd write for a month. Then we'd go to Hollywood and produce for a month. Then we'd come back to Springfield and start all over again. We were going back and forth to the West Coast like that for well over a year on those shows."[36] In 1950, the *Tennessee Ernie Ford Show* was syndicated to three hundred stations nationwide. Because the only way to broadcast the show was through RadiOzark Enterprises, it was a big moneymaker for Ford as well as RadiOzark.[37]

Another popular RadiOzark transcription project Siman produced in California was the *Smiley Burnette Show* starring the eponymous cowboy character-actor. Siman thought a variety show with Burnette might move country music toward middle-of-the-road listeners and thereby capture a larger share of the radio market. Burnette had grown up in Ravenwood, Missouri, about fifty miles north of St. Joseph. He performed in over a hundred B-movies from 1934 to 1950 as a comedic sidekick to Roy Rogers, Gene Autry, and Charles Starrett (the Durango Kid), averaging five to seven films a

KWTO Dial composite photo of Si Siman, Smiley Burnette, Gene Autry, and director John English on the movie set of *Whirlwind* (January 1951). *Courtesy of Melinda Mullins.*

year until 1952.[38] Smiley was an accomplished musician, singer, songwriter, player of one hundred instruments and builder of many, and a gourmet cook. He wrote more than four hundred songs, including several recorded by singers as varied as Bing Crosby, Ferlin Husky, and Leon Russell.[39]

Siman said he first saw Burnette perform at a Springfield theater in 1951. He went backstage after the show and asked Burnette if he'd like to do a radio show. Burnette invited Siman to join him on location for a movie he was doing with Gene Autry called *Whirlwind* (1951).[40] Siman had always wanted to see a movie in production and jumped at the chance to go. He lived with Burnette in a trailer in the California desert for a week and watched the movie crew make *Whirlwind*. Burnette did all the cooking while Siman planned the *Smiley Burnette Show* transcription series.

In May 1951, Siman went to Hollywood to begin recording the *Smiley Burnette Show* series with KWTO performer Shorty Thompson and a former KWTO hillbilly jazz group called the Whippoorwills, with Sweet Georgia Brown (Juanita Vastine) backing Burnette on the recordings. Siman thought the Whippoorwills gave the *Smiley Burnette Show* a jazzy western-swing flavor that made it a "palatable, metropolitan New York, Philadelphia, Boston-type acceptable radio show" that also promoted country.[41] The show's guest stars included Bob Crosby, Tennessee Ernie Ford, Sons of the Pioneers, Johnny Bond, Charles

Starrett, Ernest Tubb, Johnny Ukelele, Hank Williams, and Shug Fisher. During their time in Hollywood, RadioOzark transcribed 293 fifteen-minute *Smiley Burnette Show* programs. By July, Burnette was back in the Ozarks for a float trip on the White River with Siman, Mahaffey, Foster, and RadiOzark's Chicago advertising associate, Bill Ermeling. Subscribing stations reported heavy mail from listeners, indicating the *Smiley Burnette Show* was a big success.[42]

Although Siman had been working with RadiOzark for six years through his affiliation with KWTO, he was not yet an official partner in the enterprise. On May 1, 1952, he sent Foster, Cox, and Johnson a resignation letter that read: "Ever since I can remember, I have had a desire to become a partner in the business that I was a part of—probably much the same as each of you a few years back. [H]ad you stayed on the job you then had, chances are you would not be as successful as you are today. Be that as it may, for the past year I have been trying to become partner in RadiOzark, and it seems this is impossible."[43] His resignation would have been effective on June 1 but for a penciled note across the top of the letter: "Returned to Si Simon [sic] for further consideration." For the next eight years, Siman was a full partner in all the satellite companies KWTO formed.

KORN'S-A-KRACKIN'

Ralph Foster had long dreamed of creating a radio barn-dance program that would uniquely represent the Ozarks region, but he was a relative late-comer to the phenomenon. Fort Worth had debuted a barn dance on WBAP in January 1923, but the first consistently broadcast country music radio show in America began in 1924 with *National Barn Dance* out of WLS in Chicago.[44] Nashville's *WSM Barn Dance* followed in 1925, and was renamed the *Grand Ole Opry* in 1927.[45] Other notable shows during the 1930s included the *Wheeling Jamboree* on WWVA in Wheeling, West Virginia (1933), and the *Renfro Valley Barn Dance* on WHAS Louisville, Kentucky (1937).

Many other radio stations in cities large and small were cashing in on rural-oriented, local barn-dance programming during the 1930s and 1940s, including Atlanta, Dallas, Knoxville, Lubbock, and even New York and Philadelphia. Closer to Springfield, KMOX in St. Louis had the *Old Fashioned Barn Dance* (c. 1930), and KVOO in Tulsa had the *Saddle Mountain Roundup* (1939). Most radio listeners in the Ozarks would not have been able to receive the shows on KGBX/KWTO networks, but they may have tuned in to

Shreveport's *KWKH Roundup*, which came on the air in 1939 when the FCC raised KWKH to 50,000 watts of power.[46] The radio market for a local barn dance was still wide open in Springfield.

Longtime *Renfro Valley Barn Dance* performer Jim Gaskin defines the radio barn-dance formula: "There were certain classic barn dance acts: a brother duet, a sisters' group, a western group, the baggy-pants comedian who was usually a banjo picker, a quartet, the ballad singer, the love song crooner. There was also the boy/girl courtship situation. [They] always had that in the show. And all that was knitted together by the master of ceremonies, a folksy, down-to-earth kind of person."[47] All of these characteristics show up in the country music ventures that were to come to KWTO. In July 1941, the station premiered a stage version of *Korn's-a-Krackin'* at the Electric Theatre. Foster yearned to know how other stations were doing their barn-dance radio shows, so in January 1943 he sent KWTO staffers Leslie Kennon and Lou Black, performer Slim Wilson, and advertising executive Charles Brown to Nashville to "gain some firsthand information about a Saturday night barn dance of no small reputation, originating in that city."[48] Unlike the *Grand Ole Opry*, Foster planned to feature only local talent, but he hoped to learn from WSM-Nashville how a barn-dance show should work.

Christian County natives the Weaver Brothers and Elviry presented a stage version of *Korn's-a-Krackin'* from Joplin on Sunday, February 28, 1943. The celebrated "home folks of the screen" had returned to Springfield the previous year after a successful career in vaudeville and film. Their latest Republic Pictures film, *Shepherd of the Ozarks*, was still making the rounds in theaters when they appeared in Joplin. *Korn's-a-Krackin'* was so successful that it went on tour with KWTO entertainers in Kansas City, Wichita, Tulsa, Oklahoma City, and Dallas. Local KWTO staff artists on *Korn's-a-Krackin'* included about thirty-five musicians, comics, and singers, many of whom had been performing on KWTO for a decade. *Korn's-a-Krackin'* could not begin on Saturday nights until KWTO met transmitter requirements for nighttime broadcasts. The station also wanted affiliation with the Blue Network for supplementary programming. Regular radio broadcasts finally appeared on the KWTO daily schedule in March 1945, and in April it acquired a sponsor in Phillips Petroleum.[49]

The *Korn's-a-Krackin'* live radio show found a stage home at the Shrine Mosque, across from the KWTO studios on the 600 block of St. Louis Street. According to the *Dial* schedule, its first show at the Shrine Mosque was on Saturday, April 14, 1945.[50] George Earle warmed up the audience before the radio broadcast with crowd-pleasing promotions like he did with the *Breakfast* shows. He awarded prizes, chatted with audience members, and conducted entertaining events such as a bubble-gum-blowing contest where he measured the size of bubbles blown by contestants. Although KWTO was an ABC station, the larger network was not yet interested in country music. The Mutual Radio Network, however, picked up *Korn's-a-Krackin'* in January 1946. It expanded the show's broadcast coast-to-coast, making it the first regularly scheduled network radio show of its kind to come out of Springfield, Missouri.[51] By April, the *Dial* reported that *Korn's-a-Krackin'* was being broadcast to stations "as far away as Tacoma, Washington, in the northwest; Rochester, New York, in the northeast; Laredo, Texas, in the southwest, and Miami, Florida, in the southeast." New York state had the most individual stations carrying the program with six. All but two US states had at least one station carrying *Korn's-a-Krackin'*, and it was also broadcast in Canada. By July the number of Mutual stations subscribing to the show had increased to 140.[52] KWTO's radio barndance was a success, and it would become very important to Siman, since he was now a full-time employee of KWTO.

After forty-three consecutive weeks at the Shrine Mosque, the *Korn's-a-Krackin'* broadcast went on the road in July 1946. Lou Black managed and booked the tours with Siman's assistance. Ten Ozark towns received national exposure when their shows were broadcast to 140 radio stations nationwide. The seating capacities and acoustic quality of their auditoriums, as well as the availability of high-grade telephone lines, were the primary factors in choosing which towns to broadcast from.[53] The first stops were Eureka Springs, Arkansas; Warsaw, Missouri; Pittsburg, Kansas; and Carthage, Missouri. The farthest they traveled was Pampa, Texas—two hundred miles west of Oklahoma City. Sponsor organizations such as the American Legion, the Shriners, or the Chamber of Commerce often used a *Korn's-a-Krackin'* show as a local fundraising event. Chartered buses delivered the KWTO staff, including publicity director Siman, twenty-five entertainers, and the show's announcer (usually Bill Ring or Lou Black).[54] The *Dial* claimed that in some towns "hundreds of persons had to be turned away because of limited seating capacities."[55] Its Saturday night broadcast schedule put *Korn's-a-Krackin'* in direct competition with NBC's *Grand Ole Opry*.

Part of Siman's job was to sell KWTO radio and the Ozarks by taking clients, business-related people, and others on floating, fishing, and camping trips with Branson outdoors outfitter Jim Owen.[56] Siman took *Korn's-a-Krackin'* contest-winner Melvin Belew from McKinney, Texas, on a two-day fishing and floating expedition on the White River. At the end of the trip, Siman took Belew to a Saturday night radio broadcast of *Korn's-a-Krackin'* in Eureka Springs,

ABOVE

View of audience and stage during a *Korn's-a-Krackin'* broadcast at the Shrine Mosque. *Courtesy of Ralph Foster Museum.*

LEFT

Promotional ad for Korn's-*a*-Krackin', Mutual Radio Network's coast-to-coast radio show on KWTO. *Courtesy of Ralph Foster Museum.*

Arkansas. Later, in a lengthy column in his hometown newspaper, Belew wrote that Siman and a fishing guide had educated him about Ozarks streams and he had been treated to "the best fish and coffee I've ever tasted."[57] Belew's article was a successful outcome for Foster and Siman's promotion of *Korn's-a-Krackin'*, the radio station, and Ozarks tourism in general.

Beyond providing him with extra income and exciting work, Siman's association with KWTO and *Korn's-a-Krackin'* benefited him in other ways. Siman was out seeking "Queen of the Ozarks" beauty pageant contestants when he met his future wife, Rosanne Sprague, in May 1946. He suggested that she enter the contest, the winner of which would have opportunities "through radio, stage and motion picture contracts, to show the nation that the Ozarks are as famous for beautiful and talented girls as for beautiful scenery."[58] The grand prize was a Bulova watch, round-trip airfare to St. Louis, a three-day stay at the Hotel Jefferson, a complete fall wardrobe from Heer's department store, and $50 cash.[59] Sprague entered the contest and made it past the elimination judging, winning a "Reynolds Packet Pen," a record album, a glamour photo, and $10 cash.

Though Rosanne Sprague did not win the final contest, she did win Siman's heart when she went on a double date to the beauty contest's celebration dance with Junior Haden from KWTO's Haden Family band; his sister, Mary Elizabeth Haden; and Siman. As often happens with people who play music, the Hadens had never learned to dance. Siman took advantage of this situation on the double date and danced with Junior Haden's date, Rosanne. They began seeing each other regularly after that night. "I don't know about her but I fell in love ... I felt pretty bad [about the dance, but] Mary and Junior are still good friends of mine," Siman recalled.[60]

In late January 1947, Foster sent Siman to a month-long residency in advertising and sales at Simmonds and Simmonds Advertising Agency in Chicago in order to prepare him for an executive role as manager of RadiOzark and future KWTO-related projects. Daily letters to Rosanne (who was now "Rosey," "Posey," "Miss Posey," or "Miss Sprague") chronicle Siman's mission to learn advertising sales and find advertising clients. Ad executive Phil Tobias Jr. was in charge of training in Chicago. He introduced Siman to potential clients and arranged an itinerary full of options for a varied learning experience in the field.[61]

Siman's letters to "Rosie" from Chicago during February 1947 offer insights about important training that influenced his entire career in promotion and sales. On his way to Chicago, he stopped in St. Louis to have dinner with a contact in the local office of Simmonds and Simmonds. The next morning, he drove to Chicago in a snowstorm and immediately wrote to Rosie in anticipation of his first big day at the agency. On February 4, he told her that he had gotten his own office which included an electric typewriter, something he had never seen ("Boy, are they wonderful."). He used the typewriter on the rest of his letters to Rosie from Chicago.

Siman was busy with a regular schedule of learning about the various departments at Simmonds and Simmonds while also taking classes two days a week at Northwestern University. He wrote to Rosie on February 5 that he was busy every minute with a series of lectures on advertising and was grateful to Foster for providing him with the opportunity to observe a large advertising agency in Chicago: "Mr. Foster just called me and we had a nice chat regarding business etc.... I wish you could see me. I am on the 16th floor and have a very nice office of my own. This is the genuine article in the advertising field ... and I am lucky for the association." A former KWTO executive who now worked at the agency recommended him for a position. The thrill of being an important ad salesman in Chicago clearly tempted Siman for a while, but he did not want to leave Springfield. It wasn't the first time Siman passed up more money and prestige to stay in the Ozarks, nor would it be the last.

On February 11, Siman told Rosie that Foster was coming up for several days: "I will be very pleased to have him. I have several deals pending and I need his help." He pretended to pout because Rosie had not written as much as he'd like, adding: "How about you? Do I get that letter?" The next day, Siman wrote: "I have been out working on one of [the] many programs which RadiOzark has to offer and I am amazed that my success has been so good. I had lunch with so many bigshots that I was ashamed to let them know that I was little 'ole J[unio]r from the Ozarks."

During his tour of the advertising business in Chicago, Siman hoped to build contacts for selling his own shows: "I haven't forgotten [that] my mission is learning advertising and equipping old E. E. Jr. for the hard road ahead." RadiOzark's transcription business was set to expand, and Siman was already gathering ideas. On February 13, he told Rosie about touring the RCA and NBC recording studios and learning about the recording process. He also promised "many interesting stories" about television and recording. His letters suggest that Siman and Foster were already discussing possible options for their future in television. A day at RCA introduced Siman to record company and television executives who would later be helpful in acquiring recording contracts for country music performers Chet Atkins, Porter Wagoner, and the Browns.

Siman also reported on what he was learning about making effective sales pitches using printed brochures filled with facts, photos, and evidence of investment returns. He felt inadequate with this data-driven approach and admitted to Rosie that his preferred method was to make people like him enough to believe him, but: "that takes time and super salesmanship . . . and I have a lack of both. However, you can't stop ambition and already I have sold some and have 'hot' prospects for others." By the time he was preparing to leave for Springfield, Siman was telling Rosie about a lucrative partner deal for a radio show he was planning. He was excited about the things he had learned at the agency and was ready to put them to good use, but hoped his insecurities would not get in the way: "I am so in hopes that my hopes won't be throttled by my inability. Don't mistake me. I'm not suggesting that I can't do the job, but like everything I undertake, 'I WANT ACTION.'"

By the time Siman resumed his duties at KWTO in March 1947, the *Dial* was calling him "Super-salesman Si Siman."[62] Although one of RadiOzark's original purposes in 1944 was to be a booking agency, KWTO created its own "Artists Bureau," managed by Lou Black, specifically to handle bookings of *Korn's-a-Krackin'* and KWTO package shows, while RadiOzark moved on to other projects.[63] When Black took an extended leave in 1947, Siman took up the slack, handling all the Artists Bureau bookings in addition to his other duties as manager of RadiOzark. A KWTO Artists Bureau client could choose package deals with various KWTO musician groupings—three-, four-, or five-person acts—according to their event's needs. One five-person-act option was "spirituals, ballads, popular songs, hymns, and musical gems" from the Matthews Brothers, and additional talent could be added to each package.[64] The *Dial* assured potential clients that all groups had "a variety of routines and entertainment presentations that have been well worked out and put together with all the finesse of Class A vaudeville."[65]

Sometimes other entertainment events unrelated to KWTO would be sandwiched between KWTO's *Hayloft Frolics* and *Korn's-a-Krackin'*. On March 8, 1947, an African American "All-Star Colored Revue" was scheduled in conjunction with KWTO's *Hayloft Frolics* radio program and *Korn's-a-Krackin'*. On another evening, a square-dance contest between Howard Duncan's Queen City Eight and Austin Horn's Smooth Steppers occurred between the two shows.[66] On May 9, 1947, a second "All-Star All Colored" show featuring an "All-Colored Jitterbug Contest" with $50 cash prizes was scheduled before the *Hayloft Frolic*.[67] Siman likely booked all these events.

Siman's busy career took a brief recess on September 7, 1947, when he and Rosanne Sprague married, but business did not stop for long. On the way to

Si and Rosie's wedding photo. *Courtesy of Siman Family Papers, private collection of Scott Foster Siman and Jayne Siman Chowning.*

their honeymoon in Lake Geneva, Wisconsin, the couple stopped at Universal Records in Chicago so that Siman could wrangle a record deal for KWTO comedy duo Flash and Whistler. Siman liked the idea of doing business on his honeymoon, but he wasn't sure Rosie did, even though it was a "pretty quick deal."[68] He likely figured that Rosie knew what kind of guy she had married, and that she would have to get used to it sooner or later.

By October 1947 the Mutual network was broadcasting *Korn's-a-Krackin'* live from the Shrine Mosque in Springfield to 162 stations nationwide every Saturday night at ten through the KWTO studios. However, the Mutual network was slow to negotiate another contract with *Korn's-a-Krackin'* when their two-year contract expired in January 1948. KWTO broadcast a few shows without Mutual for a while with an erratic schedule, then recovered and struggled on with Mutual for another year. By June 1949, the *Dial* schedule shows *Korn's-a-Krackin'* broadcasting at 10 a.m. Saturdays without Mutual—its last days on the air.

In spite of its short network run of three years, the show contributed to promoting a "billion-dollar-a-year tourist industry" in the Ozarks, as suggested in the notes to a *Korn's-a-Krackin'* Christmas photo in the *Dial*: "Once a week during the tourist season it tells listeners from Connecticut to California about the quaintness of Eureka Springs or the charm of Bentonville, the wooded beauty of Waynesville or Gainesville, Ava or Vienna or Mount Vernon, or perhaps the scenic wonders in and near Neosho. It tells a coast-to-coast audience about its crowd of 10,000 at Rockaway Beach, 5,000 at West Plains, 3,000 at Mount Vernon."[69] *Korn's-a-Krackin'* also inspired Foster and Siman to start planning a live country music show on network television. However, according to Siman, "We didn't want another [*Grand Ole*] *Opry* because we could never catch up with them."[70] It would take several years before the *Ozark Jubilee* television adventure could begin, and the result would surprise the entire country music industry.

A GOLDEN MOMENT IN SPRINGFIELD MUSIC HISTORY

KWTO's reputation for good local country music grew after the national Mutual network broadcasts of *Korn's-a-Krackin'*. Musicians came to Springfield from other music hubs looking for better opportunities. When Chester Atkins came to KWTO in late 1946, he had worked for six radio stations in his short five-year career as a professional guitarist: WNOX in Knoxville, WLW in Cincinnati, WPTF in Raleigh, WLS in Chicago, WSM in Nashville, and WRVA in Richmond. He was poor and discouraged, and his wife Leona was pregnant. Just as Atkins was ready to go to work selling shoes in Chicago, his old friend Louis Innis called to tell him that KWTO was looking for a guitarist.[71] "People in country music were very friendly to each other. It was almost like a big employment agency; if anyone was out of work, there were a lot of people with their ears open," Atkins later recalled.[72] He traveled to Springfield and started working on *Korn's-a-Krackin'* and other KWTO radio shows with Slim Wilson and the Tall Timber Trio. He was happy to hook up with fiddler Zed Tennis, an old friend he had worked with at WLW in Cincinnati.

Born in 1924 near Clinch Mountain, Tennessee, Atkins joined his family's music-making at the age of six. As he became technically proficient on guitar, he started listening to radio programs and yearned to be immersed in music as a professional performer. When fifteen-year-old Atkins heard guitarist Merle Travis on WLW in Cincinnati, he began working on his own style of fingerpicking. He quit high school at the age of eighteen and got a job as a fiddle player and guitarist at WNOX radio in Knoxville, where he worked with future Country Music Hall of Fame members Henry "Homer" Haynes and Kenneth "Jethro" Burns. He worked with "Rambling Red" Foley at the WLS *National Barn Dance* in Chicago. Foley brought Atkins to the *Grand Ole Opry* in 1946, but he was released because the sponsor thought he didn't add anything to the show. Soon after joining the KWTO radio staff in 1946, Atkins met Siman. Atkins later recalled: "One of the real live wires on the scene was a young fellow named Si Siman. Meeting him would change my life."[73] Siman not only changed Atkins's life; he also changed his name. Upon meeting Chester, Siman said, "['Chester'] doesn't sound like a record artist to me. We're going to drop off the '-er' and [make it] 'Chet Atkins.'"[74] The name change was a welcome adjustment for Atkins: "I liked it because it was a like a nickname, something I'd never had before. The name seemed to be a natural and it stuck. Before long, everybody was calling me Chet, and I began using it myself when giving my name."[75]

Atkins loved the Ozarks and hoped to settle in Springfield: "The Ozark hills reminded me of home. Springfield was about the size of Knoxville, a small city, and I was comfortable with that. Although it was only 5,000 watts, KWTO was the dominant station of the region and a part of the Mutual Broadcasting Network, which was a national outfit. There were several good musicians on the staff: Zed Tennis, an accomplished jazz fiddle player; a good bass player, Bob White; and an excellent guitarist, "Speedy" Haworth.[76] It was a great place to work and I thought I had a chance to do something there."[77] Atkins and his wife Leona moved into a two-room tourist court cottage near Route 66. Their daughter Merle (named for Merle Travis) was born in Springfield on March 10, 1947. He felt at home in Springfield. He toured with Slim Wilson and the Tall Timber Trio during the week and played guitar every Saturday night on *Korn's-a-Krackin'*. Siman was "very supportive and enthusiastic" about Atkins's career, and Foster would always introduce him as "the greatest guitar player in the world."[78] Siman sent transcriptions of Atkins from *Korn's-a-Krackin'* performances to record labels hoping to get a contract for him.

Atkins was a big fan of guitarist Les Paul, who was working with his half-brother Jimmy Atkins in the Les Paul Trio.[79] Jimmy had told him that Paul might be coming through Springfield on his way from Chicago to California, and Atkins hoped they would meet. KWTO was familiar territory to Paul, who had performed there as "Red Hot Red" or "Rhubarb Red" before taking his ultimate stage name.[80] One day in 1947, while Les Paul and his wife, Mary

Ford, were on their way to KWTO for a visit, they heard Atkins playing guitar on Slim Wilson's show. According to Paul: "I'd told Mary the stories of how I started at KWTO with Sunny Joe [Wolverton], the programs we were on . . . So now we're driving through Missouri listening to my old Springfield station . . . and suddenly I hear this great guitar sound." Paul arrived at the station and wandered through its familiar hallways to find Atkins: "I look through the soundproof window and there's Chet playing his ass off on the air. He's got that Travis thumb thing combined with a bunch of my licks and his own stuff, and it's a great sound, a knockout." According to Paul, when Atkins took a break from playing, he came into the hall and said, "I know who you are. Hello, Les."[81]

Atkins had a different recollection of the meeting: "I looked out through the big double plate glass windows and saw this guy dressed up in a suit watching me with great interest." Atkins thought Paul might be a record producer checking him out: "I showed off some George Barnes licks, and then played Les Paul's arrangement of 'Seeing Nellie Home.' After the show I was knocked out to meet him. I think Les thought I knew it was him watching me and that I played one of his tunes as a way of saying I recognized him, but that's not the way it was."[82] According to Paul, the two guitarists talked about Atkins's brother, Jimmy, and an L-10 guitar Paul had sold to Jimmy many years ago to give to Atkins. Paul later called their first meeting at KWTO "the beginning of a very special friendship."[83]

While Siman was away on vacation, Lou Black fired Atkins from *Korn's-a-Krackin'* and touring with Slim Wilson. Siman later suggested that Atkins was fired for being late too many times.[84] Atkins thought it was because KWTO's new station manager thought his music was "too progressive and sophisticated for the KWTO audience."[85] Atkins moved to Colorado with Zed Tennis, who had also been fired, to play western swing with Shorty Thompson and his Saddle Rockin' Rhythm Band.

Prior to his firing, Siman had been working with RCA Victor's Al Hindle in Chicago to get Atkins a record contract. He had met Hindle during his residency at Simmonds and Simmonds earlier in the year and sent him a transcription of "Canned Heat" before going on vacation. Hindle forwarded the transcription to Steve Sholes in RCA Victor's New York office. Siman was thrilled to hear that Sholes was "very excited about what he heard" and hoped to make a deal soon.[86] Atkins got in touch with Sholes, who asked the guitarist if he could sing. He wasn't a singer, but he would try it out on the RCA recordings. Shorty Thompson insisted on going along to do the singing, but Atkins refused, and Thompson fired him in retaliation. Atkins sold his car and went to Chicago with Leona and Merle for his first recording session at RCA on August 11, 1947. Unfortunately, these first recordings with RCA Victor failed to show adequate sales. Atkins went back to Knoxville and worked with his old friends Homer Haynes and Jethro Burns at WNOX until May 1949, when "Homer and Jethro" moved to Springfield without him to work at KWTO.

After being fired from so many radio jobs, Atkins's move to Knoxville was a lifesaver. There he began performing with Mother Maybelle and The Carter Sisters, who recognized his brilliant musical talent and built up his wounded confidence. Mother Maybelle's guitar style blended well with his, and he liked Helen Carter's bass and accordion playing. He also loved June Carter's comedy style: "It wasn't long before she made me her straight man and I started doing comedy bits with her. She had to almost force me to do it at first, but once I got used to it, I liked it.... Working with her in that way is what finally helped me start overcoming the crippling shyness I'd always had."[87] When the Carters went to KWTO in the summer of 1949, Atkins went with them.

At KWTO, Atkins briefly overlapped with Homer and Jethro, before they returned to Knoxville in October 1949. He also reunited with his old friend Roy Lanham, a hillbilly jazz guitarist who was there with his band, the Whippoorwills. Lanham, influenced by jazz guitarists Charlie Christian and Django Reinhardt, had played with Homer and Jethro in a jazz quartet called the Stringdusters at WNOX Knoxville in 1939. He had recorded with the Delmore Brothers (with Jethro Burns) and western-swing artist Hank Penny during the 1940s and played guitar on the first studio sessions for Atkins with Nashville-based Bullet Records in 1946.[88] Before coming to KWTO in 1948, Lanham had been at WLW Cincinnati with Gene Austin, Merle Travis, Joe Maphis, Grandpa Jones, and Zed Tennis. Now it seemed like one big, happy family reunion right there at the crossroads on Route 66.

KWTO staff musicians admired the Whippoorwills' style, described in the *Dial* as experiments in "pseudo-comedy, burlesqued hillbilly numbers, exaggerated 'bop' (loosely defined as advanced jazz)" and "modern arrangements played on typically hillbilly instruments." Eventually they were working five days a week at various times of the day. The *Dial* noted that "The Drury and [Southwest Missouri State] college crowds are so Whippoorwill-happy that they keep the quartet busy three and four nights a week playing for sorority and fraternity groups."[89] The "Whips" stayed in Springfield for a year until they decided to seek opportunities in Los Angeles.[90]

Homer and Jethro on the cover of the *KWTO Dial*, August 1949. *Courtesy of Melinda Mullins.*

Atkins and his family moved into a little house on Pacific Street, about two miles away from the Carters, who were living in a large three-story brick home at 1727 E. Walnut Street, just off Glenstone. Atkins was making $50 a week at KWTO and $50 a night for personal appearances with the Carters. It was more money than he had ever made. He was riding a wave of personal and professional success: "My wife and I liked living in Springfield, we had good friends, and I was part of a successful act. This was the beginning of a good time for me. Even though our work schedule was exhausting, these were some of the happiest days of my life."[91]

The Carter Sisters and Mother Maybelle with Chet Atkins in the *KWTO Dial*, November 1949. *Courtesy of Missouri State University Digital Collections.*

The Carter Family featuring Chet Atkins became a favorite for KWTO listeners. The *Dial* expressed great excitement about the arrival of Mother Maybelle and her daughters June, Anita, and Helen. It also noted the return of Atkins, "an old KWTO favorite and an outstanding guitarist."[92] The group began performing three shows six days a week on KWTO, as part of Red Star Flour's *Cornfield Follies*. At the time, KWTO radio was broadcasting more than 150 live, weekly programs: "One group was setting up while others were leaving a studio, and perhaps a commercial was being done by a third group at the same time . . . there were two studios and an announcer's room, all continually busy," recalled Atkins. "Everybody was ambitious and each group tried to outdo the others on the air . . . We were all so busy that we had to rehearse new numbers on the road—working out a lot of them on Route 66."[93]

Atkins's stories of life on the road with the Carters are similar to those of many other musicians during the 1940s and 1950s: "We all traveled together in one car. We'd strap Anita's bass fiddle and our horn-shaped PA speakers on top, cram our other instruments, amps, stage clothes, and everything else in the trunk, pile in, and hit the road."[94] Atkins marveled at their survival, considering the large number of performers who died in car accidents on their sleepy, late-night journeys to the next gig.

Guided by audience enthusiasm, the *KWTO Dial* writers kept busy promoting their stars, Chet Atkins and the Carters. On October 12 and 13, 1949, Atkins went to RCA Studios in Chicago for two recording sessions with Helen and Anita Carter and Homer and Jethro. In November 1949 the *Dial* noted the "half-a-dozen new records to add to their growing collection of postwar RCA Victor releases, 'Kneeling Drunkard's Plea' (Helen wrote it), 'Why Do You Weep Dear Willow,' 'Walk a Little Closer,' and many others."[95] As a sign of full approval, Atkins is later called a "hill-born" KWTO star.[96]

Although Atkins was comfortable in Springfield, his gig at KWTO would not be permanent. On October 28, 1949, *Grand Ole Opry* stars Little Jimmy Dickens and George Morgan came to Springfield to do a concert at the Shrine Mosque. The Carter Sisters and Mother Maybelle with Chet Atkins shared the bill that night. Morgan was so impressed with their performance and popularity in Springfield that he went directly back to the *Opry* managers and encouraged a guest performance for Atkins and the Carters. Soon WSM was calling to offer the Carters a job—but without Chet Atkins. To the *Opry* managers, he was just another guitar player, and there were too many of them in Nashville. However, the Carters' manager and Maybelle's husband, Ezra "Eck" Carter, refused to bring them to the *Opry* without him.

Meanwhile, the group continued delighting their KWTO audiences with solid musical harmonies, creative instrumentation, and endearing hillbilly humor: "In the middle of a road show, Little Junie Carter would pluck from the audience a six- or seven-year-old girl and try to marry her off to Chet. Of course, June would admit to the little girl, Chester wasn't much to look at; [he] was, in fact, ugly as fifteen miles of bad road. But still, he needed a wife, and since the girl was already seven years old and not yet married, she couldn't afford to be choosy. Problem was, June would say, Chester didn't know how to do anything except play the guitar, so they'd never have any money."[97]

After about six months, WSM finally surrendered to the Carters' demands and KWTO offered to raise his weekly salary to $75. Atkins wanted to stay in Springfield: "After the turmoil Leona and I had been through moving from place to place, the job security at KWTO was very attractive, and something I knew I wouldn't have at WSM. Also, I had a strong feeling of loyalty toward Si Siman and Mr. Foster."[98] But an offer from songwriter and publisher Fred Rose for Nashville recording sessions ultimately broke his resolve to stay in

Cover of RadiOzark sales brochure for transcription programs of the Carter Sisters and Mother Maybelle with Chet Atkins. *Courtesy of Siman Family Papers, private collection of Scott Foster Siman and Jayne Siman Chowning.*

Springfield. In February 1950, just before the group left KWTO to perform on the *Grand Ole Opry*, Siman recorded transcriptions of the Carter family and Chet Atkins for RadiOzark.[99] The Carters took longer to do the show than most of his RadiOzark performers: "Sometimes it was Helen's nervous laughter or Anita's giggling that ruined a take, or sometimes Atkins simply called a halt to the proceedings. Where his playing was concerned, Chet was a perfectionist. Maybelle never complained, even when it took an hour to record a single fifteen-minute show. She was always happy for the chance to get it right."[100] Siman said his series with Atkins and the Carters was the most fun he ever had doing transcriptions: "We were doing it from midnight till four in the morning, and you had to laugh to stay with it and get up and not let it drop, you know. . . .

I was always in charge of comedy, trying to keep them from going to sleep on me."[101] Atkins remembered that the KWTO building had once been a mortuary, and "all of the singing jingles were done in the embalming room because of its echo-chamber effect."[102]

With Chet Atkins and family in tow, the Carters left Springfield for Nashville just in time for their first *Opry* show on May 29, 1950. Atkins said: "We didn't know it, but our years of wandering were finally over."[103] The *Dial* quoted June Carter as speaking for the whole family when she said: "Leavin' you folks is jist like leavin' a great big bowl of fried 'taters with the grease drained off! Honest—we've had the best time here, and loved every town we visited!"[104] That didn't soothe KWTO listeners, who wrote to the *Dial* in September asking why the Carters weren't on KWTO by transcription. The answer: "The Carters had time, before they left for Nashville, to transcribe only 39 15-minute programs. All these have run and no more are left."[105] Atkins paid tribute to Siman many times through the years: "He went out of his way to help me advance my career, and everything I did with RCA goes back to him. I'll always be in Si's debt for transforming me from Chester into Chet, and for helping me believe in myself."[106] Atkins and Siman would remain close friends the rest of their lives.

During a few magical months in late 1949 and early 1950, some of the greatest musical stylists of the twentieth century lived in Springfield, Missouri and worked on KWTO radio: Chet Atkins, the Carter Sisters and Mother Maybelle, Roy Lanham, Homer Haynes, and Jethro Burns. All played live music at a radio station with enough wattage and network coverage to introduce them to the entire country. Related performances at fairs and auditoriums offered them a degree of financial security, and they built lasting relationships with KWTO's "live wire," Si Siman. It had been a good time to be a musician in Springfield, Missouri. By the middle of 1950, all of them would be gone from KWTO. The next decade would bring the end of the "Golden Days of Radio," and network television would propel Springfield and the Ozarks into the spotlight as a national hub for country music.

CHAPTER THREE

The *Ozark Jubilee*:
THE CROSSROADS OF COUNTRY MUSIC

KWTO GENERAL MANAGER RALPH FOSTER'S successful experiment with the station's nationally broadcast network production of *Korn's-a-Krackin'* was proof that country music would sell to a broad listening audience. With postwar prosperity, changes in technology and transportation, and the increased interest in country music, Foster began planning for a network country music television show: what would become the *Ozark Jubilee*. He believed KWTO's *Korn's-a-Krackin'* barn dance was a model flexible enough to make the transition to a TV screen, and he had an enthusiastic partner in investor Lester E. Cox, who saw television's potential long before most people did. According to Cox's nephew Robert Lee: "I can remember his telling [me] that one day there would be a [TV] set in your house that would not only have sound but a picture to go with it. He spoke of coaxial cables and other things and my mother and dad would say that it was just 'too far-fetched.'"[1] The FCC had authorized television commercial broadcasts in 1941, but the business of World War II necessarily directed the nation's time and resources toward total war instead of television.

A few television shows had tried the barn-dance format in the late 1940s: *Village Barn* (NBC, 1948), *Hayloft Hoedown* (ABC, 1948), *Kobb's Corner* (CBS, 1948), and *Saturday Night Jamboree* (NBC, 1949). Chicago's *National Barn*

Dance also had a television version called the *ABC Barn Dance* in 1949 but, like the others, it offered only part-time or temporary coverage.[2] None of these programs achieved long-running success, likely because they lacked experience with articulating a visual presentation. Foster and Cox didn't have this know-how either, but they had Si Siman, who had become fascinated with TV while doing his Chicago advertising internship in 1947.

Although the First Golden Age of Television (1947–1960) was poised to change American life, plenty of people thought it would never last. In the 1940s, most American homes didn't have a television, and most cities didn't have a TV station.[3] Springfield's first stations—CBS affiliate KTTS and NBC/ABC affiliate KYTV—did not arrive until 1953. As soon as television became available in Springfield, Foster and Siman started the wheels rolling toward the first national country music network show by practicing on KYTV. A pool of experienced performers was already available thanks to *Korn's-a-Krackin'*, RadiOzark transcription shows, and KWTO daily radio programs.

One of the newer additions to KWTO, Porter Wagoner, had come from West Plains, Missouri. He was a meat cutter and part-time country music singer whose enterprising employer, grocery store owner Sid Vaughn, allowed him to conduct a KWPM radio broadcast from Vaughn's Supermarket. Trailways bus driver Joe Fite, who had provided transportation for the KWTO staff, heard Wagoner on the radio and told program director Lou Black about the singer's uncanny vocal resemblance to Hank Williams. Black drove to West Plains to hear Porter and talked to him about working at the station.

Meanwhile, Siman also heard Wagoner sing on KWPM when he was driving home from a Memphis business trip. "He'd take his apron off and come out behind the counter and had a microphone set up and say, 'Hello everybody! This is Porter Wagoner!' He'd do a little broadcast right from the store for fifteen minutes about big specials on pork chops and so forth. I was impressed by the way he sounded."[4] Siman stopped at Vaughn's Supermarket to meet Wagoner and asked Joe Fite to bring him to Springfield for an audition. Siman offered Wagoner $35 a week to perform on KWTO radio. Despite the fact that this was $15 less than he was making at Vaughn's, on September 29, 1951, Wagoner drove to Springfield in time to do a 5:30 a.m. radio program on KWTO the following morning.[5]

With more than forty performers doing 150 live quarter-hour shows at the station every week, KWTO must have been a thrilling introduction to the big time for Wagoner.[6] Siman thought Wagoner was as green as a country boy could be: "He was even having trouble tuning his guitar at this point in his life. He hadn't really flown yet. He'd had so little experience, but he was on the

Photo of Porter Wagoner autographed for Si Siman. *Courtesy of Siman Family Papers, private collection of Scott Foster Siman and Jayne Siman Chowning.*

shows and was very well received on KWTO."[7] A few months later, when Siman introduced RCA's Steve Sholes to a few recent recordings of Wagoner recorded at KWTO, Sholes expressed an interest in meeting him. Siman bought Wagoner a white suit and put him on a plane to New York for an audition. He came back to Springfield with a record contract for four sides.[8]

Sholes produced Wagoner's first two RCA Victor singles, "Settin' the Woods on Fire" and "Headin' for a Wedding," at KWTO in 1952. Wagoner was accompanied on piano by KWTO staff musician Paul Mitchell, a former member of Tommy Dorsey's orchestra and alumni of the Springfield Boy Scout Band; guitarist Speedy Haworth (Slim Wilson's nephew); Buster Fellers on fiddle; Bob White on bass; and George Rhodes on rhythm guitar.[9] The following year, Siman took Wagoner to Nashville for another round at RCA, but none of his first records had sold well. Wagoner continued to work on KWTO radio shows and personal appearances at full steam.

PREPARING FOR THE JUBILEE

Creating, producing, and supporting a country music network television show that would be nationally broadcast from Springfield, Missouri, was a massive undertaking for Siman and his KWTO colleagues. There was no beginner's guide to television production; it was new territory for all. It would require more than a year of preparation and planning—more talent, more equipment, more knowledge, and a lot more money—before Foster's dream could be realized. New companies that would protect the radio station from investment failure and manage an industry of artists, technicians, advertising, promotions, and publicity had to be formed. Siman entered into partnerships with Ralph Foster, Lester E. Cox, and John Mahaffey (Foster's nephew) to create several corporations with the sole purpose of acquiring, managing, and supporting a network television show.

The first of these was a firm that would license and publish original music written by local or visiting performers. In 1953, Siman was still making regular train trips to Hollywood to produce RadiOzark transcriptions of the *Tennessee Ernie Ford Show* and the *Smiley Burnette Show*. During one such trip, he happened to meet a few executives from Broadcast Music International (BMI)—the licensing company favored by the country music industry—in the dining car of the Super Chief streamliner train.[10] BMI's "broadened commercial exploitation of previously marginalized artists and sounds would have a revolutionary impact on the structure of the popular music industry" by spurring the professionalization of publishing, recording, and performance of country music and other popular forms.[11] The executives, including BMI president Carl Haverlin and BMI lyrics editor Bob Sour, told Siman they did not have a BMI affiliate in Missouri. They convinced him to start a publishing company in Springfield and volunteered to show him how to do it.

After talking it over with his partners in RadiOzark, Siman went to Nashville's leading music publisher, Fred Rose, for further advice about how to set up the publishing company. Rose ran Acuff-Rose Music, publisher of songs by Roy Acuff and Hank Williams Sr. Rose was almost like a father to Siman: "Instead of resenting competition, he was all for what I was interested in doing. So, he showed me, or taught me, a few of the who, whats, whys, and wheres" of the music publishing business.[12] Siman tried to emulate Rose: "He was, to me, the best in the business at the time, and that's what I wanted to be."[13] Using the models he learned from Rose and his new friends at BMI, Siman and his partners—Mahaffey, Foster, and Cox—signed with BMI and established Earl

Barton Music in 1953.[14] The partners then renamed KWTO's booking agency, Artists Bureau, calling it Top Talent. It was the first union booking license to be issued in Springfield.[15]

The most important link in the chain of corporations that would bring network television to Springfield was Crossroads Productions, Inc., the company that would make and manage important business decisions related to any phase of the *Ozark Jubilee*. Each of the Crossroads partners—Cox, Foster, Mahaffey, and Siman—invested 25 percent in the company. Foster was president and made major decisions about talent and personnel, Cox handled money issues, and Siman and Mahaffey, already the managing vice presidents of RadiOzark, were charged with the daily work of the *Jubilee* production. Mahaffey kept the books and made payments, and Siman managed everything else to do with the show. The partners called themselves the "four horsemen." Beyond them, Don Richardson was in charge of publicity, Andy Miller was the set designer, and Bryan Bisney was the show's director. Siman had some hand in almost everything having to do with the *Ozark Jubilee*, but always used the term "we" when talking about decisions made about the show.

Siman managed to talk his banker into giving him a $25,000 unsecured loan for his part of a $100,000 startup investment in equipment for the show. He felt vulnerable and nervous about getting a loan when the show's future was uncertain: "Had the show been canceled the first year I would have been bankrupt," Siman admitted.[16] When he brought the loan contract home for his wife Rosie to cosign, she didn't want to do it because the contract was worth more than their house. When Siman told her that if they didn't have the money for cameras they didn't have a show, Rosie conceded.

By December 1953, veteran KWTO radio performers were practicing Jubilee-style programming on local station KYTV. A weekly, hour-long *Ozark Jubilee* show began at eight on Saturday, December 26, 1953, marking the first official local *Jubilee* television performance. It featured Speedy Haworth, Bob White, Zed Tennis, the Willis Brothers (Guy on guitar, Vic on accordion, and Skeeter on fiddle), and a western-swing band called the Oklahoma Wranglers heading a cast of twenty.[17] The lead singer was Tommy Sosebee, a native of Greenville, South Carolina, who had worked on radio shows at several stations in the South.

A KWTO music program titled *The Paul Mitchell Show* soon appeared on KYTV's weekday schedule. It featured pianist Mitchell and an African American acapella group from Springfield called the Philharmonics, who had begun singing together at the Gibson Chapel Presbyterian Church in

Springfield following World War II. After winning a talent contest in 1951, they had a weekly radio show on KWTO's sister station, KGBX.[18] Yet another new live program with KWTO talent—*Home Folks Reunion*, featuring star-host Slim Wilson—began in April 1954. The resulting Saturday night schedule—*Ozark Jubilee* from eight to nine, *Home Folks Reunion* from ten to eleven, and ABC's *Royal Playhouse* and *Your Hit Parade* sandwiched in between—put KWTO in line with popular ABC network television programs, while exhibiting KWTO talent. These experiments in television would later serve as demonstrations of what could be done when Siman and his partners were trying to convince ABC-TV to sign the *Ozark Jubilee*.

THE STARS ALIGN

As Siman and his colleagues discussed future plans for acquiring a network contract, they reviewed a list of potential stars famous enough for headlining a nationally broadcast country music television show. RadiOzark had been working on transcriptions with Tennessee Ernie Ford in Hollywood, and his warm personality seemed like a good fit. Ford's top-ten hits—"Shotgun Boogie" (1951), "Mister and Mississippi" (1951), and "Blackberry Boogie" (1952)—further recommended him for the job.[19] And Red Foley's name also kept coming up. In early 1954, when Siman and his partners were considering the candidates, Foley's star was shining much brighter than Ford's. He was a star of the *Grand Ole Opry* and had a long history of hit records, starting with his own composition, "Old Shep," first recorded in 1935. His 1940s hits included "Smoke on the Water" (1944) and "Tennessee Saturday Night" (1949), while 1950 and 1951 saw four million-selling records: "Just a Closer Walk with Thee," "Steal Away," "Chattanoogie Shoe Shine Boy, " and "Peace in the Valley."[20]

Foley's solid performance history on radio shows would give him an advantage as a television host. He had started with the WLS *National Barn Dance* in 1930, helped to establish the *Renfro Valley Barn Dance* in 1937, and emceed the NBC radio broadcast of the "Prince Albert Show" on the *Grand Ole Opry* from 1946 to 1953. However, the partners worried about Foley's domestic problems—his wife had died by suicide in 1951 when Foley had an affair with a singer named Sally Sweet[21]—and his bad blood with the *Opry* management, which had contributed to his departure.[22] To make things worse, Foley had a drinking problem.

ABOVE

The Philharmonics, 1954: Eldridge Moss, Homer Boyd, George Culp, James Logan, Chick Rice. *Courtesy of Wayne Glenn.*

LEFT

Red Foley. *Courtesy of Siman Family Papers, private collection of Scott Foster Siman and Jayne Siman Chowning.*

Siman dismissed Foley's personal issues as political problems with the *Opry* and thought he simply needed a career boost: "I think Red at this point had outgrown the *Opry*."[23] In late 1953, RadiOzark decided to again try signing Red Foley for a series of syndicated radio shows. Because Siman had been to Foley's family store in Berea, Kentucky, and attended Berea College during the war, he seemed the best partner to meet with Foley and convince him to move to the Ozarks for a fresh start.[24]

At the time, Siman had a broken leg from sliding into second base during a KWTO Statics softball game, but Rosie drove him to Nashville for a series of meetings with Foley at the Andrew Jackson Hotel. Foley was feeling bad from having his teeth pulled. According to Siman: "We invited a third partner in to join us. His name was Jack Daniels, and I didn't have any pain and Red didn't have any pain."[25] On February 20, 1954, Foley signed an agreement with RadiOzark to do 156 open-end transcriptions and another agreement with Top Talent for bookings.[26] A sold-out welcoming party at the Shrine Mosque greeted Foley on April 23, with performances from Ferlin Husky, Jean Shepard, Tommy Collins, Arlie Duff, Grady Martin, and Porter Wagoner.[27] It was a new beginning for Foley and a coup for Siman and his colleagues.

Foley listed his Nashville home for sale and temporarily moved into the Siman family's ranch-style house on South Clay until he could get settled. He became a favorite of Siman's daughters, five-year-old Susan and three-year-old Jayne. He spent time with the kids, and once helped Jayne remove a baby tooth. Jayne remembers coming out of her bedroom one morning and finding Foley asleep on the couch. When she woke him up with a kiss on the cheek, tears came into his eyes. Rosie was six months pregnant with the Simans' son Scott, and Foley helped her clean the kitchen every night after dinner. Eventually Foley settled into a new home in the fashionable Brentwood neighborhood of southeast Springfield.

After Foley moved to Springfield, Crossroads partners offered him a contract for an upcoming position as the star-host of the ABC-TV version of the *Ozark Jubilee*.[28] The financial terms of this contract varied according to whether or not the network program had commercial sponsors. Commercial sponsorship of television shows was relatively new in the early 1950s. A new program might begin on a sustaining basis to attract sponsors as it became more popular. Foley's fee for such an option would be a minimum of $350 for a one-hour weekly show. With advertising, his fee would be $750 for the same show. Foley's lower sustaining fee would provide the station with a window of relief before major sponsors signed on for the entire show.[29]

Jean Shepard. *Courtesy of Siman Family Papers, private collection of Scott Foster Siman and Jayne Siman Chowning.*

Trade publications of the period took note of country performers who were migrating to the Ozarks. The music business press began calling Springfield the "Crossroads of Country Music."[30] On April 17, 1954, *Billboard* announced Red Foley's decision to headline the *Ozark Jubilee* and observed that the move was "the first step in a campaign on the part of RadiOzark and other country and western interests in Springfield to build the city into a folk capital."[31] Country music performers set their sights on opportunities in Springfield, Missouri, and began flooding into town.

Country singer Jean Shepard moved to Springfield in May 1954, with a Capitol Records contract already in hand and a smash-hit duet with Flat River, Missouri, native Ferlin Husky: "A Dear John Letter" (1953).[32] Shepard and Husky were the two best-selling country artists at Capitol Records. At nineteen years old, Shepard was the youngest female artist to have a number-one country single, an honor she held for twenty years. When Shepard felt that "A Dear John Letter" was "waning in popularity," she wanted to go her own way: "I asked Ferlin whether he was going to head to Springfield or to Nashville to try out for the *Opry*. If he decided to stay in Springfield, then I would go to Nashville. He came to Nashville and I moved to Springfield."[33] However, although Ken Nelson wanted him to start at the *Opry*, Husky did not go to Nashville right away. Instead, he came Springfield at the request of Red Foley, who wanted Husky to be his comedic sidekick similar to the role Rod Brasfield had played in the "Prince Albert Show" on the *Opry*.[34] Husky went to work on the local *Jubilee* television show in 1954, sometimes as his humorous hillbilly alter ego Simon Crum. Shepard started on the *Ozark Jubilee* local television show as soon as she got to Springfield, also in 1954, along with tall, lanky honky-tonk singer Hawkshaw Hawkins.[35]

Foley's Prince Albert Show band left the *Grand Ole Opry* to back up Foley as the "Crossroads Boys" on the local *Ozark Jubilee* radio and television shows and RadiOzark transcriptions. Foley also recorded a new album with them for Decca Records in the KWTO studios. The band kept a full calendar of performances, often appearing on the road as the Slew Foot Five. Guitarist and fiddle player Grady Martin had been recording on Decca since 1951.[36] He began his career as a teenage prodigy the age of fifteen. He played guitar on Foley's hit recordings of "Chattanoogie Shoe Shine Boy" and "Birmingham Bounce." Fiddle player Tommy Jackson also came to Springfield with Foley's band after playing on recordings for many artists, including Hank Williams. Jimmy Selph was a versatile musician and singer who toured with the *Grand Ole Opry* during the 1940s. Steel guitarist Bud Isaacs introduced the pedal steel guitar to country music and would play on Webb Pierce's 1954 hit "Slowly." Isaacs performed on the road with Foley, as well as Little Jimmy Dickens and Chet Atkins before coming to the *Jubilee*.

The stars were moving toward Springfield, Missouri, but the *Jubilee* would still need a bigger studio before it could seek a network television contract. The KYTV facilities were too small to accommodate the stage and audience for a large, live variety television show. In June 1954, Foster, as president of Top Talent, Inc., signed a six-year lease with the national Fox Theatre chain for possession of Springfield's unused, 1,100-seat Jewell Theatre, half a block south of Route 66 on Jefferson Street. Foster had big plans for the space. It would be used for "an elaborate country music show" starring Red Foley, but he also hoped to install recording studios for RadiOzark and rent the theater for conventions and other music business concerns.[37] Contractors completely

Grady Martin. *Courtesy of Ralph Foster Museum.*

remodeled the space to make room for lights and necessary studio equipment. Major expenses included getting enough electricity into the theater to originate a television show and renting a building across the street for a space to build sets for each week's show. A staff of around eighty people, including directors, musicians, and writers, was hired to get the show ready for the first broadcast.

On Saturday, July 17, 1954, Foley hosted his first KWTO radio program of the *Ozark Jubilee* from the stage of the newly renovated Jewell Theatre. The supporting cast included Hawkshaw Hawkins, Jean Shepard, Grady Martin, the Foggy River Boys, Slim Wilson, and Porter Wagoner. Other groups on the show included Wilson in his rube comedy duo Flash and Whistler with Floyd "Goo Goo" Rutledge, who had been a former colleague in musical comedy with vaudeville-and-film stars the Weaver Brothers and Elviry. The *Cash Box*—the first trade magazine to visit the *Jubilee*—highly recommended it after attending the July 17 show: "If capacity houses, a fresh format, and a well-balanced roster of top recording artists, plus a dash of Red Foley is any indication of a good show, then the *Ozark Jubilee* can easily be included as one of the top country music shows being aired today.... [It] has the strongest nucleus of any new country music show today, and from all observation should continue to grow at a record-breaking pace."[38] Two weeks later, the ABC radio network picked up the show for Springfield's first coast-to-coast live weekly radio broadcast since *Korn's-a-Krackin'*.[39]

Slim Wilson was involved in nearly every stage of the *Jubilee* radio and television shows—before and after it acquired network status—as he had been with KWTO radio shows since the early 1930s and was "the biggest star in this part of the country."[40] On the September 25, 1954, *Jubilee* radio show, Wilson celebrated his twenty-five-thousandth KWTO broadcast. Ralph Foster awarded him a gold quarter-hour transcription of his 24,999th program to commemorate the occasion.[41] A week later, Wilson signed a Decca recording contract.[42] Many other artists who appeared on the *Ozark Jubilee* were on Decca, including Roy Acuff, the Foggy River Boys, Red Foley, Wanda Jackson, Webb Pierce, Ernest Tubb, and Kitty Wells.

As Red Foley settled into the *Ozark Jubilee* stage show and radio broadcasts from the Jewell Theatre, Porter Wagoner met Springfield songwriter and milk-truck driver Johnny Mullins at a nearby drugstore lunch counter. Mullins frequently hung around backstage, hoping to sell a song or two. He became acquainted with Wagoner and pitched a song that was partly inspired by stargazing after a particularly frustrating songwriting night. That view inspired Mullins to write the remainder of "Company's Comin.'"[43] Wagoner encouraged Mullins to bring him a demo. Mullins immediately recorded it with KWTO musicians at a small local studio and presented it to Wagoner and Siman at KWTO the next day. Siman evidently brought Foley in to hear the song. "As Johnny's voice faded out, Red looked up and exclaimed, 'That's a hit if I ever heard one, Porter. If you don't record it, I will.'"[44] Siman brought RCA producer Steve Sholes down from New York to record Wagoner performing "Company's Comin'" in the KWTO studios with Speedy Haworth and Don Warden.[45] A blind man named Bill Mount provided a percussion emphasis by strapping wooden blocks onto his knees.[46] RCA released the record on September 3, 1954. It was the first hit for Wagoner, for Mullins, and for Siman and Earl Barton Music.[47] The song won Mullins and Siman a BMI award for being one of the top songs of 1954.[48]

Wagoner recorded his biggest career hit, "A Satisfied Mind," in the KWTO studios, along with another future number-one record, "Eat, Drink, and Be

Earl Barton publication of sheet music for Porter Wagoner's hit song "Company's Comin'," written by Springfieldian Johnny Mullins. *Courtesy of Siman Family Papers, private collection of Scott Foster Siman and Jayne Siman Chowning.*

Merry." Wagoner paid the musicians himself: "The two of those [number-one records]—[including] record production, musicians, studio cost, over-dubbing, all that stuff that they do today—cost me $82.80. . . . I paid union scale, and it was $40.40. I had two musicians and myself."[49] Unfortunately, the RCA contract Siman had acquired for Wagoner in 1952 had expired, meaning that there could be no distribution of the record. Siman called Steve Sholes and offered to put the record out with no expense if they renewed the contract. RCA Victor had never had a hit with an artist whose contract had expired. Siman took the master to Nashville, where Sholes arranged another agreement with Wagoner, gave him a small raise, and reissued the single. Wagoner was now known in the *Cash Box* as "one of RCA Victor's fastest-rising young backwoods warblers."[50] Once again, Siman was the spark that had started the fire.

GETTING THE ABC TELEVISION NETWORK

In late 1954, Crossroads Productions decided they were finally ready to pursue a network television contract for the *Ozark Jubilee*, but nobody on the staff knew how to begin the process. KWTO vice president Les Kennon phoned one of his contacts at ABC radio for suggestions of who to approach for a television show. According to Siman, Kennon's contact asked a lot of questions about how much experience they had with television.[51] The answer was that they didn't have any. They were assuming that there wasn't much difference between a successful, nationally broadcast radio show and a successful, nationally broadcast television show. "We [were thinking that we] would follow what success we'd had with syndicated radio and make a blueprint of it for television."[52] As Ralph Foster and ABC-TV affiliate KYTV had already pioneered the *Ozark Jubilee* on local television, they could depend on KYTV's engineers, technicians, and other people's talents to pull them through any problems.

The first step in securing a contract was to send Siman to a get-acquainted meeting with ABC-TV officials in New York, who knew very little about Springfield or the Ozarks region. Siman noted their Manhattan-centric worldview and joked that a New Yorker's vague notion of Springfield, Missouri, was that it was a place somewhere south of Times Square.[53] He realized that getting a contract with ABC-TV would require a substantial sales effort from the Crossroads team. On his next trip to New York, Siman brought with him two millionaires, Foster and Cox, and two "worker bees," Mahaffey and Les Kennon, to meet with ABC executives and the entire programming department.

ABC-TV had only been on the air since February 1953, when the FCC lifted a ban on pending station licenses and provided opportunities for new television stations all over the United States. Its New York City headquarters and studios were in the former location of Durland's Riding Academy on 66th Street.[54] Although the building had not been used as a horse stable since the mid-1940s, ABC-TV founder Leonard Goldenson claimed that it still smelled like horse manure, likely referring to the position of ABC in the network television market: "That scent was all too plain to Wall Street and to Madison Avenue, where we were regarded as a lost cause. We had no hit shows, no stars, and nothing in prospect but struggle."[55] ABC had only fourteen affiliate stations, compared to CBS's seventy-four and NBC's seventy-one, was third in the ratings, and was deeply in debt.[56] Although the cost of programming was the same for all three networks, CBS and NBC brought in five times as much advertising revenue as ABC, a distant third in the ratings and desperately in need of programming.

By 1956, ABC president Robert E. Kintner and his colleagues had created a seven-year plan to catch up to CBS and NBC by increasing billings and programs.[57] The *Ozark Jubilee* would be a survivor, as well as a victim, of this plan throughout its broadcast life.

At the moment when Crossroads was making its case to ABC-TV for a country music television show, most of ABC's programming schedule was on between six and nine in the evenings, eastern time. Country music was an inexpensive option that could be placed in a competitive time slot and would serve specialized audiences. Siman probably wasn't aware that ABC had few options and needed the money. He was focused on getting a network television contract and didn't care what network was willing to offer them one or why.

In their meeting with the Crossroads partners and associates, ABC asked specific questions about the proposed television program: How was it unique among existing shows? What was its potential for high ratings? How long would a show be and how frequently would it air? How much would it cost to produce? How much publicity would it require? What sponsorship possibilities did they see?[58] Siman and his team likely presented sample scripts and a plan for the show. A part-time KWTO engineer produced sixteen-millimeter film clips from shows on KYTV and having Red Foley as the host would certainly have been an advantage, but Crossroads partners had little else to recommend themselves for network television except enthusiasm. They had a good story about local success and a good salesman in Si Siman. "We told them how great it would be if they were the first network to do a regular country music show on network TV coast-to-coast."[59] According to Siman, the Crossroads team "really sold ABC a pig in a poke. . . . We were so positive and so excited that they bought it."[60] On December 24, 1954, ABC television network president Robert E. Kintner announced the completion of negotiations with Ralph Foster for a one-hour television program, *Ozark Jubilee*, to begin three weeks later, on January 22, 1955.[61] The contract contained a short-notice, two-week network cancellation option for six years. Siman felt like he was signing his life away, but he would not let himself think about failure. It was a dream about to be fulfilled for Siman and his partners at Crossroads Productions. They had much to celebrate.

The Crossroads partners bought three television cameras, costing around $25,000 each, and all the other necessary equipment they couldn't rent from KYTV.[62] Renovations of the Jewell Theatre were completed, the performers began rehearsing, and the press was primed. The biggest event ever to hit Springfield was going to happen in only three weeks. However, about two weeks after signing the contract with ABC, the network called to cancel the show because of transmission problems out of Springfield. There were no coaxial cables or microwave facilities in the area, and the polarity was such that transmission could come in to Springfield, but it couldn't go out. Siman explained the problem in simpler terms: "we can suck but we can't blow." This technical issue wouldn't stop them. Lester Cox had helped the University of Missouri get a television station, and it was on the cable line that ran between St. Louis and Kansas City. Crossroads would broadcast the *Jubilee* from KOMU in Columbia until AT&T installed network cables and reversed the polarity in Springfield. It was a very expensive project for AT&T, who, luckily, did not know that ABC could cancel the *Jubilee* at any time with a two-week notice. Siman likened the affair to a bunch of hillbillies "playing poker at the hundred-dollar table."[63]

THE OZARK JUBILEE GOES COAST TO COAST

The nationally televised premiere of the *Ozark Jubilee* on ABC-TV ran as scheduled on January 22, 1955, but for thirteen weeks the entire cast and crew had to travel to Columbia on a weekly basis to perform the show at KOMU. This required getting on buses at KWTO at 4 o'clock in the morning, driving three hours to Columbia, rehearsing the show they'd been rehearsing all week, going live on the air for an hour at about six o'clock in the evening, packing up, getting dinner in Jeff City at Adcock's Café, and driving three hours back to Springfield. By the time they got home, it would have been a twenty-four-hour period.[64]

In the first few months of 1955, amid the frustrations and excitement of the new *Ozark Jubilee* television show, Red Foley and Jean Shepard each had a top-five hit on the *Billboard* country chart with their recordings of "A Satisfied Mind," and Porter Wagoner's recording of the song went to number one. Although Earl Barton had not been behind these hits, Si Siman was the one who had made them happen. The *Jubilee*'s first year on ABC television would feature Wagoner singing two hit songs, "Company's Comin'" and "A Satisfied Mind."

The *Ozark Jubilee* moved into its television home—the Jewell Theatre in Springfield—on April 30, 1955. Missouri governor Phil Donnelly proclaimed it "Ozark Jubilee Day" across the state and Crossroads threw a grand opening celebration. Springfield Chamber of Commerce president Durward Hall presented US Representative Dewey Short with an Ozark Hillbilly Medallion, and a standing-room-only crowd watched as celebrities flowed into the Jewell.[65] St. Louis Cardinals baseball star Stan "the Man" Musial attended the show, as did Tennessee governor Frank Clement, a friend of Red Foley. After the *Ozark Jubilee*'s Springfield debut, Cox and Foster hosted a reception at the Colonial Hotel in honor of Foley, Siman, and Mahaffey.

Merchants used the event to advertise their products. A full-page newspaper ad for Plaster's Master Market included a large graphic of the *Jubilee* cast waving from a buckboard wagon and text congratulating the *Jubilee*: "This week-end we're celebrating the return of Red Foley, his band, The Foggy River Boys, Pete Stamper and all of the OZARK JUBILEE cast . . . by giving you some red-hot T-V SPECIALS . . . T-V standing for TOP VALUE!"[66] Another Springfield newspaper featured a two-page spread of ads for nine different television sales-and-repair businesses and one for Aunt Martha's Corn Crib restaurant at 302 South Jefferson, a few doors down from the Jewell Theatre.[67] A banner at the top of the two pages thanked the *Jubilee* for making Springfield the "T-V COUNTRY MUSIC CENTER OF AMERICA," and the Corn Crib ad invited readers to "Come on over and join the crowd after the show."[68]

A *Springfield Daily News* columnist pronounced the *Jubilee* "a major 'first' for Our Town": "What with its TV rating rising higher and higher with each network telecast, *Jubilee* officials see the program as one of the city's major tourist attractions."[69] The estimated audience for each week of the hour-long network portion of the show was twelve million viewers.[70] Tickets cost one dollar and could be purchased by mail, but the *Ozark Jubilee* became so popular that they were sold out a year in advance as Springfield motels, hotels, and tour bus companies bought them for customers who used their services. The *Jubilee* became a "major shot-in-the-arm to the tourist industry of the Ozarks," attracting tourists coming by bus tour and car. Often, thirty-five to forty different US states were represented by auto license plates around the Jewell Theatre.[71] Audience members at the broadcasts held up signs identifying their hometowns. Audience member Randle Chowning, future co-founder of the rock band the Ozark Mountain Daredevils, remembers his cousin tearing up a bed sheet and using black shoe polish to write "Ulysses, Kans" on it so they could have a sign for the cameras.[72]

In the 1950s, an indication of a television show's success was a full mailbox. Following the first *Ozark Jubilee* broadcast, viewers from forty-five states

Ozark Jubilee USA audience members holding up signs identifying their hometowns. *Courtesy of Siman Family Papers, private collection of Scott Foster Siman and Jayne Siman Chowning.*

sent more than 25,000 cards and letters to the show.[73] The producers put up a real mailbox on the set, with piles of real letters flowing out onto the floor. The show averaged 6,000 letters a week.[74] Siman claimed that they "did listen to the mail; we did review every piece of mail that came in, and it was monstrous."[75] He had to hire part-time workers to sort through the letters.

Siman attributed the *Jubilee*'s success to a combination of luck and good timing; television was new, and people wanted to watch country music shows. Syndicated urban columnists reported on the *Jubilee* as a trend-setting television phenomenon and local success story—sometimes, during its early years, in rural or hillbilly terms.[76] New Yorker Charles Mercer wrote: "A fellow who galloped in from the Ozarks the other day reported that the city of Springfield, Mo., used to be noted for butter, eggs and country music. Now, says he, it's noted for country music, tourists, eggs, and butter."[77] An article about the *Jubilee* in *TV Guide* was titled "'Tain't Hillbilly, Neighbor! It's 'Country Music' That's Making a Splash on TV."[78] Gossip columnist Earl Wilson visited the *Jubilee* and commented, "Down in the catfish country, I got some good news for Jackie Gleason and Perry Como. They needn't worry about their TV rating battle here because many Ozark folks don't watch either one of them."[79] And columnist John Lester wrote that KWTO was "dedicated to the complete over-running of all radio and TV by country music" and "making Springfield, MO., the world-center of hillbilly, folk or country music."[80]

Red Foley and the Crossroads staff open mail from fans of the *Ozark Jubilee*. *Courtesy of Siman Family Papers, private collection of Scott Foster Siman and Jayne Siman Chowning.*

Springfield was a hub of exciting activity during the mid-1950s, with performing artists, national advertising agency personnel, sponsors, and ABC executives flying back and forth between Springfield and New York, Nashville, or Los Angeles. One observer commented that "more cowboy-booted guitar players breeze around in Cadillacs in Springfield than in any other place its size,"[81] and some of these had one—or a few—million-selling records. The regional Springfield airport was small, with limited flights serving what became a heavy influx of travelers. On Saturday nights the streets were packed with cars before and after the *Jubilee*, and excited tourists from dozens of states and local towns milled about on the sidewalks. Route 66 ran straight through downtown on St. Louis Street, half a block from the Jewell Theatre. Combined with normal through-traffic on Route 66, congestion could be a nightmare for drivers as well as Springfield police. Auto traffic and parking were significant problems downtown.

OZARK JUBILEE PICKERS AND SINGERS

Hopeful talent who came to Siman for a slot on the *Jubilee* had increasingly slim chances of getting on the show unless they had a recording contract or a successful performance history. When Siman interviewed young or inexperienced candidates, he asked them what they could offer the show or how their performance could fit a concept: "They had to have a real reason. I would tell them, give me an idea why I should put you on. If you've got a new record or a new song, and you're trying to pitch it to the public, I'm interested. But I want to picture it as the viewer will see on television, and since we're going to do the whole song, it has to fit the format that we're doing."[82] *Jubilee* performer Billy Gray encouraged his friend Willie Nelson to audition, but Nelson was rejected for lack of experience and ended up working as a dishwasher at Aunt Martha's Corn Crib restaurant until he could get enough money to go back to Fort Worth, Texas.[83] Sometimes the team planned the entire show around bigger stars such as Eddy Arnold, Gene Autry, or Ernest Tubb.

One of the *Jubilee* performers who came to Springfield was guitarist John "Bucky" Wilkin, whose mother, Marijohn Wilkin, had quit her teaching job in Texas to become a songwriter and tour with Foley. Marijohn and Bucky Wilkin traveled from Texas to Springfield once a month so that Bucky could perform in a spinoff program for younger entertainers, the *Junior Jubilee*, which premiered in November 1955.[84] "A lot of us came to Nashville by way of Springfield, Missouri," Wilkin recalled, "because that was where the big country music show was."[85] Wilkin got her start writing for *Ozark Jubilee* performers Foley and Wanda Jackson, and was soon serving as the artists' contact for Earl Barton Music nationwide.[86] She met Decca recording artist Mitchell Torok in Springfield, and he recorded the first of her many songs. *Junior Jubilee* booking agent Lucky Moeller got Marijohn an interview with Jim Denny, who signed her with Cedarwood Music in Nashville, where she wrote "The Long Black Veil" with Danny Dill for Lefty Frizzell. She also wrote Stonewall Jackson's "Waterloo" with John D. Loudermilk. Wilkin, Dill, and Loudermilk are all now in the Nashville Songwriters Hall of Fame.

Managing *Jubilee* performers was a challenge, but competition ensured a constant supply of good talent from other country music shows around the country. A path to success for many country music performers of the era was from regional barn-dance radio shows to Springfield's *Ozark Jubilee* to Nashville's *Grand Ole Opry*. Several acts came from the *Louisiana Hayride*, a weekly radio barn-dance show that began in 1948 as a live stage broadcast from Shreveport,

Louisiana's KWKH AM.[87] *Hayride* producer Horace Logan constantly competed with the *Grand Ole Opry* by taking chances on new talent, resulting in an entirely different "style and attitude."[88] The *Hayride* cast included Hank Williams and Elvis Presley at varying times.[89] Logan viewed the *Opry* management as being closed-minded and petty, and he bitterly claimed that "never once in its long, glorious history has the *Opry* ever created a single star or launched a single career that I know of. The *Hayride*, on the other hand, created dozens of stars and launched hundreds of careers."[90] However, Shreveport could not support *Hayride* artists with booking agencies, music publishers, or record companies, and didn't have a television broadcast to compete with the *Ozark Jubilee*. Thus, many *Hayride* performers drifted north to Springfield: "From the point of view of its artists, one of the greatest mistakes that KWKH management made was its failure to enhance the station's outreach through the use of television."[91]

The career path of *Louisiana Hayride* member Billy Walker was familiar to many Texas performers from the 1940s and 1950s.[92] Influenced by a Gene Autry movie, Walker began singing at age thirteen. He hung out in Texas dance halls where Bob Wills and His Texas Playboys were performing; there, Playboys guitarist Eldon Shamblin gave Walker his first guitar lesson. At the age of fifteen, he entered and won an amateur talent contest at KICA radio in Clovis, New Mexico, and was soon doing his own radio show at the station while he played in various bands around Texas. In 1949 he joined the *Big D Jamboree* live broadcast on KRLD in Dallas.[93]

Walker signed a contract with Columbia Records in 1951, and moved to Shreveport the following year, after *Louisiana Hayride* member Webb Pierce influenced Horace Logan to hire him. While Walker soon had his own live television show airing three days a week, he could see that things were happening in Springfield. Performing at an *Ozark Jubilee* radio show in the fall of 1954, he saw that "thousands of people were moving through there. I could see the future was TV."[94] He transitioned to the network television show on its first bus trip to Columbia but kept his contract at the *Louisiana Hayride* until July 1955 while still making regular trips from his home in Waco for the *Jubilee*.[95] In November, Walker finally moved to Springfield; he toured with *Jubilee* performers and did several KWTO radio shows a day. Walker was a regular performer on Saturday night's ABC-TV *Jubilee* show until he moved to Nashville to work on the *Grand Ole Opry*, the next big thing on the path after the *Jubilee*.[96] Billy Walker was a cast member in four of the most important southern barn-dance variety shows of the mid-twentieth century, but only one of them, the *Ozark Jubilee*, was on network television.

Jim Ed and Maxine Brown. *Courtesy of Ralph Foster Museum.*

The Browns—Jim Ed, Maxine, and Bonnie—joined the *Hayride* in 1954 as regular cast members under contract and had two top-ten hits, "Looking Back to See" and "Here Today and Gone Tomorrow." For a while they traveled back and forth from Springfield to Shreveport, doubling-up on appearances on the *Ozark Jubilee* and the *Louisiana Hayride*. Ultimately, a move to the *Jubilee* was worth risking backlash from embittered *Hayride* producer Horace Logan, who had given them their first break and considered them "ungrateful." The *Ozark Jubilee* was the group's "real breakthrough," as they received the national television exposure that KWKH could not offer. Siman was excited to add them to his list of regular guests; he called them on the road after their first appearance and said, "You Browns were the hit of the show last week. You should see the fan mail that's waiting for you. It's stacking up all over the place."[97]

The Browns came to the *Jubilee* in 1955 with a Fabor Records contract, but the company wasn't paying them. Siman approached the group and said, "I hear you kids are looking for a label. Maybe I can help. Which label do you prefer?" Jim Ed Brown answered, "Any good one that'll take us." According to Maxine, "Si looked at me with a twinkle in his eye, as if to say that he knew all about the hard times we'd been through." Before Siman shopped other labels for them, he asked Capitol producer Ken Nelson if he would pick up legal fees involved in getting the Browns off Fabor. Although Nelson liked the Browns, the label did not want to get into a legal fight over them. Siman had a good relationship with Steve Sholes at RCA and felt loyal to him for their work with Atkins and Wagoner. When he suggested RCA to Maxine, she thought he was joking; RCA was the "big-league" label that their friend Jim Reeves was on. But Sholes, who had signed Elvis Presley the year before, was interested in more country music talent from his friend Si Siman. Jim Reeves had also encouraged Sholes to sign the Browns in 1956. Sholes agreed to pay for their move from Fabor to RCA. A few days later, an RCA contract—"big, fat, and solid as a brick outhouse"—was waiting for them at home in Pine Bluff, Arkansas.[98] The Browns were ecstatic.

In March 1956, the Browns recorded their first single for RCA in the KWTO studios. The song, "I Take the Chance," had been written by Ira Louvin especially for Maxine. Local fiddlers Harold Morrison and Jimmy Gately, both *Jubilee* regulars, played on the recording. The song quickly moved to the number-two spot on *Billboard*'s country chart and stayed there for twenty-one weeks.[99] Maxine Brown vividly remembers receiving the group's first royalty check for $3,000: "We were more than thrilled—we had finally proven ourselves as recording artists. Having a number-one record is wonderful, but having a record company that will actually pay you for it is even better."[100] They had yet to receive royalties from their first two singles with Fabor, but after signing with RCA the Browns had a long run of success.[101] Maxine Brown recalled: "I don't think Horace ever forgave us for quitting the *Hayride*, but like Jim Reeves, Elvis, and many others, we had done as much as we could on the *Hayride*. We simply couldn't afford to turn down this big opportunity, not after the many bumpy roads we'd already traveled."[102]

One of the less attractive features of being a successful entertainer, especially during the 1950s, was traveling the literally bumpy roads to gigs, and travel could be more difficult—even dangerous—for women. When Jim Ed Brown was drafted and went to boot camp in 1957, Top Talent booked Billy Walker to sit in for him on a tour with Maxine and Bonnie Brown. They had never traveled with anyone other than their brother and felt vulnerable on the road alone with Walker. Without being too specific, Maxine wrote in her autobiography that on one leg of the tour, her sister Bonnie started driving at high speeds around curves as a way to keep Walker "in his place," implying that he was making unwelcome sexual advances toward her in the front seat.[103] The Brown sisters ultimately took Walker to the Washington, DC, airport, gave him the money due to him, and canceled the rest of the tour.

On their long drive home to Arkansas, the Brown sisters happened to run into their old friends Ira and Charlie Louvin and joined them in a caravan as far as Nashville. Ira Louvin had been writing a song for the Browns called "The Last Thing I Want" and saw the chance meeting as a sign of success. Maxine said of the song, "The words always remind me of that scared, lonely time on the road." The Browns recorded the song for RCA, and it became the B-side to their top-ten country hit "I Heard the Bluebirds Sing" in September 1957. The Brown sisters stayed off the road until their brother Jim Ed was transferred to the Pine Bluff Arsenal in Arkansas and could easily travel with them again.[104]

SI AND THE WOMEN

Maxine and Bonnie Brown's experience on the road with Billy Walker is one of the many unfortunate issues that women in country music faced during the 1950s. In addition to sexual harassment, they often had a difficult time trying to meet cultural expectations of marriage and motherhood while navigating the lifestyle of an entertainer. Siman respected women, and he was not afraid to help them develop their careers in music. Some already had a good start when they came to Springfield. Colleen Carroll, a singer from northeastern Oklahoma, had a contract with Cardinal Records when she came to the *Jubilee* in 1955. The *East Oklahoma Tribune* called her July appearance on the *Jubilee* a move to the "Big Time," a call "up the stardust trail to nationwide recognition."[105] Carroll performed on the *Jubilee* until 1958 when she decided to go back home to Oklahoma to be with her children. Four years later she gave birth to one of the world's best-selling performers of all time, Country Music Hall of Fame member Garth Brooks.[106]

For Oklahoma native Wanda Jackson, the *Ozark Jubilee* was like another home, but it helped that her father was her road companion. She came to the *Jubilee* at the same time as Colleen Carroll, soon after her first hit single on Decca, "You Can't Have My Love." Jackson was only seventeen years old and barely out of high school when she made her first *Jubilee* appearance in July 1955. Being among the *Jubilee* stars was a learning experience. Jackson recalled that "because it was such a high-profile TV program, every major

Wanda Jackson. *Courtesy of John Richardson.*

country star wanted to work on the *Jubilee* . . . I got to stay right there in one place and work with them all!"[107] She turned down opportunities for better-paying jobs, including being the girl singer with Ernest Tubb's band, because she didn't want to leave the *Jubilee* where she had developed close friendships with Porter Wagoner, Bobby Lord, and Brenda Lee. Jackson wasn't tempted to quit such a comfortable environment: "It was getting closer to the time I had to make a final decision, but every time I'd think about leaving the *Jubilee* I would just cry and cry. It seemed like the Nashville people had a clique, and it was easy to feel like an outsider. At the *Jubilee* we were a smaller group and, gosh, if somebody got a hit, we were just tickled to death for them. It seemed that Nashville was more competitive and there was more jealousy going on, while the *Jubilee* cast was a family."[108] Show performances boosted demand for an artist on the road and could produce substantial earnings. Top Talent booked Jackson on *Jubilee* package shows across the United States.

In addition to her bookings, Jackson's hectic schedule during 1955 and 1956 included tours with her part-time boyfriend, Elvis Presley. Following an appearance on the *Jubilee* in early October 1955, Jackson and her father headed out for a series of one-night performances in Oklahoma City, Tulsa, Wichita Falls, Fort Worth, and Lubbock. After a night at home in Oklahoma City, she was back at the *Jubilee* in Springfield. The next day she was out for a six-day tour with Elvis, followed by two tours in Nevada, California, Arizona, New Mexico, and Colorado before flying back to Springfield for her third *Jubilee* performance that month. "Daddy and I racked up over 8,500 miles on the car that month alone, which was not atypical during that period. In fact, the following month, we put another 10,000 on it."[109] She compared coming home to a "race car driver pulling in for a pit stop. All hands were on deck, to turn us around and get us back out there in record time!"[110] Her hard work paid off—by December, the *Country and Western Jamboree* 1955 reader's poll listed Jackson as the "Best New Female Singer," undoubtedly aided by her road gigs and frequent television exposure on the *Jubilee*. The following year, Jackson's new manager, Jim Halsey, consolidated her bookings, and she made over $15,000 (about $166,000 in 2023): "I wasn't exactly living in the lap of luxury, but I was working hard, living my dreams, and making a very good living—especially considering I was still a teenager."[111] When Jackson moved to Capitol Records in 1956, she wrote and released many charted singles and became a powerful rockabilly performer. After her first Capitol hit, "I Gotta Know," the *Grand Ole Opry* invited her to join the cast, but still she refused to leave the *Jubilee*. "I loved my *Jubilee* family," she said.[112] By 1957, she was known as the "Queen of Rockabilly" with several hits on both the country and pop charts.[113]

One of Siman's most promising *Jubilee* artists during the mid-1950s was eleven-year-old Brenda Lee. Her first contact with the show occurred in Augusta, Georgia; Red Foley was headlining a show at the Bell Auditorium on February 23, 1956, and the show's emcee, Peanut Faircloth, had arranged for Lee to perform as a guest. When Foley met Lee after the show, KWTO's Top Talent manager Lou Black was with him. Foley described being transfixed by Lee's talent: "I still get cold chills every time I think about the first time I heard that voice. About midway through the show, we put her on, and she reared back and let go. One foot started patting rhythm like she was putting out a prairie fire, and not another fiber of her little body moved. And when she did that trick of breaking her voice, it jarred me enough to realize I'd forgotten to get off the stage after introducing her. There I stood, after twenty-six years of supposedly learning how to conduct myself on stage, with my mouth open and a glassy stare in my eyes."[114]

Brenda Lee. *Courtesy of Ralph Foster Museum.*

Lee credits Foley for discovering her that night, but Crossroads had already gotten information about her from a variety of sources before Foley returned to Springfield. *Jubilee* director Bryan Bisney claimed that he was the one who discovered Lee having received a letter from Lee's stepfather, Buell Rainwater, and a tape of her singing on an Augusta radio show: "After listening to her tape, I decided to have her come on the *Jubilee*. That's how she got started on network television."[115] Bisney doubted that Lee remembered such details, considering her age at the time.

Siman sent bus money for Lee and her mother to come to Springfield for her first *Jubilee* performance on March 31, 1956. Siman said that his first thought after hearing her perform was "How did all that talent get in such a little girl?"[116] Siman went to work on his friend Paul Cohen at Decca Records and arranged a recording contract for Brenda in May 1956. According to Lee, however, Foley staged a performance for her at the Country Music Disc Jockey Convention and pressured Decca, his label, into signing her.[117] Her first Decca recording session produced seven songs, including her first single,

"Jambalaya," and "I'm Gonna Lasso Santa Claus." Lee's first performances were scheduled for September's monthly *Junior Jubilee*, ostensibly to help her gain confidence and experience. Lee was ready for her first big spotlight on national television by October 21 when *Jubilee* scriptwriter and publicity director Don Richardson took her to New York to appear on the *Perry Como Show* and do a round of interviews with magazine writers and syndicated columnists who were fascinated by her youthful talent.[118]

Siman recalled that Lee was an "instant smash, with the big voice [and] dead-pan face, and not bigger than a penny. We used to say we found her in a box of Cracker Jacks."[119] After the school year was out, Lee and her family moved to Springfield and began touring with Foley and the *Jubilee* between television broadcasts. She recalled that "the musicians in the band would get a kick out of teaching me dirty jokes, which I would merrily repeat to get a laugh without understanding the meaning behind any of them."[120] In the fall, Lee started attending the Phelps School in Springfield during the week and kept a busy weekend schedule with road tours and *Jubilee* broadcasts.

On November 10, 1956, Lou Black took Lee to the Country Music Disc Jockey Association convention in Nashville and managed to get her on stage with Bob Wills and the Texas Playboys. "Everybody seemed to be amazed at me up there singing, and I was really happy to be there," she recalled.[121] However, after the Saturday night festivities, Siman found Black dead from a heart attack in his hotel room. Only four days earlier he had resigned from Top Talent to manage Lee full-time under a new five-year management contract. Lee and her mother had been scheduled to depart with Black on a flight to New York the next day for another appearance on the *Perry Como Show*. The young star had to continue her bookings schedule without a manager.

When Siman booked Lee in Las Vegas for a show with the Ink Spots in December 1956, she became the youngest headliner ever to perform in Las Vegas. *Time* and *Life* magazines wanted to do stories on her, so Siman arranged a birthday party for her at the Flamingo Hotel as a publicity stunt. Even though she was turning twelve years old, Siman recalled, "[we said] 'We're celebrating Brenda's ninth, tenth, and eleventh birthday in Las Vegas' . . . [We] got more publicity out of it that way."[122] More appearances followed on the *Perry Como Show*, the *Steve Allen Show*, and CBS Radio's *Robert Q. Lewis Show* in February 1957. She was a showstopper and attracted huge crowds everywhere she went. One appearance with pop singer Teresa Brewer at the Kansas City Auto Show in March 1957 set an all-time attendance record of 12,500, and the following night she did a solo show that drew 11,000.[123]

Brenda Lee's birthday party in Las Vegas. *Courtesy of Ralph Foster Museum*

Crossroads hoped to maintain their investment in Lee by filling Black's management spot with someone on the *Jubilee* team. However, Red Foley's manager Dub Allbritten stepped in, signed Lee to a new personal management contract, and got his friend Charlie Mosley to be her legal guardian in charge of her finances in 1957. According to Lee, her singing career was bringing in considerable income at this time; each Steve Allen show paid more than $2,800 and Perry Como paid $2,000. Her recordings on Decca Records earned her $1,773 and stage performances brought in about $1,000 per show. While Lee's annual income had increased to over $36,000, the money was deposited into a trust fund after 30 percent was taken out by Allbritten and Mosley for management and expenses. Lee would be unable to access the trust funds until she turned twenty-one. Until then, she lived on a weekly allowance of $75 awarded by a probate court judge.[124]

When Lee and her family moved to Nashville in July 1957, Crossroads filed a lawsuit against Allbritten, Mosley, and Brenda's mother, Grayce Rainwater, for breach of contract. In her autobiography, Lee implies that Crossroads cashed in on her increased income by taking 25 percent management commission rather than the customary 10 or 15 percent, and claimed that it was taken out of her fees for personal appearances rather than from her net income after expenses. She added: "On top of everything else, I had been paid only $850 for six months' worth of weekly appearances on the *Ozark Jubilee*."[125] The Crossroads contract signed by Lee's mother claimed 25 percent of Lee's performance earnings beyond the *Jubilee* show and committed her to *Ozark Jubilee* performances "not less than twelve times per year" for two years, at a minimum of $50 per show.[126]

However, Grayce Rainwater was apparently unable to understand the contract. She testified that when she asked how much time she had to look over the contract before signing it, Crossroads management told her "two minutes." When she asked for a lawyer to review it, they said "any attorney in Springfield will approve this contract." Grayce's story is plausible, considering the diffidence often expressed by women trying to navigate such negotiations. *Jubilee* scriptwriter and frequent Crossroads critic Bob Tubert claimed that *Jubilee* contracts "were just unconscionable ... They had dual contracts on the acts, taking commissions for [both] management and booking."[127] Allbritten and Mosley argued that Missouri law required that contracts with minors be approved by a court and an appointed guardian, thus the contract was illegal.

The feud between Crossroads and Allbritten, Mosley, and Rainwater continued, with arguments over damages. According to Lee: "Crossroads maintained that it had advanced money to Mother, bought me clothes, booked me on network TV, arranged for concert tours, arranged for my recording contract and, in short, made me a star. It claimed its booking division had arranged for more than thirty concert appearances across the United States, plus the three-week Las Vegas engagement and the Como and Allen TV shows."[128] Rainwater insisted that Decca, not Crossroads, had arranged the network TV appearances for her daughter, and that it was Red Foley who had gotten her the record contract. Allbritten and Mosley sued Crossroads for $50,000 in damages and asked for a full accounting. Crossroads tried to get an injunction to prevent Lee from performing until they were paid off.[129]

Siman was silent about these painful negotiations. Author Steve Eng confirms that "although his name does not appear in the pages of depositions, insults, and counter-insults," Siman was there.[130] Ultimately, all parties had to let the case go after hearing Davidson County Chancery Court Judge Ned Lentz's conclusion: "If I grant this injunction it might injure this little girl who may be at the height of her career. I am not interested in the dollars and cents angle but in what is best for the little girl."[131] Eng reports Siman's final word on the case: "We put our tail between our legs and got on our chartered airplane with three attorneys, and headed our ass back to the hills of the Ozarks. It just shows you a contract ain't worth the paper it's written on sometimes."[132]

After Lee left the *Jubilee*, she recorded songs from several songwriters she had met in Springfield. Her first Decca chart success occurred in early 1957 with her third release, "One Step at a Time," written by Hugh Ashley, an Earl Barton publishing client from Searcy County, Arkansas.[133] Siman's rockabilly protégé Ronnie Self wrote Brenda's first top-ten song, "Sweet Nothin's" (1959). Her first big hit was "I'm Sorry" (1960), written by Self and Lee's new manager, Dub Allbritten. The Grammy-nominated song was number one on the *Billboard* charts during the summer of 1960 and stayed in the top ten for more than six months. It made Brenda Lee an international recording star, and was her biggest moneymaker, with over 15 million dollars in sales worldwide. When she toured Europe in the summer of 1960, the Beatles were her opening act.[134]

Patsy Cline was among the more difficult *Jubilee* performers for some staff members, but not for Siman, who considered her his top female vocalist. The first of Cline's sixteen appearances during the show's network run was in January 1956. She asked Foley what she could do to advance her career. He assured her that things would happen soon and encouraged her to continue on the path she was taking. He was right about her career, which rapidly took off a year later after she sang "Walkin' After Midnight" on the nationally televised program *Arthur Godfrey's Talent Scouts* and "effectively used television to become a national star."[135] Decca Records rushed to release the single a few weeks after the performance, and it became her first national hit on both the country and pop charts. She was a celebrity by the time she returned to the *Jubilee* on March 2, 1957.

Since meeting Foley in 1956, Cline had become confident about her performance and appearance on stage. However, she offended Foley with her take-charge attitude (and probably her "tough-girl" language). After one of her *Jubilee* appearances, Foley ran to Siman and said, "next time she's on the show, she can do it by herself."[136] His strong dislike for Cline is evident in their duet of "Walking in a Winter Wonderland" on the *Jubilee* broadcast of December 12, 1959.[137] When one is aware of the problems that existed between Cline and Foley, the stiffness and discomfort being felt by both is painfully noticeable in their performance of the cheerful Christmas song.

The *Jubilee* production team also had problems with Cline. They didn't like one of her blouses because of its glitter and asked her to change. *Jubilee* director Bryan Bisney's brisk approach toward her did not help. Cline would not give in, and she wore the blouse. Siman thought the problem was with the crew rather than Cline. He was not threatened by her style and praised her records as some of the greatest he'd ever heard. He reasoned that "if you don't want Patsy Cline, don't get her."[138] Siman knew she was fighting for what she thought was right, and he wasn't going to try to change who she was. For him, it was just a matter of understanding and accepting personal preferences.

As a *Jubilee* newcomer, singer Norma Jean had trouble with some of the production team's song choices and staging decisions. "They had me do some things like sitting on a fence singing 'Don't Fence Me In' when I wanted to sing the 'Window Up Above.'"[139] Although she acknowledged and appreciated Crossroads for giving her a start in the music business, she felt threatened by Bisney. Scriptwriter Bob Tubert stated that "Bryan had network television that had to be on the air, and he was not a nice, patient person. I understand he had to be that way, but he should have understood it bothered her."[140] According to publicity director Don Richardson, Bisney had "great personal dislike" for Norma Jean; in his diary entry for April 12, 1960, he quoted Bisney as saying of Jean "She treats me like dirt!!"[141]

Siman liked people who made him laugh, and Minnie Pearl was one of the best at it. She certainly didn't need any help from Siman with her career. As a well-educated aspiring actress, Sarah Ophelia Colley was the daughter of a Tennessee mill owner and grew up in a privileged home. In 1940, twenty-eight-year-old Colley became a member of the *Grand Ole Opry* as "Minnie Pearl"—the only female cast member at the time. She was influenced by June "Elviry" Weaver of the Weaver Brothers and Elviry of Christian County, Missouri, and appeared several times on the *Ozark Jubilee* and its later rendition, the *Five Star Jubilee*. She and her husband Henry Cannon invited Siman and Foley to visit their two-room cabin on Eddy Arnold's farm in Brentwood, Tennessee. They ended up staying three or four days at the farm, where Siman learned how to cook Minnie Pearl's special country ham. The recipe became a favorite in the Siman household. Cannon was a pilot and insisted on flying Foley and Siman back to Springfield in his private jet after their visit, instead of letting them take a commercial flight home.[142]

KEEPING THE STARS HAPPY

When celebrity cowboy singers such as Gene Autry or Tex Ritter performed on the *Jubilee*, the staff created special themes tailored to their reputation. Siman had met Autry in 1951 while working a RadiOzark transcription deal with Smiley Burnette in California. Autry already had a strong connection to the Ozarks having been a relief telegrapher for Frisco Railroad in Oklahoma while writing songs and singing with his boss, native Springfieldian Jimmy Long. When the railroad transferred Long to Springfield in 1928, Autry went with him to sing and write songs before going to work at the WLS *National Barn Dance* in Chicago.[143] The two wrote Autry's first big hit, "That Silver Haired Daddy of Mine," in Long's Springfield home in 1930.[144]

Jimmy Long and his children, Jack and Beverly, performed as the Long Family on KWTO in the early 1930s, during which time Autry fell in love with Long's niece, Ina Mae Spivey, who was a singer studying music education at Southwest Missouri State Teachers College in Springfield.[145] When Gene and Ina Mae married on April Fool's Day 1932, Autry's address on the marriage license was Springfield, Missouri. As an actor in ninety-three "singing cowboy" films, he helped to introduce country music to a mass audience. Autry made 640 recordings as a singer—300 of them he wrote or cowrote—and more than a dozen reached gold or platinum status.[146] He had a successful weekly television show on CBS called *The Gene Autry Show* when he was appearing on the *Jubilee* in 1956.

Siman thought Tex Ritter was one of the "brightest artists" he ever worked with.[147] After studying pre-law at the University of Texas, Ritter entered law school in Chicago while working in the entertainment business singing cowboy songs. Eventually he pursued an acting career and moved to Los Angeles, where he acted in seventy movies and sang on the soundtrack of seventy-six films, including the theme song for the 1952 western *High Noon*. Ritter's recording of "The Ballad of High Noon" won an Oscar for Best Song, and Ritter performed it at the first televised Academy Awards program in 1953. He had starred in a western movie with Red Foley in 1941, and the two toured together in 1954, just before Ritter came to the *Jubilee* in 1955.[148] He was also a *Jubilee* guest performer in 1959 and 1960, and one of the five star hosts of the 1961 Crossroads production on NBC, the *Five Star Jubilee*. Ritter and Siman were founding members of the Country Music Association.

Another favorite performer of Siman's was *Grand Ole Opry* star and honky-tonk music pioneer Ernest Tubb. The "Texas Troubadour" was an early proponent of electric guitars in country music, and his biggest hit before coming to the *Jubilee* was "Walking the Floor Over You" in 1941.[149] Siman appreciated him as a stylist, rather than a great singer. Like many country music singers of Tubb's era, he was a fan of Jimmie Rodgers, whose wife Carrie helped Tubb get a recording contract with RCA in 1936. He joined the *Grand Ole Opry* in 1943 and became friends with *Opry* host Red Foley. He opened downtown

Publicist and scriptwriter Don Richardson, Gene Autry, and announcer Joe Slattery on the set of the *Ozark Jubilee. Courtesy of John Richardson.*

Nashville's landmark Ernest Tubb's Record Shop in 1947 and showcased *Opry* talent on his *Midnight Jamboree* radio show for many years.

Although Siman was an amateur songwriter, he was not a musician or a singer, and the relationship between performers and executives could be as difficult as privates and generals. Not all artists appreciated their time at the *Jubilee* or wanted to be friends with Siman. Some had complaints about money or Siman's management style. With so many artistic perspectives and egos, problems were bound to occur.

Band musicians working on the *Ozark Jubilee* television show earned union wage as they did on radio barn-dance shows, but the salary included rehearsal hours and they were not paid extra for promotional appearances. This policy sometimes created friction. The local musicians union lacked funds and commitment and did not enforce union scale. Recording artists could negotiate salary and non-performance hours, depending on their status, for amounts anywhere from $100 to $1,000. Siman offered contracts for big-name performers such as Red Foley and Brenda Lee. Legendary guitarist and songwriter Merle Travis came to the *Jubilee* for $100.[150] One of Patsy Cline's arrangements combined $175 for transportation and $100 for her performance. Carl Smith made $500 for sitting in as emcee for Foley on May 18, 1957.[151]

Spring Fork, Missouri, native Leroy Van Dyke was frustrated by the salaries at the *Jubilee*. In a telephone interview in 2021, he argued that Siman should have offered him more than union wages because of his growing status as a recording artist at the time. He felt Siman had not been fair in his negotiations: "I had had a million-seller record ["The Auctioneer," 1956] before I ever got down there, and I was in the $75 [pay scale], which still was very, very cheap. And this went on for a couple of years or so. Then he [Siman] said, 'We're cutting you to $25.' I said, 'Si, we had an agreement.' It was just a handshake deal. We didn't have anything on paper. But I grew up [learning] that [when] you make a deal, your word should be your bond, you know.... I said, 'Si, we had a deal: $75.' He said, 'Well, if you don't like it, we'll just call the dogs and you can go somewhere else.'"[152] Van Dyke was also miffed that Siman hadn't published and recorded "The Auctioneer" when he first approached him with the song in 1956 before coming to the *Jubilee*: "Si said, 'Well, we don't have anybody here that can do it.' I said, 'Si, that's not what I'm interested in. I can do it. I wrote it. I can do it.' 'Well,' he said, 'we're not interested.' He turned down a million-seller."[153] "The Auctioneer" was more than a million-seller; it was a 2.5 million-seller. Despite this, Van Dyke stayed with the *Jubilee* from 1957 to 1960.

Billy Walker was a chronic grumbler who charged Siman and his staff with increasing his workload for the same pay: "Once they got you over there, you were doing other things like radio shows, etc. So by the time I got done, I was doing a network TV show for $25."[154] Siman knew the extra radio shows promoted artists as well as the televised *Jubilee* and reasoned that such events provided opportunities for financial gain that could not be compared to a static weekly fee. As usual with show producers, even today, musicians were expected to appreciate "opportunities," but Walker claimed that these reduced his paycheck. His complaint is reasonable, considering the *Louisiana Hayride* union hourly performance rate given to new artists for three- or four-hours' work on each Saturday night show was $18 for a soloist, $12 for a backup musician, and $24 for a bandleader with at least five group members.[155] Siman's perspective on Walker was that they had hired him when he needed exposure during a lull in his career, but they did not guarantee him a regular spot.[156]

Walker said there were "different kinds of contracts. But mostly it was a word of faith. You said, 'Here's what I'll do for you.' We didn't have lawyers or know about legal contracts. Most of us doing something were guys that grew up on a farm and knew nothing about contracts except recording. I didn't have everything in writing with the *Ozark Jubilee*."[157] Horace Logan's system for awarding contracts at the *Hayride* seems less stable than Siman's "gentleman's agreement" because it depended on the mood of a particular night's audience. Logan allowed a new artist one song on the CBS network portion of their show and two songs for the live audience at a later segment: "If the audience applauded loudly enough after an artist finished his two numbers . . . he could come back for one or more encores. The artists who encored regularly were obviously the audience's favorites, and they were the ones we tried to sign to long-term contracts with the show."[158] As producers and employers, Logan and Siman had budget concerns that determined how much to spend on any particular artist, and income from the network varied. The inconsistency could understandably cause confusion and hard feelings.

Billy Walker boiled it down to the management's greed that "eats everything that means the most . . . But they've got all the smarts and you don't know anything."[159] Walker thought producers such as Siman and Logan were greedy and denied him profits he thought he deserved. To Walker and others like him, Siman was just an executive who pulled the strings—an officer among privates, detached and inaccessible. Walker said he enjoyed living in Springfield, but he "just never got to go where the Coxes and Fosters and the Simans hung out. The power brokers thought we were dumb hillbillies. We thought we were entertaining people."[160] Siman's after-show parties for guest stars and television executives, sometimes held at the Hickory Hills Country Club, made the class division Walker described evident. Siman was a salesman at heart and recognized the value of schmoozing with out-of-towners and people in charge of the show's future. Rebellious cast members were the least of his concerns on those occasions.

Like Van Dyke, Walker felt cheated by Siman and the *Jubilee* because they did not honor their contract, even though they technically didn't have one. *Jubilee* scriptwriter Bob Tubert had a different perspective; he accused Crossroads of making money off Walker through ABC without raising Walker's pay. Crossroads might pay Walker $25, while charging ABC $500 for him as production costs.[161] Although Walker praised the *Ozark Jubilee* because it "kept country music alive, 'cause nothing was happening in Nashville," he was still bitter about Siman many years later. In a 1993 interview he stated: "Si was very congenial. He was the one who booked all the shows. The con man is always nice."[162] At one point, Walker and Tubert claimed that the *Jubilee* staff performers were going to stage a revolt and named the culprits as Foley,

Van Dyke, Marvin Rainwater, Bobby Lord, and "at least ten or fifteen acts with the musicians." However, the revolt never happened because "the hierarchy buffaloed the rest of us and said, 'You can find you a new TV outlet.' "[163]

Other problems with performers occurred because of complications introduced by television cameras. Most singers and musicians at the time had never been on television and therefore didn't understand how to dress for filming. They came with what they wanted to wear without knowing that they would have to be coordinated, that stripes were especially problematic, and that glittery costumes reflected too much light into the cameras. The network required makeup, but some performers didn't like makeup or the look it created. The biggest problem was choreography. Most country performers without a guitar didn't know what to do with their hands when on camera. Siman fought against having what amounted to a stand-up radio show on television, but it was difficult to get the artists to do anything except stand in front of a microphone and sing.[164]

Siman viewed himself as a mediator between Crossroads and the artists: "Any major contribution that I made [to the *Jubilee*] was to be able to mediate and negotiate [on the performers' behalf] and give them the feeling that they were really wanted and are really welcome and we're not going to try to stuff something down your throat, but this may make it look better. Our bottom line was [we're going to] try to show [them] off the best way we know how, and not have their feelings hurt, and not to have them say, 'Well, we're not coming back here again.' "[165] The production team's bottom line was to display the performers at their best, but Siman acknowledged that at least a couple of them left with hurt feelings.

Siman had to deal with a wide spectrum of personalities on the set: "It's kind of like getting on an airplane. You may not know the pilot, but you're trusting your life to him. In television, unless you're an expert, which I've yet to find one, you necessarily need to put yourself in the hands of the producers and the directors and the writers, because they do this for a living." If there was a problem on the set, decisions had to be made immediately by Siman, as the executive producer, director Bryan Bisney, and floor director Fred Rains. If there was a script problem, writers Bob Tubert or Don Richardson would be called in immediately: "[A script problems is] not something you can do tomorrow; it has got to be now . . . We tried to be as nice as we could be, but sometimes you can't. So, it wasn't always easy."[166]

Although the *Ozark Jubilee* ran year-round, artists had other opportunities for stardom through replacement shows for other programs during their

Slim Wilson. *Courtesy of Ralph Foster Museum.*

summer off-season. In 1956, ABC approached Siman about doing a weekly, live, 30-minute television show starring Eddy Arnold at the Jewell Theatre, with Chet Atkins as a regular guest. "When [ABC] looked at all the talent lists that were made available from producers like us, they came to me and said, 'If you can deliver Eddy Arnold and Chet Atkins, you've got the contract.' I could, and I did."[167] Siman admired Arnold's talent and had worked closely with Atkins in the past, so a show with them seemed like a natural fit. ABC's *Eddy Arnold Show* ran on Thursday nights from April through September 1956. Headliners included popular television entertainers Vaughn Monroe, Helen O'Connell, and Foley's son-in-law, Pat Boone. Atkins and Arnold commuted from Nashville to Springfield weekly to rehearse for the show on Wednesdays and returned to Nashville on Fridays after the Thursday night broadcast. The show was only open to about five hundred ticket holders, but KYTV put reruns of the program in its Saturday night schedule. Slim Wilson hosted *Talent Varieties*, a weekly half-hour country music talent show produced by Siman, that aired on ABC-TV from June to November 1955. Wilson, backed by his Tall Timber

Trio, introduced amateur and professional talent on the show. *Jubilee* music director Bill Ring conducted talent auditions, while Bryan Bisney took his place in September as producer and director. ABC radio carried the program as *Talent Round-Up*, with an additional half hour.

In addition to being involved with the network summer replacement shows, *Jubilee* performers were on several local KYTV country music programs and a local version of the *Ozark Jubilee*, while also going on the road in various groupings. According to publicist and scriptwriter Don Richardson, Top Talent booked Ozark-based performers in arenas, auditoriums, stadiums, and grandstands in forty-two states, the District of Columbia, Canada, and Alaska. In 1957, "*Ozark Jubilee* units played to more than two million people in person ... for every type of event from a fund-raising in a one-room Missouri schoolhouse to such famous annuals as the Ohio State Fair."[168]

Crossroads continued to create a lively business environment for the country music industry in Springfield, enabling *Jubilee* artists to take advantage of network programs originating in other cities. Crossroads made a demo for a pop-variety show titled *Snooky Lanson Time* in January 1960. Lanson was the popular host of *Your Hit Parade* on NBC-TV. In October 1960, NBC executives hired Siman as the talent coordinator for a new series called *Today on the Farm*, originating in Chicago and featuring Eddy Arnold. Siman was responsible for booking *Jubilee* artists Johnny Horton, Tex Ritter, Chet Atkins, Brenda Lee, Bobby Lord, June Carter, and Minnie Pearl on the show.

HANDLING RED AND THE AFTER HOURS

Red Foley was a calming presence on the *Ozark Jubilee* set, as well as the show's greatest asset. His fame as a country music recording and performing star attracted viewers, advertisers, and network executives to the show. Those who knew him personally found Foley's warmth and casual demeanor appealing. Dickson Terry of the *St. Louis Post Dispatch* wrote that Foley was "to country music what Louis Armstrong is to jazz": a good singer and entertainer and a "very likable character."[169]

When asked what they remembered about him, music business colleagues often described him in terms of authenticity, selflessness, and easygoing nature. Porter Wagoner said that what he learned from Foley influenced the rest of his career: "He could communicate with an audience as well as anybody I've ever known. He taught me how to speak to an audience." Wagoner recalled that Foley "always thought of the other people around him,"[170] and Norma Jean said she was blessed "just to know him."[171] Brenda Lee credited Foley for her career: "Without him, his kindness and his belief in me, I never would have had the career I've had. There's no question in my mind about that. He's the one who opened the door and unselfishly nurtured me during what I now realize was the most pivotal moment of my childhood career."[172] Siman said that "nobody ever had a better friend than Red Foley."[173]

Jean Shepard was thrilled to work with Foley and thought he was the "ultimate entertainer."[174] One time, he wanted her to do a duet with him on the *Jubilee*, a song that he had recorded with Kitty Wells titled "One by One." "I told him I couldn't sing in the same key Kitty did," recalled Shepard. "He insisted. Well, it was just too high for me. Right at the end of it—I was so embarrassed—my voice broke. Red just put his arms around me, right on television, and he laughed and said, 'Don't worry about it, sweetheart. It lets them know that you are human.'"[175] Foley had plenty of experience with human flaws.

The entire *Jubilee* staff, as well as some locals, knew that Foley had problems with alcohol. Maxine Brown of the Browns said that Foley's alcoholism "was a well-kept secret among all the entertainers because we all loved him so much."[176] Siman dealt with Foley the same way he dealt with everybody else: by working with him as a unique person with unique problems. "Well, let's face it: he had an alcohol problem. And if you don't understand putting up with that, then you might as well get out of the business, because if you're doing anything like we were doing, where you're dealing with hundreds of people, you're going to have beaucoup problems."[177] Some thought Foley was often drunk while on the air, but Siman swore that it never happened during the show. Whether or not this was the case, Foley missed cues, mispronounced words, and frequently appeared to be sluggish. Sometimes *Jubilee* announcer Joe Slattery introduced a guest emcee sitting in for a "vacationing" Foley, when he was really in St. John's Hospital drying out.

Siman viewed Foley as a complicated, but talented person, and felt that he was worth the trouble: "What I came up with was, here's a man who thrived on crises. If he didn't have one, he'd create one. It could be self-induced. Then when he'd have a crisis, that would call for going out and getting drunk, and that was his excuse for drinking."[178] No evidence confirms Foley's exposure to Alcoholics Anonymous, which had been active in Springfield since 1945. A.A. members might have called on him in the hospital. However, with the *Jubilee* cast and management covering for him and his fame a constant companion, recovery might be difficult, even with A.A.'s tradition of anonymity. Don Richardson wrote in his diary that Foley worried the production team, and that he didn't like the way local gossipers talked about the performer's drinking. Foley's unanticipated absences due to binges, followed by drying-out spells in a hospital facility that Richardson called the "flu" ward, caused scheduling problems and the crew would have to hustle to reinvent the show. A guest host would have to be rounded up. Porter Wagoner, Webb Pierce, Eddy Arnold, Rex Allen, Carl Smith, and Jim Reeves served in this capacity for Foley at different times in the show's history.[179] Everybody wanted to buy him a drink and dinner, and Siman couldn't protect him all the time.

Foley wasn't the only one with a drinking problem. Years after she left the *Ozark Jubilee*, Norma Jean admitted to having a drinking problem during her days on the show.[180] Gossip around Springfield kept track of *Jubilee* stars who frequented local bars, and Siman claimed that the *Jubilee* staff would "keep a little posse on their trail. We had the Springfield Police Department subsidized to the extent of being our buddies for how important the show was to this area. So, we generally knew where all the principals were at any given time during Thursday, Friday, and Saturday, when we were in the big rehearsals on commercials and the show."[181] These including singer Webb Pierce, as noted by Richardson in his diary: "Webb loaded tonight at Rendezvous, arguing with Faron Young."[182] Pierce sought treatment for alcoholism at Springfield's Burge Hospital in 1960. Gene Autry was also on the *Jubilee*'s list of entertainers to corral. Richardson suggested to Autry that he write Foley a "keep-your-chin-up letter" before an upcoming income tax evasion trial, and found it ironic that Autry volunteered to be a character witness for Foley.[183]

Siman had a lot of experience with talented people and tolerated their uniqueness. He thought it would be hard to get along with a talented crew if he expected them to be like other people: "You don't treat people equally, because they're not equal. Where one may be very eccentric, another may not be. One may be totally offensive, and others are not.... Some people you can just order around; other people, you've got to figure out how to get it done so it doesn't sound like that."[184] Siman didn't always get it right, but he felt that he had enough experience to make suggestions that would help each artist accomplish what they wanted.

Siman was usually good at spotting talent. As he said many times, "if I had any talent at all, it was to recognize talent in others." He helped many *Jubilee* artists achieve success or expand their careers in the music business. Because performers couldn't live off of what they were making on the *Ozark Jubilee*, Siman explained, "enhancing their potential income through records and promotions was a very important part of the job." Siman's connections with Steve Sholes at RCA resulted in record contracts for Chet Atkins in 1947, Porter in 1952, and the Browns in 1956—and all three stayed at RCA for at least twenty-five years.[185] It was a pretty good record.

CHAPTER FOUR

The *Ozark Jubilee*:
PRODUCING A NETWORK TELEVISION SHOW

A LTHOUGH CROSSROADS CHARGED ONE DOLLAR for admission to the *Ozark Jubilee* stage shows at the Jewell Theatre, their operating money came from the ABC television network, which made its money from advertisers brought in through various agencies or their own sales department. The *Jubilee*'s overall budget from ABC varied because ABC network reps dictated the show's length from week to week. The weekly budget given for a half-hour show would be doubled if an hour show was scheduled, and two-and-a-half-hour shows had bigger budgets, accordingly.[1] Crossroads could never count on the schedule nor the budget. They would prepare for the maximum air time but were sometimes preempted by special programming such as an awards show. In such cases, Crossroads would record the live stage performance on kinescope to use in place of the network feed when necessary.[2] The *Ozark Jubilee* went on at the Jewell Theatre every week, with or without the live network feed.

Crossroads was more concerned with staying on the air than making big money, but with the show's continued success, the network offered more money and travel expenses. Siman's initial salary guarantee was $250 per week, which he felt was "not much for an executive producer of a weekly network TV show."[3] The amount of advertising money increased after the first year and so did his salary, but the future of the show was never guaranteed.

Country music was becoming a big business in the Ozarks, and the music business press reported on its every move for at least the first two years. Dickson Terry of the *St. Louis Post Dispatch* claimed that the "production of country music, as carried on in Springfield, is estimated to be a $2,000,000-a-year business . . . [*Ozark Jubilee*] is drawing all the top talent in the country music field. In fact, they say now that all a man has to do is appear on *Ozark Jubilee* and he's made, so far as record sales are concerned."[4] The producers had to maintain the momentum by keeping the network interested in the show.

In June 1955, *Billboard* proclaimed that "hillbilly music TV shows have more friends than anybody," and *Jubilee* publicist/scriptwriter Don Richardson fanned the fire with weekly press releases boasting of high ratings.[5] Two commonly used research companies gathered the numbers; American Research Bureau (Arbitron) collected data by putting diaries—for viewers to keep track of shows they watched during the first seven days of the month—in 2,200 homes, and A. C. Nielsen installed devices based on radio "Audimeters" to record television usage in more than 1,000 homes.[6] Other television research was available from Pulse, based on personal interviews in sixty-four markets, and Trendex, a company that conducted telephone interviews in fifteen cities in the eastern and central time zones.[7]

The ABC-TV research team did its part to demonstrate high numbers for its programs by drawing from specific demographic categories to show the *Jubilee*'s success with male, female, or youth viewers in different time slots. An overall score was all categories combined. The results would influence advertisers' decisions about where and when to advertise their products. ABC passed ratings in different configurations on to Crossroads, and Don Richardson used them to write press releases used by local media and national country music outlets. But the high ratings numbers put forth by ABC-TV could be misleading, then as well as now. For instance, the Wikipedia entry for "*Ozark Jubilee*" states that "by early 1956, the *Jubilee* had earned a 19.2" Nielson rating.[8] The source of this figure is a full-page, 1956 *Billboard* ad, purchased by Crossroads and ABC Television to celebrate the *Jubilee*'s first birthday.[9] The ad prominently displays the latest Nielsen rating of 19.2, but this was not the show's overall rating; a fine-print paragraph at the edge of the ad reports high Arbitron numbers, but lists demographic categories for the show's popularity. The *Ozark Jubilee*'s overall rating in 1955 was 11.2, and it remained within two points of this throughout its history.[10]

Since 1955, the *Jubilee*'s first year with ABC, the network's primary goal had been to catch up with CBS and NBC. By 1956, ABC founder Leonard Goldenson knew that the network "was still struggling mightily."[11] From 1956 to 1960, ABC sought to outdo CBS and NBC by attracting younger audiences, and they expanded their programming options in this direction accordingly. An awareness of the network's position in these years partly explains the network's intervention in *Jubilee* production decisions. A look at ABC-TV programming from 1953 to 1959 reveals frequent program cancellations as the network experimented. Country music remained constant because it was inexpensive to produce and "quite salable."[12] The *Ozark Jubilee* cost the network $8,000 per month in its first year, while other shows contracted during the same time—the *MGM Parade*, *Warner Brothers Presents*, *Wyatt Earp*, and the *Mickey Mouse Club*—cost considerably more.[13] The most expensive program was *Warner Brothers Presents* at $58,000 per month.

During its first year on television, the *Jubilee* faced serious competition from WSM's *Grand Ole Opry*. Although WSM had been the first Nashville station to acquire a television license in 1948, the *Opry* managers hadn't been interested in TV at first, thinking it was a passing fad.[14] In addition, WSM president Jack DeWitt was worried about the massive expenditure involved with TV: "Television would require new studios, built from scratch, with sets, lights, backdrops, props, wardrobe, makeup, and other things one didn't need for even the most elaborate radio shows." Another consideration was the problem of WSM's national and regional advertising base: clients wouldn't be interested in buying ads for local television. Yet Nashville was a "conspicuous blind spot on the television map of the United States."[15] Once DeWitt and his associates decided to give country music television a try, they faced significant, expensive technical problems getting the show on the air.

ABC-TV had the Ralston Purina Company on board for a country music show, and Purina first considered sponsoring KWTO's *Ozark Jubilee*. But "RadiOzark execs chilled when Purina insisted that the deal be an exclusive, with no other sponsors being eligible for the remaining three weeks in each month."[16] With a weekly program to support, this was not an option for the *Jubilee*, but the *Opry* could become a testing ground for WSM. They signed on with an ABC-TV Ralston Purina show from the Ryman Auditorium. On October 15, 1955, the premiere of ABC-TV's *Grand Ole Opry* was broadcast live to 130 ABC television stations and WSM radio listeners.[17] It featured Carl Smith as host, Les Paul and Mary Ford as special guests, and *Opry* regulars Minnie Pearl, Justin Tubb, Lonzo and Oscar, and the Wilburn Brothers, who were from the Ozarks.

From October 1955 until September 1956, the *Opry*'s ABC Ralston Purina show replaced one hour of the *Ozark Jubilee*'s ninety-minute slot on the fourth Saturday of the month, claiming almost a quarter of the *Jubilee*'s monthly airtime. When the ABC contract with the *Opry* expired, it was not renewed. The *Opry* would be absent from network television until 1978 because "the *Opry* did not concentrate on TV the way the Springfield group did, preferring to stick with radio and its live shows."[18] A syndicated program, *Stars of the Grand Ole Opry*, was also available on film, but this option was not a threat to live television. The *Ozark Jubilee* remained the dominant country music show on all major TV networks.

MOVE OVER, NASHVILLE!

In 1956, the *Kansas City Star* proclaimed Springfield as "television's country music capital" because of the *Ozark Jubilee*, and the show's success translated into dollars for the entire city. Springfield city manager Irving McNayr told the *Star* that the show was "one of the biggest tourist attractions in Missouri. In the last year Springfield has voted to annex territory equal to what it previously had, and we have voted 10 million dollars in sewer bonds and 11 million in electric utility bonds. Springfield is on the move, and this show helps."[19]

Life magazine acknowledged Springfield and Shreveport as the country's "two thriving centers for rustic music makers." Shreveport's *Louisiana Hayride* did not have television exposure, but its 50,000-watt radio signal could broadcast the weekly show far across the South. *Life* ranked Nashville in third place because of its historical significance and superior recording industry: "the rugged pioneers—the self-styled hicks, hayseeds and fiddling fools who put country music on a paying basis 31 years ago—are still operating out of their home base, Nashville, Tenn."[20] In spite of its new recording industry, the article categorized Nashville as old-school, confirming the city's unstable position as a music center during the 1950s. Springfield may not have had Nashville's recording studios or its *Opry* tradition, but it had Siman, who, as the producer of the *Ozark Jubilee*, had become a spokesperson for the country music industry, and was busily trying to promote its growth and shape its future. Responding to the trend in listener preferences for pop and rock and roll during the mid-1950s, he became a founding member of the Nashville Music Association, as well as the first trade associations formed to promote a particular genre of music: the Country Music Disc Jockey Association (CMDJA) and the Country Music Association (CMA).

The roots of the CMDJA went back to a November 1952 convention related to the *Grand Ole Opry*'s twenty-seventh birthday celebration. Eighty

PRODUCING A NETWORK TELEVISION SHOW 109

Crossroads advertisement promoting the *Ozark Jubilee. Courtesy of Siman Family Papers, private collection of Scott Foster Siman and Jayne Siman Chowning.*

country music disc jockeys had attended. The following year, the convention expanded and became the CMDJA. Its approximately one hundred charter members hoped to stabilize and promote country music and country music radio programming.[21] Its tagline, "The Voice of America's Music," is echoed in a comment Siman made to the press regarding expanding the image of country music: "When I say 'country music,' I mean the country of the United States, not just the bare feet and hayseed stuff south of the Mason-Dixon line. We include music from the Canadian Rockies, sea songs from the Atlantic Coast, southern spirituals, western cowboy songs. It could be called mongrel music—it comes from all parts of the country."[22] Although in its first few years the *Jubilee* featured stereotypical hillbilly sets and props, such as barns and rail fences, Siman's selection of artists and music styles was relatively wide-ranging. By 1957–58, *Jubilee* set designs and performers' costumes reflected more cosmopolitan conventions.

Left: Si Siman, circa 1963. *Courtesy of Siman Family Papers, private collection of Scott Foster Siman and Jayne Siman Chowning.* Right: Ralph Foster. *Courtesy of Ralph Foster Museum.*

Siman's response to evolutionary trends in country music was evident in his tendency to hire rockabilly performers such as Wanda Jackson, Sonny James, Brenda Lee, and Carl Perkins, whose television debut was on the *Ozark Jubilee*. James's 1956 hit "Young Love" became the first teenage country crossover single, and Perkins performed his biggest hit record, "Blue Suede Shoes," on the same day he became the first country artist to reach number three on the rhythm and blues charts.[23] Traditionalists viewed movement toward pop and mainstream genres as abandoning country music, but Siman knew that change had to happen in the music and entertainment business. Some observers feared the end of country and western music altogether, but Red Foley saw the need to blend country with other musical forms: "It's just like we had a dress store and saw all the customers going to a store across the street where they had newer styles. We've got to sing the newest styles. So, lots of country and western singers are gradually switching to rhythm and blues."[24] Siman's suggestion for solving the "problem" of rock and roll was not to fight it, but to get more country music on television. He knew that record labels reported immediate sales boosts when their artists performed on the *Ozark Jubilee*. The show's presence on national television was doing more to help country music survive than rock and roll was damaging it.

Siman's perspective about country music's strength and versatility was on display when Top Talent and Crossroads hosted the CMDJA's first convention on June 14-16, 1956. They produced a "Country Music Carnival" at the Colonial and Kentwood hotels in Springfield to coincide with RadioOzark's Ozark Square Dance Jubilee at Marvel Cave Park (now a part of Silver Dollar City). Crossroads handled tickets, publicity, local arrangements, and talent for the event.[25] The 220 members attending included country disc jockeys from Florida to Canada, among them Tom Perryman, "Ramblin' Lou" Schriver, Nelson King, Connie B. Gay of the Town and Country Network, "Cracker Jim" Brooker, and Don Ramsey. Also attending were representatives from BMI, Acuff-Rose Publishing, Peer International, Tannen Music, Cedarwood Publishing, Town & Country Network, Showcase Music, Columbia Records, Decca Records, Mercury Records, Capitol Records, RCA Victor, Philip Morris, *Country Song Roundup*, *Jamboree Magazine*, *Billboard* magazine and the Charles Lamb Agency. The main purpose of the gathering was to raise funds for the organization and plan future meetings.

The *Ozark Jubilee* sponsored a Friday luncheon of chicken and dumplings for participants, and the Springfield Chamber of Commerce awarded CMDJA president Nelson King the Ozark Hillbilly Medallion reserved for distinguished visitors. Performers during the luncheon were Foley, Johnny Horton, Brenda Lee, the Browns, Billy Walker, Johnny Cash, Smiley Burnette, Chet Atkins, Audrey Williams, Roy Drusky, Jerry Reed, Slim Wilson, and other *Jubilee* staff artists. Crossroads also organized a four-hour, Friday night country show hosted by Red Foley and Sonny James at the Jewell Theatre for a paying audience of 1,200 people. Two weeks before the show, *Cash Box* reported that "four of the country's leading recording stars have already assured the association of their desire to appear . . . Since the public is going to pay the association wants to give it the best possible line up of talent."[26] The show netted over $1,200 for the CMDJA.

On Saturday evening, conventioneers attended the ABC broadcast of the *Ozark Jubilee* at the Jewell Theatre. Visiting deejays and their families, performers, and music business professionals had reserved seats, and an after-show party hosted by Red Foley Enterprises and Decca Records capped off the conference activities. *Billboard* pronounced the festival a success, with the exception of a "few slip-ups in arrangements" and a "bit of moaning" from BMI tradesmen about a lack of business-oriented activities.[27]

The following year, the CMDJA held its annual meeting in Kansas City. Although negotiations for a nationally televised broadcast of the meeting's main concert event fell through, Crossroads brought the *Ozark Jubilee* cast to

Lou Black (center) with disc jockeys attending the Country Music Disc Jockeys Association meeting in Springfield, June 1956. *Courtesy of Siman Family Papers, private collection of Scott Foster Siman and Jayne Siman Chowning.*

entertain attendees for more than three hours at the Arena of the Municipal Auditorium. The show featured the Browns, Billy Walker, Slim Wilson, Faron Young, Jimmy Skinner, Webb Pierce, the Blackwood Brothers quartet, and Bobby Lord. Despite this lineup, ticket sales were "optimistically described as 'fair,'" and the convention only a "scant forty registrants."[28] The CMDJA was declining due to conflicts over who should control the country music industry and a lack of funds.[29] In 1958, the board of directors unanimously voted to disband the CMDJA and transferred its remaining $1,200 to the new CMA.

Early discussions about the CMA's purpose reflected a desire to distance the organization from the CMDJA's divisive political struggles. "Instead, it would be industry-wide and would be led by a board of directors, elected by the membership and representing every facet of the business. The board would devote attention to only those projects that would benefit every aspect of the business."[30] As the CMA had money troubles for a while, fundraising became a central topic of discussion for board members. In September 1959, Siman and Crossroads TV hosted the first CMA quarterly board meeting ever held outside Nashville, at the Kentwood Arms in Springfield. Fifteen members from New York, Nashville, and Miami attended the meeting. Crossroads brought the board members to Ralph Foster's farm for a Friday evening barbecue, and Eddy Arnold and Ernest Tubb provided entertainment for weekend events. Arnold's smooth, Nashville-sound vocals and Tubb's hard-core country demonstrated a successful combining of contrasting styles, one that represented the range of the country music industry.

DAILY WORK OF THE JUBILEE

The *Jubilee* production team had the same routine seven days a week, every week of the year. Mondays and Tuesdays were planning days, when Siman would meet with the production staff.[31] Siman was first in the chain of command, followed by Mahaffey, who was in charge of payroll. Then came Bryan Bisney (the director), Bill Ring and Slim Wilson (alternating between assistant director and music director), and Don Richardson (scriptwriter, later with Bob Tubert).[32] Bisney had final script approval. The meetings also included floor director Fred Rains, set designer Andy Miller, KYTV manager Carl Fox, chief engineer Dennis White, and band leader Slim Wilson. The group had a lot of fun, and became a family unit, according to Siman. They had nicknames for each other: Rains was "Freddy Floor," Mahaffey was "John Payroll," and Siman was "the Sergeant" in charge of detail.[33]

On Wednesdays or Thursdays, advertising executives from either ABC-TV or ad agencies would come to Springfield to rehearse commercials. Music rehearsals were also on Thursdays, and show walk-throughs on Fridays. Performer Billy Walker complained about the long Friday rehearsals: "There was no such thing as time calls. You had to be there from about noon till about four or five in the afternoon. When they pointed their finger at you, you better be ready to go."[34] Because artists were not always in town on Fridays due to their personal appearances, a final music rehearsal was always scheduled for ten o'clock on Saturday mornings.

The *Jubilee* program followed a general pattern. Red Foley or the guest host would begin with three or four up-tempo, good-feeling songs to get the audience excited and happy. Guest stars might join Foley in a duet, a lively song, or a comedy skit during the course of the show, and the last number of the show was always Foley's song of inspiration. Siman aimed at building every unit up toward a crescendo ending.[35] The team worked through program concepts, choreography, dialogue, flow, and procedures. They created transitional devices Siman called "cowcatchers" to announce what or who was coming next on the show: "Rather than just putting a name up, we might do a little piece of them doing something," such as a clip of Gene Autry riding his horse Champion, to attract attention and bring the viewer into the next hour if it was a longer show.[36] Other examples include a comedy bit, or a film clip of a sunset, flowers, or water running over rocks. The technique may sound a bit corny today, but Siman claimed it was original to the *Jubilee*.

Siman and his team tried to create specific themes for each week. If the talent booked for a show leaned toward a western style, they might have a real chuck wagon on the set. Eventually they learned that having a theme narrowed their field of performers; there weren't many theme options and artists wanted to do things that were new and different. They instead started emphasizing transitional devices that would thematically tie individual acts together and create a smooth production. When a guest star signed up for the show, Siman asked for the songs that he or she would be doing. The team would then plan an efficient schedule around these, and the band could work through the songs before formal rehearsals with the artist.[37]

Following every week's show, Siman would get a call from someone at ABC critiquing the broadcast—noting mistakes but also praising the crew for what worked. A memorandum would follow, with instructions about how to improve staging, lighting, makeup, costuming, and other details: "Don't ever light anybody from below the chin because it shows shadows. Don't light them directly overhead because it does the same thing and makes their eyes [look] hollow. . . . Do something about the square dancers. Put them in gingham dresses. Tell the cowboys to lean their hat[s] back because they're hiding their face[s]."[38] Right after each show, Siman would schmooze with the ad agency people and their clients by taking them out to the Hickory Hills Country Club or the Grove Supper Club for dinner and a little party with Red Foley or some of the other stars.[39] On Sunday morning, Siman would get a group of staff members together and start shuttling people to the airport. On Monday morning he would be back at the weekly meeting, planning a new show. There was no day off for Siman.

To avoid problems when the show went live, the production team would work three weeks ahead. Despite this, Siman claimed they "were never ready." There were always problems when the cameras went on: "They'd be putting makeup on Red Foley and he'd still be rehearsing lines, or something was wrong with one of the songs and we were trying to work with the guest stars that were there," he recalled.[40] Don Richardson or Bob Tubert wrote scripts for every show. They were available on studio monitors, and everybody on the

Ozark Jubilee rehearsal. *Courtesy of Ralph Foster Museum.*

set had a mimeographed copy, but they rarely followed them.[41] Anything could happen on live television, but Siman found this exciting. He believed that mistakes could sometimes turn into assets because they made stars more human to audiences. Regardless of advance preparation, acts of God or "self-imposed acts of God" (personal problems) might interrupt the plan.[42] When illness or performance schedule conflicts intervened, the staff might have to scramble for a substitute performer, which might mean that sets for certain songs or acts would have to be redone. Live television was an intimidating format—when something unexpected happened on stage, there was no time delay, no rewind-and-do-over. And the show would end at its scheduled end time whether they were ready or not.

The *Jubilee* performers could reach more people in a moment on television than in personal appearances over their entire lives, but it kept Siman and his team on their toes. Once, during a cowboy song duet, Red Foley and Ernest Tubb fell backward off the bench they were sitting on. The audience went into hysterics, while Siman "about had cardiac arrest in the control room."[43] Foley and Tubb simply got up and acted like nothing had happened. It was funnier than many planned routines by comedy acts. In another cowboy routine, a suction-cup arrow was supposed to hit the wall beside Tex Ritter's head. The shooter's aim was bad, and the camera had to be adjusted to show where the arrow actually had hit and stuck. "It broke everybody up ... laughing and [it] just ruined the effect," recalled Siman.[44] After the scene, Ritter said "I'll tell you one thing. That ain't the way I shot that six-shooter." Apparently shooting techniques on set did not improve; in the middle of a rehearsal of "High Noon," a suction-cup arrow intended to hit a board stuck to Ritter's chest instead, prompting him to say, "What in the hell are you trying to do? Kill me?"[45] Siman loved the spontaneity of it all.

Nothing could be taken for granted with the cast, or with the equipment. For instance, on opening night at the Jewell Theatre, a slide projector used to introduce commercials and promos had an electrical short and burned the power supply. Engineers put out the fire, but smoke filled the control room. One engineer ran a couple doors down the street, found a tractor battery in storage, and wired it up to the slide projector. The show carried on. When it was over, ABC called and complimented Siman on the show. He responded, "Well, I'm sure glad you liked it, because we fed it to you on a piece of barbed wire."[46] He never explained the reference.

Advertisers bought commercials during the *Jubilee* because it reached more people for less money than other shows. Sponsors included Dickies Work Clothes, Rolaids, American Chicle (makers of Dentyne and Clorets), Regal Pale Beer, Carter's Pills, Dristan, and Johnson's Wax. To promote advertising sales for 1957, the ABC marketing department boasted about the impressive accomplishments of the *Ozark Jubilee* during its first two and a half seasons on the network. These included increasing numbers of personal appearances and higher performance fees for *Jubilee* artists; high ticket sales to fans from thirty-four states; articles about the *Jubilee* in major national publications, including *Time*, *Newsweek*, *TV Guide*, and *Business Week*; and multiple honors received by the show.[47]

While advertisers were a blessing, they were sometimes a curse. Siman learned to be careful with advertising agencies, as they wanted to control more of the show's content. Siman reasoned that the advertisers hadn't gotten the *Jubilee* where they were; they had gotten themselves there. His feelings about advertisers were: "You're buying a commercial, and we want to work with you, and we want you on our team, but don't tell us how to run the show."[48] The agencies would write the commercial copy and the production team would approve it or not during the commercial rehearsals, held ahead of the show rehearsals. If Crossroads voiced objections to the copy during rehearsals, an on-site agency representative might rewrite the copy received from the sponsor on the spot. They tried to tie commercial content into the *Jubilee*, but it didn't always work out.

As producer of the *Ozark Jubilee*, Siman had his hands full. The show ran fifty-two weeks a year, with no summer break or seasons. He had to keep three shows going at a time: "the one that we're buying talent for that's coming up three weeks from now, the one we're building sets for that's coming up two weeks from now, and the one that we're in production on that's coming up Saturday night."[49] When he wasn't planning shows, he was dealing with clients, advertising agencies, talent, and artist managers. "You inherit other people's problems whether you want them or not." He might get a two-week vacation, but it would be consumed by phone calls about problems on the show. If he left town, it would be for a business trip to Nashville. Even camping and fishing trips sometimes became business trips.

Siman frequently entertained television network and music business executives from New York, Chicago, or Nashville on floating expeditions on the White River with popular Ozarks outfitter Jim Owen. Siman said that the executives "really fell in love with that river. Every second you were floating, you were looking up at God's wallpaper."[50] Owen used nineteen-foot, shallow-draft, wooden john boats for floating and fishing on the upper White River. Before the US Army Corps of Engineers started building dams that turned the White River into a series of lakes in Missouri and Arkansas during the 1950s and '60s, it was "the best smallmouth bass stream in the whole United States."[51] In 1958, *Daily Oklahoman* Outdoor Editor Vernon Snell recommended Siman to readers as a fishing guide for their next trip to Bull Shoals Lake.[52] He claimed that Siman once posed as a guide for anglers from Kansas City and St. Louis while they "spilled their business troubles all over the boat." Siman told Snell he now had a new philosophy: "Any time you have a problem bothering you ... don't give up. Just change jobs for a day."[53] While such tall tales make for fun reading, the column was also giving Siman—as well as the *Ozark Jubilee* and Bull Shoals Lake—free publicity, and selling the benefits of an Ozarks vacation to urban readers in Oklahoma City, just a few hours away.

The Simans took family camping trips with their neighbor John Morris, who had two daughters about the same age as Jayne and Susan Siman, and a son, Johnny Morris, who hung out with Susan and Jayne's younger brother, Scott.[54] The kids swam and floated in the river while the elder Morris and Siman would try to solve the problems of the world. Their wives would set up a card table right in the river and play cards while cooling their feet in the water. Meals were cooked over a campfire. Siman also tried to make time for his family by taking them with him on Nashville business trips. His daughter Jayne remembers begging her father to let her come along on his meetings in Nashville restaurants because she loved to listen to the southern accents. His wife Rosie would take the kids to Andrew Jackson's home, the Hermitage, and give them history lessons. "That was the big vacation, although I know Daddy was doing business while we were there."[55]

At home, Siman purchased an old seven-room farmhouse on ten acres near Springfield Lake for about $40,000. They named the place "Rosi Acres" at the suggestion of KWTO/*Ozark Jubilee* announcer and performer Bill Ring, who said the word "Rosi" was a perfect combination of the names Rosie and Si. Siman tried to avoid doing business at home in Rosi Acres, but the phone still rang. Calls often came from *Ozark Jubilee* entertainers and colleagues, or from promoters wishing to book *Jubilee* talent. The Siman family had a tradition of uninterrupted dinners together: "No phone . . . but lots of conversation about life in general. Daddy always said the prayer, which was thoughtful each night. He loved his family and loved his home life."[56] Domestic life was not always fun for Rosie, who managed everything at home—from sick children to a snake in the house—so that Siman could manage his work. Jayne remembers standing at the door crying out for her father not to leave. Siman tried to make amends for his absence by bringing gifts for the kids when he returned.

One winter while Siman was out of town, Rosie and the children were snowed in and lost power. Rosie was very sick, and Scott had pneumonia. Young Jayne and Susan fed them by heating soup in the fireplace. It was three days before help arrived. When Siman was at home, Rosie was responsible for cooking and providing hospitality for a variety of *Jubilee* stars, many of whom stayed with the Simans, and other people who came for socializing or business. Jayne remembers getting off the bus excitedly one day after school and running down the lane to welcome Tennessee Ernie Ford. Though Rosie and her mother made most of the kids' clothes, the youngest child, Scott, was a "trial kid" for *Ozark Jubilee* sponsor Dickies Jeans: "They'd send him jeans and see how long it would take him to wear the knees out." The Siman children had ponies, a big barn, plenty of room to roam, holiday celebrations like Easter egg hunts and Halloween parties, a large circle of family and friends, "and lots of company, including stars from the *Jubilee*."[57] Jayne learned to play piano, and her mother often joined her playing both ragtime and classical music. They sang around the house and in the choir at St. Paul United Methodist Church. Overall, the Siman children apparently had normal—if privileged—childhoods during the *Ozark Jubilee* days.

KEEPING THE NETWORK

In spite of its good ratings and low production costs, the *Ozark Jubilee* was almost canceled many times during its five-year run. Siman felt that the network's reasons for wanting to cancel were unfounded and suspected that some ABC executive's wife didn't like country music because it was degrading for the network.[58] Yet Siman had enough experience with ABC by now to understand their need to respond to shifting audience interests. Siman became a road warrior for the *Jubilee* as he fought to broaden the program's viewer base. He racked up air miles negotiating agreements with network executives in New York, especially after ABC-TV became more popular and they no longer had to depend on the *Jubilee* for programming.

A bewildering series of near cancellations, schedule changes, and show-title modifications indicates the anxiety felt by network executives trying to exact ratings from what they perceived as a rural program supposedly designed to attract viewers in the rural South, when the number of television owners in the South were minimal compared to the rest of the country: "Even accounting for the 'southern diaspora,' the estimated 20 million white and African American migrants who left the South between 1900 and 1970, there were not enough southerners to shift [the region] into a position where they could dictate national tastes."[59] Southerners owned a small percentage of the nation's television sets (about 14.4 percent), an inadequate number to register viewer preferences in the ratings. "A network needed to win 34 percent of the viewership to secure first place in the ratings, and the South could only provide a fraction of that number, even with every set tuned to the same station. Therefore, the South was a niche audience at best and certainly not large enough to commandeer a network's program schedule for nearly a decade."[60] Thus, ABC had no way to get a demographic reading on the *Jubilee*'s popularity or what its viewers wanted. The network's narrow, damaging perspective of country music was what Siman and his colleagues at the CMDJA and the CMA had been trying to adjust.

On August 16, 1957, ABC issued a two-week notice of cancellation to the *Jubilee* after *Your Hit Parade* producer Dan Lounsbery spent a week in Springfield trying to "streamline" the show.[61] Siman made a trip to New York to get it back on the air. Consistently erratic, last-minute schedule changes made it difficult for the crew, as well as members of the press in charge of TV schedules, to keep up. A year later, ABC moved *Jubilee* from Saturday nights to Monday nights, but advance ticket sales made it necessary for the

Jewell Theatre shows to continue on Saturday nights. Undoubtedly frustrated by the possibility of doing two full shows a week, the team negotiated for a revised Saturday night schedule, with the live show being "kinescoped over lines to Hollywood for delayed broadcast over ABC network stations, mostly on Monday nights."[62] The *Jubilee* stage show had to be moved to an earlier time on Saturday nights for "a period of four to six weeks," but KYTV's airtime was still undetermined because local programming had to be rearranged. The shifts were chaotic for all involved: advertisers, Crossroads staff, performers, and KYTV personnel.

ABC further confused things by changing the program's name from the *Ozark Jubilee* to *Country Music Jubilee* in July 1957, ostensibly to broaden the show's geographical relevance and increase market share, although it continued to play to sellout crowds at the Jewell. On October 19, the show welcomed its 200,000th visitor.[63] Then on August 2, 1958, the *Country Music Jubilee* became *Jubilee USA*. Siman said the name changes were a result of "poor thinking on the part of the network. They thought they had better sales appeal if we called it *Jubilee USA* and not just *Ozark*, which [they thought] was too local."[64] But fans never let go of the original name—it was always the *Ozark Jubilee* to them. The network simply didn't know how to make country music appeal to their interpretation of what mass audiences wanted, and didn't think anyone from the Ozarks knew, either.

From his first contact with ABC-TV, Siman was the appeaser who navigated attempts by network missionaries such as Don Lounsbery to make the *Jubilee* fit New York and Los Angeles television models. A review of changes made to the *Jubilee* during its last three years reflects the network's efforts to shift away from idealized rural settings and music toward a modern look and pop sound. These efforts included modifying country-styled songs and instrumentation for a more pop sound; moving the bands off camera; replacing country-themed set designs with abstract backdrops; asking singers to perform without their guitars; replacing women's western or country apparel with slick, modern styles; exchanging men's cowboy costumes for suits and ties; reducing or cutting off Foley's relaxed banter with the audience; and using heavily scripted introductions and transitions between acts. The result was a network television variety show that was at times indistinguishable from others except for its cast of country stars. The *Ozark Jubilee*'s freshness and intimate qualities gradually disappeared.[65]

Singer Wanda Jackson blamed ABC for the *Ozark Jubilee*'s decline and felt the show was better with a more traditional presentation: "ABC didn't think a country music show could hold its own if they didn't bring in some pop performers . . . We country folks started the show, and it was getting more and more popular. Why did we need pop artists to come in and to help us or make us more legitimate? Well, we didn't! . . . After a while, it began to feel like it just wasn't really going anywhere. We stopped getting the really good country guests when the flavor of the show changed."[66] Her comment is ironic, considering her influence in rock and roll as the "Queen of Rockabilly." The *Jubilee*'s novelty as a live TV show had not only worn thin, parts of its broadcast were obviously lip-synched or prerecorded.

Nevertheless, the *Jubilee* coasted along as the only country music show in the ABC schedule while adventure dramas such as *Zorro*, *The Walter Winchell File*, and *77 Sunset Strip* met ABC's goals to outdo CBS and NBC by capturing a younger audience: "The young housewife—one cut above the teenager—with two to four kids, who has to buy the clothing, the food, the soaps, the home remedies. It's this woman in the twenty- to thirty-year-old age that the action appeals to most. The heroes are all good-looking, virile types. The women like to look at them. And the husbands go along for the self-identification with the he-man type."[67]

THE END IN SIGHT

Continuing problems with Red Foley—which began as early as April 1957, when the IRS filed tax liens against him for $270,000 in unpaid income taxes from 1948 to 1957—contributed to ABC's final cancellation of the *Ozark Jubilee*.[68] Don Richardson tried to keep gossip about Foley's alcoholism, marital disputes, and tax problems from spreading outside the Crossroads family by feeding the press a good supply of news about his successful performances. The IRS was relentless in seeking its due, however, despite the fact that Foley and his wife Sally insisted that incomes determined by the IRS were "fictitious, erroneous and arbitrary."[69] In December 1959, the IRS issued an indictment on two counts of income tax evasion for $28,500 in taxes for 1954 and 1955. Foley was arrested and released to Foster and Siman with a $2,500 bond.[70] He pled not guilty at the trial that began in Springfield in March 1960.

The word was now out, and sponsors became jittery. According to Siman, "they might have bailed out if our team hadn't put a measurable amount of effort [in] saying 'We know the guy's innocent and he's going to be proven innocent.'" Siman had witnessed Foley's casual attitude toward money; he had once given Foley a check for his television appearance on the *Dinah Shore Show* in Hollywood, and later found Foley at the Corn Crib restaurant getting ready to autograph the back of that check for an adoring fan—it was just another piece of paper to him.[71] Despite this incident and Foley's inefficient bookkeeping skills, Siman was convinced that he was incapable of what the IRS charged. The trial went on for a year and a half while sponsors and the network edged away from the *Jubilee*. Foley's alcoholism progressed, and his health became a serious problem. On Thursday, February 4, 1960, Don Richardson noted in his diary that "Red did a wig-flip last night, with [Dr.] Ginger H'Doubler saying our boy would have to remain in [the hospital] until Friday the 12th, which leaves us with a not unfamiliar last-minute situation on the *Jubilee*. Slim [Wilson] scheduled to emcee, with Carl Smith and an as-yet-unbooked second guest."[72] Foley missed an important *Jubilee* troupe show, sponsored by client Massey Ferguson, in Denver early the following week. The morning of the show, Richardson had to write a script for Foley to record on the telephone "from his bed in the 'flu' ward," for a broadcast in the 9,000-seat Denver Coliseum later that day.[73]

Upon Foley's release from the hospital, he took off for Nashville and failed to return for a scheduled taping of Massey Ferguson commercials a week later.[74] He finally flew in late that evening but "tied one on after flying in" and didn't make it to bed until eight the next morning. The *Jubilee* crew "had a rough time getting him up at 11 for rehearsals" and he was "3/4 shot at rehearsals, in very weak voice," said Richardson, who added: "What the hell, it's just my living, that's all."[75] If Foley started a song in the wrong key, he would stop singing and ask Slim Wilson to start over. Audiences seemed to forgive it all. "We in the control room went into apoplexy over how he was ruining the show's timing," said Richardson, "but folks at home shrugged and smiled [and said], 'Well, that's just ol' Red for you.'"[76] In April, Foley was back in St. John's Hospital—"in the padded job" for drug and alcohol addiction—after being flown back from Oklahoma City by a friend.[77] Siman went to Foley's house and cleaned out all the prescription bottles, to little effect. Siman claimed that Foley "lost his ambition to do the show, so we were in a different ball game altogether."[78] Sponsors didn't want to renew. To make things worse, the *Jubilee* also started mysteriously losing its network connection in the middle of a broadcast. The show began to miss commercials because of the unexplained signal break, and when they got it back the transmission was bad. Siman blamed it on union problems, but "couldn't prove anything."[79] Despite this, the show went on.

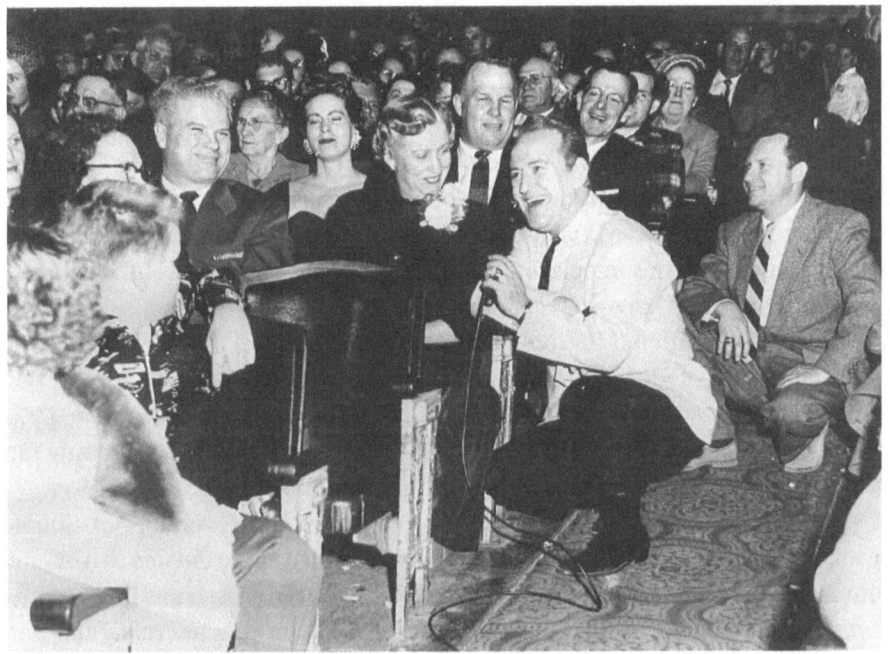

Si Siman (far right) assists Red Foley as he works the *Ozark Jubilee* crowd.
Courtesy of Ralph Foster Museum.

Things seemed to be running smoothly again until ABC wanted to put a Madison Square boxing program in the *Jubilee*'s Saturday night slot. *Jubilee USA*'s ratings had risen to 12.2 by March 1959, and ABC had renewed it, but someone at the network wanted to program sports in that time slot and canceled the renewal.[80] Crossroads then got another cancellation notice from ABC-TV. This one was permanent. On September 18, 1960, the *Springfield Leader and Press* announced that "a made-in-Springfield product which in its lifetime has been loved, lauded, laughed-at and loathed, is on its deathbed. . . . With it will go the rather unexpected label—from its birth—of being one of the ten oldest programs on network TV."[81] Siman liked to say that they got canceled due to illness: ABC got sick of them.[82] Ralph Foster had a more practical view of the situation when he said the *Jubilee* had been reduced to a "necessary casualty."[83]

The last *Jubilee* show at the Jewell Theatre—its 297th consecutive stage performance—was on September 24, 1960. The *Jubilee USA* radio show continued, but even that soon went off the air. It was the end of an era. For at least a year after the *Jubilee*'s final show, Crossroads turned away orders for between 150 and 300 *Jubilee* tickets a week from fans who didn't know it had been canceled. Crossroads issued certificates of thanks to the *Jubilee* cast and crew in recognition of their talent, patience, understanding, and warm cooperation. Siman didn't know what they were going to do, but he wanted to keep the team together. He told an interviewer, "Country music has a place today on network TV ... It may not be the *Jubilee*, but there's going to be a country music show on the network from someplace."[84] *Jubilee* performers used the show name to market themselves in personal appearances throughout the region.

Springfield officials demolished the deteriorating Jewell Theatre in February 1961. RadiOzark had purchased the Landers Theatre around the corner two years before for $65,000, thinking they would move *Jubilee USA* to the new location. They had spent $4,000 on remodeling to get it ready for the move, but the show ended before the renovations were complete.

The community grieved over its loss of status and revenue, but Siman would not give up. He considered negotiating a return of the *Jubilee* to ABC-TV after other thirteen-week network contracts expired. A second idea was to syndicate previously filmed programs. A third option was to create another country music show for a different network. This time Crossroads could negotiate with experience and a proven record of success, in spite of the *Jubilee*'s final cancellation. They would not have to start from scratch; they could tap into the fame of the old *Ozark Jubilee* while continuing its recent evolution into a more sophisticated variety-show style of country music for a new era.

Another network *Jubilee* show seemed possible on NBC, with the Landers Theatre being its home. Crossroads approached Red Foley about hosting the new show, but the IRS trial and Foley's drinking problem were ongoing. Cox demanded that Foley make a pledge not to drink any more on the job, but Foley refused and said drinking didn't have anything to do with the job. Cox disagreed, and told Foley that drinking was indeed his "number-one problem."[85] On March 10, 1961, Siman announced to the press that a new weekly half-hour variety show for NBC-TV called the *Five Star Jubilee* would begin in Springfield.[86] Two days later, NBC-TV brought multi-million-dollar mobile units to Springfield in two large buses and parked them outside the Landers Theatre to broadcast the show, which was scheduled to begin in five days. As with the *Ozark Jubilee*, Siman had technical issues getting the show on the air. Signal interference from KTTS radio across the street disrupted the television picture from the Landers. For two weeks, the evening broadcast show had to be taped for rebroadcast at one-thirty the next morning until technicians could

On the set with the *Five Star Jubilee* broadcast in 1961, featuring hosts Carl Smith, Snooky Lanson, Tex Ritter, Rex Allen, and Jimmy Wakely. *Courtesy of Ralph Foster Museum.*

arrive from New York to fix the problem. Sponsored by Massey Ferguson, the *Five Star Jubilee* featured five celebrity hosts in alternating weeks: Rex Allen, Snooky Lanson, Tex Ritter, Carl Smith, and Jimmy Wakely. It was the first regular network television country music show in color ever produced outside New York or Hollywood.

The *Five Star Jubilee* did not lack star quality, but as a taped program it lacked the raw excitement of live television. Guest performers included Roy Acuff, Jimmy Dean, Flatt and Scruggs, Minnie Pearl, Ray Price, Barbara Mandrell, and Faron Young. The *Five Star Jubilee* looked like every other variety show on network television, far removed from the Ozarks identity that had made it unique just over five years before. Yet, the affiliation with NBC looked like a success. Crossroads owned the theater, had a staff of eighty people, and "everything was going to be just fine," until NBC decided to withdraw their color cameras for the upcoming broadcast of the 1961 World Series.[87] The sponsors got shaky again, NBC didn't renew its contract, and the *Five Star Jubilee* was over in only six months. Its last broadcast was September 22, 1961. Crossroads was left with the Landers Theatre and all the production equipment not owned by NBC.

In 1963, Siman and his Crossroads colleagues formed a new company called Tele-Color to produce similar shows in the future. In his grand style, Foster told the media that Tele-Color would be a "special-projects service, specializing in the creation and design of unique uses of color," a "marriage of film and electronic-camera techniques to introduce a whole new era of economy and utilitarian use of color."[88] Tele-Color went to work filming ABC's *Wide World of Sports* in 1964. Siman had hopes of staying in the television business, but his Crossroads team "started losing players because of no television show, and first thing you know our team was kind of falling apart."[89]

AFTER THE JUBILEE

Top Talent continued to book *Jubilee* artists for years after NBC canceled the *Five Star Jubilee*. Red Foley was still a star among his fans, who didn't care about the gossip that surrounded him. He sold his Springfield house in November 1962 and worked on an ABC television version of *Mr. Smith Goes to Washington*. From July to September 1963, Siman booked Foley on shows in Colorado, Texas, Florida, Kansas, Minnesota, and Arizona as a featured artist with *Jubilee* performers. His personal earnings for the shows ranged from $500 to $2,500 per show.[90] Foley continued to perform throughout the country until his death on September 19, 1968—a year after being inducted into the Country Music Hall of Fame—at the age of fifty-eight. The official cause of Foley's death was respiratory failure, but the raw truth of Foley as an alcoholic dying alone in a motel room is far less decorous. Jean Shepard was one of the last people to see Foley on the night he died.

In spite of his frustrations with Foley's problems, *Jubilee* publicity director Don Richardson wrote a fond memoriam for Foley after his death:

> Chain-smoking Camels, worrying his tongue over an upper plate that never seemed to fit right and smoothing back his hair with the heels of his hands, he was a good audience in any conversation. A companionable sort who laughed louder than anyone at Bill Ring's jokes in the office, who teased Siman over a highly touted guest singer on the *Jubilee* who went sour on the air, who intently lived every impassioned moment of Ralph Foster's play-by-play account of landing a big fish two days ago in Canada. Red exhibited a puppy dog affection for those he liked.[91]

Siman also paid tribute to Red Foley after his death in 1968 by setting up a memorial fund at Berea College to endow a perpetual music scholarship for students who wish to pursue a career in the music business. Berea College students have been receiving Red Foley Memorial Music Awards every year since 1970.

Cancellation was not the end of the line for *Jubilee* performers. "Most of them were so talented it was just a matter of movement and readjustment. Some of them went to Nashville. Some of them went to Branson and started their own show[s]. Some went back to the West Coast."[92] *Jubilee* announcer Joe Slattery became a celebrated announcer in Chicago. Leroy Van Dyke recorded another album and had a number-one hit, "Walk on By," in 1961 with Mercury Records. Harold Morrison, Jimmy Gately, Bill Ring, and other staff performers sought opportunities on local TV programs as entertainers or announcers.

Slim Wilson celebrated twenty-nine years with KWTO in 1961. He traveled to Chicago every week to star on NBC-TV's weekly Saturday show called *Today on the Farm* with Joe Slattery and Eddy Arnold.[93] After the contract ended, Wilson had a Saturday morning radio show at KWTO while resuming a regular performance schedule. From 1964 to 1975 he had a local television show called the *Slim Wilson Show*, featuring the Tall Timber Trio with Bob White and Speedy Haworth. In keeping with his characteristic humility and humor, someone asked him if he knew how to read music, and he responded, "Not enough to hurt my playin'."[94] Siman respected Wilson for staying in the Ozarks: "I think I understand humility. It's being big and not knowing or caring about how popular you are. Slim Wilson was such a person. The reason Slim Wilson was so big is simple: If you want to be big you have to be big yourself."[95]

Jubilee scriptwriter and publicist Don Richardson moved forty miles south of Springfield to the Branson area, where he worked as publicity director at a new theme park that opened in May 1960. He was the creative force behind naming the new park Silver Dollar City. *Jubilee* set designer Andy Miller became Silver Dollar City's art director and replicated *Jubilee* sets all over the park. Richardson helped bring the CBS-TV series *The Beverly Hillbillies* to the Ozarks by inviting the show's producer, Paul Henning, to visit. After the entire cast and crew of television's popular show came to Silver Dollar City in 1969 to film the first of five episodes, the rest of the world came to Missouri to bask in the beauty of the Ozarks and attend one of many country music variety shows modeled after the *Ozark Jubilee*.[96]

In the early 1960s, former KWTO and *Jubilee* performers Bob Mabe and Lloyd Presley opened the first country music shows south of Springfield in nearby Branson.[97] One variety show after another popped up on Highway 76, locally known as "the strip," making the town a mecca for country music fans during the 1970s and 1980s.[98] The shows closely followed the barn-dance format developed on the early *Ozark Jubilee* shows, blending country, bluegrass, and gospel with hillbilly comedy. In the 1990s, many of the Branson theater shows shifted from Ozarks and country-styled programs to glitzy, Vegas-style performances of cover tunes. By the 1990s, "a stampede of past-their-prime country legends threatened to remake Branson in old Nashville's image," until the "Branson blitz plateaued."[99] Only a few country shows remain, along with high-impact venues such as the Branson Star Theater. Missouri's official ragtime piano player and former *Junior Jubilee* square-dance caller Gary Ellison claims that "the fingerprints of the *Jubilee* are still here," and *Presley's Country Jubilee* provides the evidence in its name.[100]

After the *Jubilee* era, Si Siman was at another crossroads. ABC-TV offered him a high-paying job in production if he would move to New York. "That was hard to turn down," he said. "But I couldn't see me, with my deep roots in Springfield, and my family and Rosie's family, picking up and going to, of all places, either Hollywood or New York."[101] Affiliations with Crossroads, RadiOzark, Top Talent, and Earl Barton had to be reconfigured. When Lester E. Cox died in 1968, the Cox family bought his shares of Crossroads from Mahaffey, Siman, and Foster.

Siman and Mahaffey had started Earl Barton Music in 1953 and established its affiliation with BMI. They had also purchased radio stations together in Shreveport (KCIJ); Waynesville, Missouri (KYSD/FM); and Fort Leonard Wood, Missouri (KJPW). The division of investments was simple: Siman traded his stock in the three radio stations for Mahaffey's stock in Crossroads TV, Top Talent, and Earl Barton. Foster remained as an investor in Siman's companies until his death and left his portion of the company stock to Siman. Mahaffey left to buy more radio stations and continue in broadcasting.[102]

Siman wanted to work with songwriters and took Rosie on a house-hunting trip to Nashville. According to Siman's daughter Jayne, "They had a house picked out, and we were going to move, but us kids cried."[103] Siman and Rosie decided they would wait a year before making a decision. If nothing happened in his new music publishing business after a year, they would revisit the possibility of moving to Nashville. He just didn't know how long it would take to start over. Siman was grateful that "God didn't put all the talented people in one place."[104]

CHAPTER FIVE

AWARD-WINNING MUSIC PUBLISHER

ALTHOUGH THE STAGE WAS EMPTY at the Landers Theatre, the sense of music happening in Springfield still lingered. Siman had demonstrated his undeniable instinct for talent by advancing the careers of Chet Atkins, Brenda Lee, Porter Wagoner, the Browns, and others. The *Ozark Jubilee*'s longevity on network television and the sellout performances of the show, both at home and on the road, confirmed his skills as a promoter and pioneer television producer. The question now boiled down to whether Siman's ear for hit songs would be enough to sustain a career as a music publisher. Siman thought he might try songwriting, but he wasn't satisfied with the results. He and Porter Wagoner had often brainstormed ideas for songs while driving to and from Nashville "to stave off boredom and keep awake."[1] Siman said the ideas would come, but he just couldn't meet his own expectations.

Siman now had full control of Earl Barton Music and thought about moving to Nashville, but he and Rosie decided to give the publishing business in Springfield a year before leaving the Ozarks.[2] There were plenty of songwriters in the region to work with, including former *Jubilee* artists who wanted to stay and work from Springfield. However, Siman's one-year plan to make Springfield, Missouri, a hotbed for his music publishing business slowed to a five-year crawl. He learned the hard way that the music publishing business was an endurance test requiring patience, perseverance, and a positive attitude. But Siman had an easygoing nature that paid off when dealing with personalities most people found difficult or temperamental.

A ROCKABILLY ICON: RONNIE SELF

One of the most interesting and troubled early songwriters Siman worked with was rockabilly singer Ronnie Self. Music journalist Bruce Eder believes that Self could have been bigger than Elvis Presley: "Why Ronnie Self never made it as a performer is one of the great mysteries and injustices of pop music history ... He should have been there, thought of in the same breath as Perkins or Jerry Lee Lewis; instead, he's a footnote in rock and roll history outside of Europe, where he's treated as a legend."[3] Siman thought Self was "the most uninhibited writer" he had ever met.[4]

Ronnie Self was born in 1938 in a small community called Tin Town, Missouri. He was a wild child whose interest in music and songwriting began as a teenager. Self wrote his first song at the age of fourteen. In 1956, he signed his first songwriting contract with Dub Allbritten, who managed Brenda Lee and Red Foley. Allbritten put him on the Phillip Morris Caravan package show as the rockabilly option, where he "he quickly began attracting attention with his wild and highly animated stage act, not to mention the nature of his songs, which combined the intensity of R & B with high-energy rockabilly."[5]

The same year he recorded his first single on ABC Records, "Pretty Bad Blues," with the B-side "Three Hearts Later." Columbia Records took note and signed him to a recording contract in 1957. Self married in 1958, and his wife was pregnant with their first child soon after his Columbia recording of "Bop-a-Lena," written by Mel Tillis and *Jubilee* guest artist Webb Pierce. Because of his popularity in the Phillip Morris Caravan, Self had been asked to do a screen test for the movie *Rally Round the Flag, Boys!*, but he never appeared because of his child's birth, and he quit the Phillip Morris Caravan. When "Bop-a-Lena" came out on the charts, nobody would book him on television variety shows "for fear that he wouldn't turn up" and "Bop-a-Lena" "stalled low on the charts and disappeared soon after."[6] Other recording contracts with Decca and Kapp were unsuccessful.

Self's hopes for a more lucrative career in songwriting were promising. Jim Denny at Nashville's Cedarwood Music published two smash hits for him: Brenda Lee's "Sweet Nothin's" (1959) and "I'm Sorry" (1960). Si Siman

Johnny Cash and Ronnie Self at the *Ozark Jubilee*. *Courtesy of Country Music Hall of Fame and Museum.*

published "Home in My Hand," recorded by artists such as 1950s country singer-songwriter Dallas Frazier, Welsh singer-songwriter Dave Edmonds, and legendary late-1960s country-rock band, Commander Cody and His Lost Planet Airmen. However, Self had no career success after 1961.

Siman thought Ronnie Self was a genius, but he was a very expensive investment. Drug and alcohol addiction deteriorated his ability to live any sort of normal life, and his erratic behavior became increasingly worse. Self's sister, popular Springfield vocalist Vicky Self, said that "Si had a way about him that he could control Ronnie without hardly saying anything, by just saying, 'Hi, how are you?' and that's saying something with Ronnie."[7] However, Siman's power over Self could only go so far. Tragically funny stories about Self still circulate in the Springfield music community.

A few of Self's seven children usually tagged along with him to gigs and recordings. Springfield drummer Bobby Lloyd Hicks recalled being at a session in the late 1960s to record Self's "Waiting for the Gin to Hit Me": "Ronnie was singing and strumming and he would get the time all mixed up and these little kids are like sitting [cross-legged] on the floor ... singing 'Waiting for the gin to hit me / Mama say a prayer for her bad boy / Waiting for the gin to hit me.' There were just these three cherubic voices singing about being absolutely blasted."[8]

Self was notoriously bad with money. Journalist Mary Sue Price suggested possible causes for his financial woes: "In the moneyed 'I'm Sorry' days, he bought and wrecked three cars in one day."[9] One time, Self came into Siman's office on Friday afternoon to get a $10,000 royalty payment. Knowing Self's inclination to throw money away, Siman suggested that he take only a portion of the payment and save the rest. Self argued that $10,000 was enough to last him the rest of his life. Against his better judgment, Siman wrote him a check for the entire amount. On Monday morning, Self was back in Siman's office asking for another advance to pay his rent. Siman said, "Well Ronnie, you told me that money I gave you last Friday was enough to last you the rest of your life." Ronnie lowered his sunglasses and looked Siman in the eye and replied, "Well, Si, I done lived longer than I thought I was going to."[10]

Despite Self's instability, Siman reached out to Louisiana rocker Dale Hawkins to produce and release several singles for him, including Wayne Carson's "The Road Keeps Winding" and Self's "High on Life"—with no success.[11] Siman set up a music publishing company with Self called Table Rock Music, only to be left in the hole: "I had spent about $25,000 before [Ronnie] came in and said 'Si, it's splittin' time.' I said 'Well, what do you mean? I give you an office, I give you half the company, put up the money to run it.' He said, 'I'm sorry, it's splittin' time.' It was. He left."[12] Self's recordings remained collector's items among rockabilly fans long after his August 1981 death in the Silver Saddle Motel at the age of forty-three from an apparent heart attack after mixing alcohol with pills. He was buried with his sunglasses on.

HITMAKER WAYNE CARSON

The publishing business was slow for Siman until young singer-songwriter Wayne Carson promised to turn things around. His parents were Odie and Olivia Head, who had a long history at KWTO as staff musicians known as "Olive and Odie" or "Shorty and Sue Thompson."[13] Shorty had been a staff artist on KGBX/KWTO in the early 1930s. He had left in 1937 to work at

KMMJ in Nebraska. There he met Sue, a radio veteran who had performed with her sisters on WNAX in Yankton, South Dakota. The two married, moved to Colorado, and had two sons. In six years in the armed forces, Shorty Thompson did more than 1,400 stage shows and appeared in a motion picture titled *Eldorado Pass* with Charles Starrett and Smiley Burnette.[14] In 1948 he returned to Springfield, where he and Sue did transcriptions for RadiOzark and with their western-swing band, Saddle Rockin' Rhythm. They arrived just before Mercury Records released his first single in November 1948. Shorty and Sue played on *Korn's-a-Krackin'* before it ended in 1949, and Saddle Rockin' Rhythm had a regular radio show on KWTO in the early 1950s. During the *Ozark Jubilee* years, Thompson rejoined Slim Wilson as a member of the Tall Timber Trio and worked many shows booked by Top Talent. When the Thompsons brought their family to KWTO radio, their two young sons, Gary and Wayne, became the darlings of the *KWTO Dial.*

His family's experience with performing, publicity, and life on the road provided a solid education about the music business for young Wayne Carson.[15] When he was fourteen, Carson bought a thirty-dollar guitar, started playing it on the back porch after school, and soon was playing club dates.[16] He decided that instead of covering other people's songs, he would write his own. Shorty Thompson asked Siman to help with his son's career, and Siman officially started working with him as a songwriter in the early 1960s.[17]

Siman saw in Carson a gifted songwriter with a unique guitar style, one he had learned by emulating Merle Travis and Chet Atkins. More than anything, he saw an intangible thing that people in the music industry refer to as the "it factor." Carson just needed time to develop it and put all the pieces together, and Siman thought he was the man who could make that happen. Early in their early partnership, he had a great deal of success, including a Decca recording contract, through Red Foley, for Carson at age nineteen and an MGM contract at age twenty-two. He put Carson on the road with Foley, of whom Carson said, "Every human being on this planet should be like him. Red taught me how to be a professional."[18] Carson also performed with his group called the Travelers, named after his Decca single, "The Traveler."

Carson later recalled that in 1962 he was "playing every damn toilet in the country . . . I had to scuff around in a lot of clubs and beat away the cockroaches for a lot of years, but I had Si to believe in me."[19] Carson's band played fairground shows and rodeos such as the Jaycee Bootheel Rodeo in Sikeston, Missouri, in 1966, where he appeared with *Beverly Hillbillies* star Buddy Ebsen. According to the Sikeston *Daily Standard,*

Left: Photo of eight-year-old Wayne Carson autographed for his "manager," Si Siman. *Courtesy of Ralph Foster Museum.* Right: Wayne Carson as a young songwriter. *Courtesy of Siman Family Papers, private collection of Scott Foster Siman and Jayne Siman Chowning.*

twenty-two-year-old Carson was an "MGM rising recording star" and songwriter with more than 150 published songs, including "Blue Feeling," "The Traveler," "There's No In-Between," and "It's You, Always It's You."[20]

Carson honed his chops, wrote songs, and recorded demos at KWTO for Siman to pitch to artists, record producers, and label executives in Nashville. Sometimes his demos were simple guitar and vocal versions of songs, but if Siman thought the song had potential, he would do a full-band production. Carson once said, "Si knows his way around Nashville and he worked hard to get my songs recorded and played. And I worked my butt off singing anywhere they'd let me, and I kept on writing, and finally it worked."[21]

On their first trip to Nashville, Carson and Siman were accompanied by country singer, songwriter, and television entrepreneur Stan Hitchcock, who later recalled: "Wayne and I shared a hotel room, and I was a witness to raw genius in Wayne. He sat on the bed, chain-smoked, and wrote songs the whole trip. Si was the only one that could handle Wayne, and they made songwriting history together . . . [Siman] was a father figure to a lot of us in those years," Hitchcock recalled.[22] However, a lot of the songs Siman pitched for

Carson were passed on. Publishing was proving to be a difficult profession that involved much travel, handshaking, and rejection.

Siman's song-plugging trips to Nashville in the mid-1960s followed a typical pattern. First, he would make a couple of key phone calls from home to see if he could get a list of who was looking for songs or had a recording session coming up so he could tailor his pitch. He would then pack his suitcase, gather up reel-to-reel tapes of new demos from Carson (and occasionally other writers), load up his Wollensak T-1500 reel-to-reel tape player, and drive eight hours to visit a list of decision makers in Music City. Many of them were friends of his from the *Jubilee* years.

One of those calls was always to Siman's golf buddy Bob Beckham of Combine Music, one of the top publishing companies in Nashville, with writers including Kris Kristofferson. Beckham had had several minor hits as an artist on Decca Records. When he and Siman first met, he was an opening act for Brenda Lee. When Beckham's performance career faltered, producer Owen Bradley suggested he move to publishing. Beckham made a list of artists' needs for whenever Siman came to Nashville. It dawned on Beckham that he should make a list like Siman's every week, thus inventing the "pitch sheet" still in use in Nashville.[23]

Another call was usually to Siman's old friend Chet Atkins, to see who was on his production schedule for RCA. In 1964 he got Atkins interested in producing Della Rae (Moore), a young singer from Missouri. Atkins liked her sound and produced her initial singles for release on RCA. Several of them had been written by Carson, including "Hurry Up Summer," "Someone Sometime," and "That's The Way a Man Is." Unfortunately, none were hits.

Carson's cycle of writing, recording demos, and pitching songs went on for about four years with little sign of a hit record. He had enough confidence to know he could write a hit song, but he had a lot to learn before he could get out of the pattern of near-misses. Siman pitched Carson's song "Turn Around and Look Again" to Roy Clark through producer Ken Nelson. Clark's recording of it wasn't a chart hit, but it was a sign that they were on the right path with Carson's music. They needed to get a major artist on a major label.

In 1966 Siman went to Atkins at RCA with a Carson song he thought would be perfect for Eddy Arnold, who had been on the *Ozark Jubilee* several times and had starred in *The Eddy Arnold Show*, the ABC replacement show Siman produced in the summer of 1956. Arnold was one of the biggest country acts of all time after much pop-crossover success on RCA. Siman played Arnold a tape with Siman's proposed song on it, but Arnold turned it down. The tape kept rolling to a Carson song called "Somebody Like Me." According to Siman,

Arnold quickly said, "Turn that back! Play it over again!" Siman played the song three or four times until Arnold responded, "Man, that's for me!"[24]

Despite his initial enthusiasm, Arnold felt there was not enough of a song in "Somebody Like Me" to make a record, and started to have second thoughts about recording it when his next session came up. Atkins and Arnold got Carson on the phone and asked if he would consider writing another verse. Carson knew if he took too long to write the new verse, he risked Arnold finishing the recording project without his song because another publisher might pitch Arnold a song that would knock Carson's out of consideration. According to Siman, Carson calmly said, "Well, the third verse goes like this," and he wrote it "right there, over the phone."[25] The new verse was "I hope you listen to now / each word that I've told you now / these things you better do now / or you won't have her long." Arnold was practically speechless, but he liked it. Atkins produced the new version, and in September 1966 RCA released "Somebody Like Me" as a single. It spent four weeks at number one on *Billboard*'s Hot Country Singles chart, and eighteen weeks on the chart in total. Siman and Carson had their first real hit together, and Siman was back on the country music charts as a music publisher for the first time since the 1950s.

Country music was now in a traditional, "hard country" phase, with Merle Haggard, Porter Wagoner, George Jones, Tammy Wynette, and Loretta Lynn topping the charts. Because of this, many Nashville producers resisted Carson's creative perspective. Though grounded in country music, the style and technique on Carson's demos had pop, rock, and R & B influences, and his melodies were more intricate than most songs on country radio at the time. Siman had long been promoting the acceptance of pop influences in country music, as he felt that there was a "demand for good country songs [that are] middle of the road, as well as for pop and rock songs that are written by country-oriented writers—by writers who have a good understanding of soul and earth. The world is our market."[26]

Siman and Carson had several record deals in Nashville not pan out, so in 1967 they went to Memphis to work with producer Lincoln Wayne "Chips" Moman. He was an R & B and pop guitarist and singer who worked as a recording engineer and had helped to make Stax Records a major player in the early 1960s. He had established American Sound Studios in 1964 and recorded a slew of pop hits that dominated the *Billboard* Hot 100 charts.[27] When Siman and Carson started coming to Memphis, they were entering a bustling, regional American music center for pop and soul hits. Its long music history starts with W. C. Handy playing the blues in Beale Street clubs in the early 1900s.

Independent record companies thrived in Memphis during the 1960s: Sun Records had Jerry Lee Lewis and Johnny Cash, Willie Mitchell at Hi Records had Al Green and other artists, and Stax Records and its East Memphis Music publishing company had Carla Thomas, Otis Redding, and Sam & Dave.

Carson fit right in with Moman's writer-musician focus at American Studios while Siman wore holes in his shoes in Nashville trying to pitch one specific Carson song called "The Letter." Carson said the idea for the song came from his father, Shorty Thompson: "My dad had a song called 'Her Last Letter,' and the first line was 'Give me a ticket for an airplane.' I thought that was corny, but I got to looking at the thing, and worked up the song. My wife had given me a pump organ for Christmas and I wrote the song on it."[28] The Vietnam war was a grim context for many soldiers coming home or getting letters from home during the 1960s. Siman knew "The Letter" was a sure hit, and he decided to bring it to Moman.

Carson played some songs for Moman and his new producer protégé, Dan Penn, at American Studios and left them a demo tape that included "The Letter." Penn gave a copy of the tape to a local rock group with a sixteen-year-old white soul-singer named Alex Chilton. Penn asked them to work up the songs for a session and gave Chilton free rein with his natural abilities. The group was disappointed about not getting "state-of-the-art professionalism" with Moman. Instead, they got Penn, a "novice producer who slouched and wore old plaid Bermuda shorts, taped-up sneakers, and kept a pack of cigarettes rolled up in the sleeve of his baggy T-shirt." They found the studio "littered with dirty dishes and ashtrays and leftover food from the previous night's session." Chilton was hung over, and Penn had to work with him to get a good performance of "passion and conviction."[29]

After recording a basic track of "The Letter," Penn asked future Musicians Hall of Fame member Mike Leech to add a string and horn arrangement to create a fuller sound. According to Roben Jones, "Mike's sweeping string melodies, carrying forward the ideas implicit in the basic tracks, became a trademark of the American Studios sound." Leech would create instrumental and string arrangements for over 200 artists in his career. Carson's song was his first. In a moment of inspiration, Penn tacked on a jet airplane sound borrowed from a sound effects record as a "literal illustration of the story." Moman wanted it deleted, but Penn responded, "That's my record, and I'm gonna get a razor blade and cut this tape up into a million pieces if you make me take that airplane off."[30] Fortunately, Moman surrendered. Carson later claimed that Moman liked the song so much he tried to buy Siman's songwriting contract for $25,000, but Siman assured him it wasn't for sale, and $25,000 wasn't nearly enough anyway.[31] The rock group who recorded the song changed their name to the Box Tops, and Bell Records released "The Letter" as a single in the summer of 1967, the "Summer of Love." At first Siman worried about the song's success on an unknown label, but happily realized that "we could no more stop that from being a hit then we could make it a hit. It just immediately took off. Unbelievable."[32]

"The Letter" reached number one on the *Billboard* Hot 100 chart on September 23, 1967, and stayed there for four weeks. *Cash Box* ranked "The Letter" as the number-one single of the year, and *Billboard* ranked it as number two. It was an international hit, charting in Australia, Belgium, Canada, Ireland, Netherlands, and the UK. "The Letter" is in the Rock and Roll Hall of Fame's list of "500 Songs that Shaped Rock and Roll," and in *Rolling Stone*'s list of the "500 Greatest Songs of All Time." The record received two Grammy Award nominations and was inducted into the Grammy Hall of Fame.[33] Carson's career had finally taken off, with Si Siman as his pilot.

Within just a few months in 1967, Siman and Carson had topped both the country and pop singles charts with "Somebody Like Me" and "The Letter."[34] Siman was pleased when the Box Tops also recorded his favorite Carson song "Neon Rainbow" in November, but he thought the band made a huge mistake by not releasing "Mr. Busdriver" as their second single; Carson had written the song as a follow-up to "The Letter," and Siman thought the song could propel them to yet another level. In the summer of 1969, the Box Tops issued Carson's "Soul Deep" as their last charted song before breaking up. It was a top-ten hit around the world, selling over six million records worldwide within three years.[35] The Arbors capitalized on the psychedelic era in 1969 with another version of "The Letter" that timed out at almost twice the length of the original single.[36]

Siman and Carson wrapped up the 1960s with a banner year in 1969. Merrilee Rush recorded two Carson songs, "Every Day Livin' Days" and "Your Lovin' Eyes Are Blind," for her hit album *Angel of the Morning*; Waylon Jennings recorded Carson's "Tulsa," a top-twenty country single; and Dale Hawkins produced "Keep On" for former *Louisiana Hayride* member turned pop artist Bruce Channel. The latter song peaked at #12 on the UK Singles chart, and Channel's album *Keep On* included multiple Carson-penned tunes, including "Nobody," "Instant Reaction," "Mr. Busdriver," "Try Me," and "On a Rainy Day." Hawkins also wrote songs with Carson, and their "Heavy on My Mind" was included on Hawkins's critically acclaimed album *LA, Memphis & Tyler, Texas* on Bell Records in 1969.

Any doubts about Siman's ability to mine songwriting talent from the Ozark hills disintegrated after 1969. He opened an office in Nashville and made periodic trips there from Springfield for a week of pitching songs, but he remained close to his base in the Ozarks. Former *Jubilee* staff member Bob Tubert managed Siman's Nashville office for a while, and later Stan Hitchcock took it over.[37] Carson spent his most productive years in Springfield with Siman: "I wanted to be around Si. We played so much golf together, hunted and fished together. I didn't move to Nashville because I didn't want to leave my best friend."[38] If Carson needed to pitch songs or cowrite with a larger songwriting community, he commuted to Memphis or Nashville—often with Siman. A golf course served as an auxiliary office where Siman could pitch songs to record producers and maintain his presence in music business centers outside the Ozarks.

Hit songs from Siman and Carson during the 1970s added consistency to the previous decade's sporadic but powerful successes. Their first big '70s hit was a "blue bird"—a recording that just happens because someone professionally unconnected to a song loves it and finds a way to get it recorded or brings it to the attention of someone who will. Leon Russell was the impetus for a monster blue-bird event, the recording of "The Letter" by Woodstock star Joe Cocker. A&M Records had signed the raspy-voiced English rocker in the late 1960s and reaped the rewards of his debut album released in May 1969 when it went gold in the United States. Cocker's American manager Dee Anthony advised him to put a tour together, if for no other reason than to keep the immigration authorities from kicking him out of the country.[39] Cocker reached out to British producer Denny Cordell, who booked him into Woodstock, and Leon Russell, who coproduced his second album with Cordell.[40]

Russell is credited with the idea of Cocker doing a cover version of "The Letter" for the tour. It was a risky proposition, since the song had already been the record of the year and a top-twenty hit within a two-year span. Nevertheless, Cocker recorded "The Letter" on March 17, 1970, during rehearsals for his upcoming Mad Dogs and Englishmen tour.[41] Russell and Cordell produced the recording, with Russell providing backup with his group, the Shelter People. A&M elected to release "Space Captain" from the rehearsal sessions as Cocker's next A-side single, believing it could be the long sought-after chart breakthrough. Fortunately, they put "The Letter" on the B-side. Disc jockeys, who had more autonomy in 1970 than they do today, rejected "Space Captain" and literally flipped the record over and started playing "The Letter." As a result, the song was again a hit, appearing in *Billboard's* Hot 100 within two weeks and eventually reaching #7. A&M then released Cocker's live album in August, and it went to #2 on the *Billboard* album chart.[42] The Mad Dogs and Englishmen experience became a classic rock event for fans of three generations as rereleases of its album, related concerts, and movie soundtracks appeared into the twenty-first century.

HONKY-TONK GARY STEWART

In the 1970s, Siman and Carson had their biggest run of success with songs recorded by legendary honky-tonk singer Gary Stewart. A native of Kentucky, Stewart was writing and playing in Florida club bands when he met country singer-songwriter Mel Tillis, who suggested he move to Nashville. RCA's Jerry Bradley signed Stewart as a songwriter for Forest Hills Music. A few Stewart songs recorded by Billy Walker, Cal Smith, and Nat Stuckey achieved moderate success, but his own recordings on Cory and Kapp labels went nowhere.

In 1970, Motown Records gave Stewart $30 to demo some of their classics, hoping to interest country artists in doing cover versions. Stewart became frustrated with Nashville, the labels dropped him, and he moved back to Florida. The following year, Stewart heard the Allman Brothers for the first time and became "determined to merge the new southern rock with his love of honky-tonk."[43] However, RCA staff producer Roy Dea heard Stewart's Motown demos and convinced Bradley to sign him.[44] Stewart moved back to Nashville in 1973, where a new and exciting future with RCA awaited.

Carson met Gary Stewart through Siman's old friend Bob Beckham, who suggested RCA's Roy Dea as a producer for Stewart's first album. Carson's songs "Drinkin' Thing" and "I See the Want to in Your Eyes" were exactly what Dea was looking for, and Stewart had his first hit when his recording of "Drinkin' Thing" reached the top ten in 1974.[45] Country music historian Bill Malone remarked that "Drinkin' Thing" earned Stewart "critical praise as a worthy heir to George Jones and other honky-tonk greats. Hard-core country fans found Stewart's clear and pleading tenor voice, with its pronounced and breathy vibrato, immensely appealing."[46]

Dea planned for the B-side of the single, "I See the Want to in Your Eyes," to be Stewart's next hit. In the meantime, Stewart had been opening for Conway Twitty shows, and Twitty heard the B-side and asked Stewart if he could record the song.[47] Stewart approved. Twitty's version featured Nashville keyboard player "Pig" Robbins, bassist Bob Moore, and guitarist Grady Martin. It became Twitty's eleventh number-one country hit, and it stayed on the *Billboard* country chart for thirteen weeks in 1974.[48]

Cover of sheet music for Gary Stewart's number-one single, written by Wayne Carson. *Courtesy of Siman Family Papers, private collection of Scott Foster Siman and Jayne Siman Chowning.*

After "Drinkin' Thing," Stewart's career mushroomed into a feast of Carson-penned country radio hits, including his first and only number-one single, "She's Actin' Single (I'm Drinkin' Doubles)," in 1975. Carson composed the song while sitting with friends in a Springfield bar; he noticed an older man sitting at the bar drinking double shots as his young female companion was "acting single" by checking out other men.[49]

Both of Carson's songs ended up on Stewart's 1975 debut album, *Out of Hand*, which climbed to #6 on the *Billboard* country album chart and became one of the most critically lauded country albums of the 1970s. Music critic Geoffrey Himes claimed that Stewart's albums were "live and wild by the standards of mid-1970s Nashville," and they widened the range of country music for younger audiences.[50] Thom Jurek of *AllMusic* gave the album five out of five stars and stated that a "strong case could be made for *Out of Hand* as one of the top one hundred country records of all time."[51] Stewart scored additional hits in the 1970s with Carson's "Oh Sweet Temptation," "Whiskey Trip," and "Ten Years of This." He found a niche singing some of the biggest and most timeless drinking songs, perhaps because he knew about drinking firsthand. He struggled with alcohol, drugs, and depression, and died by suicide in December 2003—one month after the death of his wife of forty years, Mary Lou.[52]

THE MONSTER HIT

A dead-end record contract became the beginning of a long journey for Siman and Carson's biggest hit. In the late 1960s, Chips Moman had produced several unsuccessful sides with Carson for Monument Records, including a song called "Always on My Mind." The nucleus of the song came easily for Carson in Memphis, following an argument on the phone with his wife Bridget in Springfield about his lengthy absences from home. "She was pretty damned irate about it," he recalled. "So, I tried to calm her down. I said, 'Well, I know I've been gone a lot, but I've been thinking about you all the time.'—and it just struck me like someone had hit me with a hammer. I told her real fast I had to hang up because I had to put that into a song."[53] Carson wanted to record the song on the Monument project, but Moman thought it needed a bridge. Mark James, author of Elvis's "Suspicious Minds" and B. J. Thomas's "Hooked on a Feeling," wandered into the studio at some point, as did songwriter Johnny Christopher. They came up with the bridge Moman wanted. Two hours later they were ready to cut the song.[54]

Moman was impressed with the rewrite, and they went into the studio to record the song. After the session, Carson and Moman were so excited that the next day they hopped on Moman's plane and flew to Nashville to play it for Monument's label head, Fred Foster. Unfortunately, Foster didn't think it was a hit. On the trip back to Memphis, Moman told Carson that Foster was going to regret it. Monument eventually shelved the entire project, including "Always on My Mind." When Siman asked the president of Monument why, he said, "I wish I could answer that."[55] American Studios artist B. J. Thomas recorded a version of the song in Memphis, probably produced by Moman, but it was never released, either. Siman was an aggressively committed believer when he heard a hit. He never gave up on "Always on My Mind" and decided to pitch it to his former *Jubilee* star Brenda Lee through her producer Owen Bradley. Lee recorded it in 1972 and this became the first officially released A-side version of the song. A few months earlier it had been released as a B-side by R & B artist Gwen McCrae. Seven years later John Wesley Ryles also recorded the song.

Carson became acquainted with Elvis Presley in Memphis when he was recording a massive comeback album produced by Moman titled *Elvis in Memphis*. Despite the career boost the album provided, Presley insisted he never wanted to work with Moman again because of events and misunderstandings that had occurred during the sessions.[56] Presley went to Nashville producer Felton Jarvis to record "Always on My Mind," and Jarvis brought in players from Memphis for style continuity with the *Elvis in Memphis* album. When "Always on My Mind" was released as a single in 1973, a poll by ITV in the United Kingdom chose the song as Presley's most popular single of all time. Despite this, the song only topped out at #16 on the *Billboard* Hot Country Songs chart in the United States.

Almost ten years later Carson and Siman got a break with "Always on My Mind." Willie Nelson had been recording a series of duet albums with artists who had helped him along the way, such as former *Jubilee* performers Ray Price and Webb Pierce. On one of the duet albums, titled *WORLD WAR II*, Chips Moman produced Nelson with Waylon Jennings on a recording of Carson's "No Love at All" as a token of gratitude from Jennings to Siman's son Scott, a Nashville music business attorney who had settled a legal dispute with Jennings over royalties.

Moman was working on another of Nelson's duet albums and called Siman to get a Carson song that the artist could do with Merle Haggard. Siman suggested "Always on My Mind." Haggard thought the song was too pop and didn't want to use it. Siman understood Haggard's loyalty to traditional country, but he thought Haggard might get a career boost with the crossover play the song was likely to get. They finished the album without "Always on My Mind," but Moman kept thinking about the song that Haggard had rejected. CBS Records were complaining to Nelson's managers about his lack of a solo album, so Moman cobbled together a Nelson solo project that included "Always on My Mind" and released the song as a single on March 6, 1982. Ironically, Nelson was now giving Siman, who wouldn't hire him for the *Jubilee*, one of the most awarded records in country music history.

Willie Nelson's version of "Always on My Mind" immediately raced to number one on *Billboard*'s Hot Country Singles chart in May 1982, staying in that position for two weeks and remaining on the chart for twenty-one weeks. Top 40 radio stations also loved "Always on My Mind"—it was #5 on the *Billboard* Hot 100 for three weeks and stayed on the chart for twenty-three weeks. It was the best-performing single on the *Billboard* Hot Country Singles year-end chart of 1982 and also charted in a number of other countries. As author Roben Jones notes, "Under Si's guidance and advice, Wayne [Carson] became

BMI award winners for "Always on My Mind" celebrating in 1982: Ed Cramer of BMI, Scott Foster Siman, songwriter Wayne Carson, producer Chips Moman, and cowriter Johnny Christopher. *Courtesy of Siman Family Papers, private collection of Scott Foster Siman and Jayne Siman Chowning.*

the foremost writer in a style Nashville was just beginning to call 'advanced' or 'progressive'—going beyond the classic drinking and cheating songs . . . and discussing all aspects of life through music."[57] The Recording Industry Association of America certified "Always on My Mind" platinum—signifying one million in sales—on October 7, 1991.

In 1982 and 1983, Siman and Carson picked up trophies at almost every award show in the music business—Siman for publishing and Carson for songwriting. Willie Nelson won Single of the Year and Album of the Year in 1982, and songwriters Johnny Christopher, Mark James, and Wayne Carson won CMA Awards for Song of the Year in 1982 and 1983. At the 1983 Grammy Awards, "Always on My Mind" won Song of the Year and Best Country Song for Christopher, James, and Carson, and Best Male Country Vocal Performance for Nelson. In his 1983 acceptance speech for the top CMA Song of the Year, Carson said that country music had been "his life" and, "without Si Siman, it wouldn't have been much of a life."[58] The National Music Publishers Association also named "Always on My Mind" Song of the Year and Country Song of the Year in 1983, and the Academy of Country Music named it Single of the Year and Album of the Year. "I've been at it for almost forty years and had lots of rewards, but nothing like this," Siman gushed.[59] "Always on My Mind" was inducted into the Grammy Hall of Fame in 2008.

Carson was inducted into the Nashville Songwriters Hall of Fame in 1997. In 2011, the Country Music Hall of Fame and Museum saluted Carson as part of its "Poets and Prophets" series, honoring songwriters who have made significant contributions to country music. While interviewing Carson at his home in Nashville for the series, the museum's editor, Michael Gray, happened to see a home computer that had 8,500 recordings of Carson's songs by other artists. "And those were just the ones Mr. Carson knew about," wrote Julie Thanki in the Nashville *Tennessean*.[60] Stephan Thomas Erlewine proclaimed that "Always on My Mind" was "virtually the definition of a modern pop standard—a song that resonated with both artists and audiences, spawning a surprising number of cover versions, by a surprisingly diverse list of musicians."[61] Over three hundred versions of the song have been recorded.

SIMAN THE PROFESSOR

A successful career of finding hit-producing songwriters didn't mean that Siman could always recognize one. According to Carson, he and Siman were once sitting at a bar when "a couple of guys from Sikeston, [Missouri,] walked in the door . . . They were DJ's down there, and they came in with this little bitty cassette player and played us some songs that were real hard-core country. We said we weren't into that at the time. Si and I talked it over, and we just didn't hear anything in their songs. Well, it happened to be Jerry Foster and Bill Rice, who went on to write about eighty-seven Top 10 records."[62] On another occasion Siman and Carson were headed out to lunch in Nashville with Chet Atkins and Bob Beckham. A "kid" approached him with a song for Beckham, but Siman passed on it because they were late for their lunch date. The kid was Jerry Jeff Walker, and the song was "Mr. Bojangles." Carson said "That's the way it is. Nobody's above making a mistake."[63]

These instances aside, Siman got it right plenty of times, and stories about his successes kept his Springfield office humming with songwriters writing, calling, and arriving in person seeking advice. Siman viewed the music publisher's job as more than a person who files a copyright and collects royalties; he adopted the role of a professor who taught writers how to make hit records. He admitted that finding hit songs was not a science: "I've missed a lot of hits, and I'm going to miss a lot more. You just fly by the seat of your pants and hope that you're right."[64] One of the songs he most regretted missing was Brenda Lee's biggest hit: "I'm Sorry" by Ronnie Self. He learned that there is no secret pathway to a hit song, although he spent much of his life trying to find it.

Siman decided that the way to help his writers have successful careers was to find out what not to do. He often referred to songwriting as a craft. His emphasis on craft, as opposed to art, meant that writers needed to work hard to master the nuances of songwriting. Anyone could write a song (art) but not everyone could write a hit song (craft). To perfect a craft takes hours of hard work and a touch of luck, but even hours of work and immense talent don't always pay off in the music industry.

Writers seeking advice and song critique from Siman often had little musical knowledge or experience with making demos. Songwriter Ronald Johnson, who worked as a disc jockey for Springfield radio stations as "Woody P. Snow" or "Jay Stevens," appreciated the free access to Siman and was open to Siman's advice for writing hit songs. According to Johnson, Siman's Rule #1 for songs involving women or romance was "Don't put the lady down. Put her on a pedestal. If you gotta have a bum or a wolf, you be it."[65] Siman wasn't interested in self-indulgent, musical meditations—he was looking for hits: "You have to have hits. It's a kind of [an] eat-what-you-kill business. If you don't get any hits, there's no money."[66]

Johnson recalled Siman's patience: "He'd listen to everybody. If he didn't like it, he'd say, 'That's interesting.' You knew that he didn't like it when he said that."[67] One writer who submitted a song for Siman's opinion received the following letter in response: "I listened to both songs very carefully and they are both above average, but not good enough to get us a hit. The ideas are okay but there's too much rambling. Keep in mind you are getting one opinion and there are 38,000 Si Simans yet to try. Good luck. Sinceriously [sic], Si."[68] He taught writers how to create lead sheets—musical notations—and often suggested specific revisions. Sometimes the songs weren't worth the trouble, but he listened anyway. He believed it took writing at least one hundred songs to find a "voice," but he knew that nothing could substitute for talent. He felt that real talent came with real responsibility to work and fulfill that gift. In Siman's view, artists who descended into drugs and alcohol in a fog of romanticized decadence had lost their clarity and ambition. It was a waste of talent.

Once writers got past the one-hundred-song mark, Siman thought they needed to learn lessons about getting to the point, developing strong melodies, and crafting good lyrics. He advised songwriters to "try to get a strong idea and then figure out how it's going to end. Then back up just as little as you can and write to that end."[69] Siman had learned a lot about being a successful publisher: do your homework and stay ahead of the market; pay attention to music trends; be very honest, but try not to hurt people's feelings; learn when to police your writers and get them to conform; learn when to push your writers forward; and help writers see the difference between commercial and hobby writing. Siman knew that not everyone can write hit songs, but he allowed that sometimes a person can write just one: "I think everybody is basically at heart a songwriter." However, Siman added: "I've seen mothers and daddies mortgage the farm to get an album out on their son or daughter when I really didn't feel like it was going anyplace and I'd tell them so. And they would go ahead and do it anyway. All I could do was give them the best counsel I know how." Siman could only offer his opinion: "I know that there's people who will disagree with me, but that's what makes the world go 'round."[70] On the other hand, he felt a responsibility to help a sensational writer hone his or her skills for the commercial market. Siman often asked his writers to try writing positive songs—he thought that put him ahead of others in the music business and claimed the technique was a turning point in his publishing career—but he never wanted to kill anyone's originality for the sake of a positive message.

THE SPRINGFIELD MUSIC SCENE

After their success with "The Letter" in 1967, Siman and Carson wanted to create a home for musicians in the Ozarks like Moman had done at American Studios in Memphis. In 1969, Siman, Foster, and Mahaffey established the Sound of Springfield recording studio, later called Top Talent Studio, at 1763 E. Elm Street. They bought a building, consulted with the engineers at American, and acquired a state-of-the-art eight-track recording machine. Multi-track recording on magnetic tape was on the rise during the 1960s, and Siman wanted to be on the forefront of developments in the recording process. Carson viewed the studio as his "baby": "I designed the building and

Lewie and the 7 Days. *Courtesy of Larry Lee.*

I told the architect what I wanted."[71] The studio featured two echo chambers for reverb effects. The *Springfield Leader and Press* reported that "the orange brick building houses some $150,000 worth of sophisticated electronic equipment—equipment which dwarfs other facilities previously available locally."[72] Carson became the studio arranger and production manager "after Hollywood songwriting success that has netted [him] record sales [of] over six million worldwide in the past three years."

Top Talent's main fare were jingles, radio shows, and music recordings. In an interview published upon the studio's opening in 1969, Siman said, "We hope our studio will be a creative workshop for the many talented writers, performers, and groups of the entire Ozarks area."[73] Siman joked about not seeing Wayne for a couple of years, as Carson immersed himself in the studio, tweaking his songs and working with local musicians. Top Talent Studios never became nationally known, but its impact on the next generation of Springfield performers was undeniable. Siman and Carson influenced an entire generation of local musicians, singers, and songwriters who still talk about them as conductors of the golden years of the post-*Jubilee* music scene.

Former Ozark Mountain Daredevils drummer Larry Lee was in high school when he met Siman in the '60s.[74] He recalls frequent visits to Siman's office at KWTO: "He was just very kind, and he would let me hang out. I was just a kid." He appreciated the open-door policy and the fact that "Si would share stories and play some of the new songs Wayne [Carson] had written or songs that people were sending to him." Lee liked to flip through the trade magazines lying around Siman's office and soak up as much about music as he could. As *Billboard* and other trade publications were well beyond the financial reach of most musicians, Siman's office was an educational resource for them.[75]

Lee's best friend in high school was fellow Springfield musician Mike Bunge, who was the same age as Lee but became his mentor in the music business. He invited Lee to watch Carson recording demos in the KWTO studio: "Wayne was just a sweet guy, a little older than Mike and [me]. He was the first person I met who was writing songs. I didn't know anything about what that was." Lee began touring with Carson on weekends during his senior year in high school. "I learned a lot from . . . just watching [Carson] and how he interacted with people. Wayne was always very good at that." At a rodeo performance in Oklahoma City, Carson's band performed one set on a flatbed truck parked at the edge of the ring, and another two sets in an adjacent pavilion. Lee said it was an interesting education for a seventeen-year-old: "They actually had chicken wire around the bandstand. I heard a lot of ruckus and fights going on that night . . . I had never experienced anything like that before . . . Wayne showed me the evils of music all right."[76]

In the fall of 1965, Lee began playing in a Springfield-based R & B band called Lewie and the 7 Days.[77] Siman managed the group, and Carson recorded them on Skipper Records, a label named after KWTO manager Ralph Foster, who was nicknamed "Skipper" by Siman and his colleagues. Everyone in the group was a college student hoping to avoid the draft. They did backup demos for Carson and Ronnie Self and performed on the road at gigs booked by Carson's brother Gary. In 1966, Siman booked the 7 Days on a tour in Vietnam sponsored by the US Defense Department. The group had to compile a sixty-minute show and get matching stage costumes for the tour. Siman had big plans for the group and wanted to record a demo tape for them in Memphis to present to United Artists when they returned from Vietnam.

The Vietnam tour had a big impact on the band, not because of the music, but because of the war. Saxophonist Bill Jones said he was just "three weeks out of high school" and found himself "in Vietnam on the front lines where we could hear gunfire between songs." Jones had been playing music in nightclubs since he was fifteen with popular Springfield singer Benny Mahan, who frequently appeared at the Rendezvous in the Colonial Hotel and the Esquire. A tour in Vietnam was a totally different music experience, and eighteen days in the middle of a war was plenty.[78]

Larry Lee was also traumatized by the visceral threat of war during the tour. He often spent time getting acquainted with soldiers who were about his age. "We'd be sitting there drinking beer in these little huts and these flares were going off, going *dat-data dat-data dat-data dat*. They were having a war two hundred yards away." The band played at field hospitals, where they saw men who couldn't walk without crutches and some in wheelchairs. They went into hospital wards where wounded soldiers were bandaged up so thoroughly he couldn't tell what they looked like. "It was frightening, very depressing. And [they were] all kids that [were] maybe my age or a little older . . . Every one of them said, 'Whatever you have to do, do not come back over here.'" A letter from the selective service was waiting for Lee when he got home. Remembering the advice from soldiers in Vietnam, and knowing that "Vietnam just didn't look like the scene that I wanted any part of," he enlisted for four years in the navy, instead of eighteen months in Vietnam, and served most of his time in Puerto Rico.[79]

Going to Vietnam had been a traumatic experience, but Lee's anxieties were partly healed during his navy years, especially when he got letters from Si Siman back home. Having also been a navy man, Siman knew what it was like to be in the military. "Si just really kept me connected by sending me little articles every once in a while, [and] little notes saying, 'How you doing? Everybody is fine back here and waiting for you to get home.' He was like my second dad." More than anything, being in the navy and hearing from Siman made Lee want to spend his life playing music and writing songs. One day when he was on shore duty, he went to a chapel on the base and started writing songs after plinking on the piano a bit. He had never played a piano or written a song before that day. He didn't know where the songs came from or know why he started writing them, but the experience sealed his commitment to be a songwriter.[80]

In July 1967, Siman booked Wayne Carson with Lewie and the 7 Days on a month-long US State Department tour to the Caribbean.[81] It was "more of a vacation" for Bill Jones, who was glad to be out of Vietnam. Drummer Bobby Lloyd Hicks replaced Lee, who left for the navy in September 1966. Lewie and the 7 Days backed Carson for a twenty-minute set and performed for another twenty minutes on their own. Jones thought Carson was a great entertainer who filled his set with good jokes and a lot of interaction with the audience.[82]

When Lee returned from the navy in June 1970, Mike Bunge was waiting for him at the airport and took him to Carson's studio where he could record some of the new songs Lee had started writing in Puerto Rico. Lee began playing with Bunge's popular new rock band called Granny's Bathwater, which included Bobby Lloyd Hicks, bassist Dave Pease, and Springfield songwriter John Dillon. Bunge wrote almost all the songs for the band.[83] "Bunge brought the band from a blues unit into a horn-blazing gang of collaborators, grooving on funk, R & B, jazz and blues."[84] When Dillon went to Siman for advice on the band's music, Siman told them they lacked an identity: "Who are you? You can't tell by your music. You've got some rock, some jazz, some blues, but [listeners] can't tell who you are. You need to find some way to combine your rock with your country roots. . . . You've got to be true to yourselves. You're not from England, Memphis, or New Orleans. You've got to sell the Ozarks."[85] Dillon left Granny's Bathwater because of "creative differences" with Bunge.[86] The wisdom of Siman's advice became reality when Buddy Brayfield, Steve Cash, Randle Chowning, John Dillon, Michael "Supe" Granda, and Larry Lee started a band that epitomized the Ozarks' country-rock sound: The Ozark Mountain Daredevils.

The group's history began in 1971 when Dillon and Lee hooked up with Chowning at the New Bijou Theatre, a music venue on E. Trafficway under the Route 65 overpass in Springfield. Steve Canaday and Curt Hargis owned the Bijou, a 6,000-square-foot converted warehouse with high ceilings and a good sound system. They booked progressive bands such as acoustic-based rocker Dan Hicks and His Hot Licks, blues harp player Sonny Terry and guitarist Brownie McGhee, blues violinist Papa John Creech, and the blues/rock band Pure Food & Drug Act. Up to four hundred people could be packed into the Bijou, although it was legally restricted to 250. Hargis claimed it "wasn't a dive bar: it had nice tables with candles, and the beer was 3.2 percent."[87] The low alcohol content didn't keep anyone away, especially musicians who gathered there to try out new songs.

"Randle was the one that really was pushing the idea of the three of us writing together," Larry Lee recalled.[88] In the spring of 1972, Chowning and his brother Rusty rented a farm house in Aldrich, Missouri, from a former university professor for $20 a month. At that time, members of the group called themselves Family Tree and camped out at the house to solidify their sound, write songs, and loosen their minds. Later that year they were on their way to international success as the Ozark Mountain Daredevils with a million-selling album on A&M Records guided by famed rock and roll producers Glyn Johns and David Anderle.

The Ozark Mountain Daredevils. *Courtesy of Dwight Glenn.*

On November 24, 1973, *Billboard* included the new Daredevils' album on its "Recommended LPs – Pop" list, noting that it started with the "familiar lyrical Eagles-type sound" and that the "countryish southern rock band... the Daredevils play a lot of different textures of music and have much to say."[89] When the band started to get national attention and needed a manager who wanted to work with them, Larry Lee reached out to Siman for advice on a proposed management contract. Siman told him it wasn't a great contract and that the commission was too high. He did not make the obvious pitch to publish their songs himself. Chowning said that the group was "not in Si's formula" for love songs.[90] However, Siman advised the group to hold on to their publishing rights, knowing the fleeting nature of pop radio success. Lee notes that he is "still getting publisher royalties on the songs, thanks to that advice."[91]

The Daredevils scored two major hits: "If You Wanna Get to Heaven" (1974), written by Cash and Dillon, and Lee's "Jackie Blue" (1975), which hit number one on the *Cash Box* and *Record World* singles charts in and continues in rotation on classic rock radio stations today. The group recorded six albums on

A&M Records and two greatest hits collections. Eclectic songwriting and varying levels of ambition among the members gradually caused the original band to disintegrate, but other Springfield musicians stepped in to keep the group going. Lee spent twenty-three years working as a songwriter and producer in Nashville before returning to Springfield in 2006, and Michael Granda moved to Nashville permanently to be around the music scene but regrouped with Dillon and Cash for touring and recording.[92]

Wayne Carson told everyone that the Daredevils were like his kids: "Those were kids who used to hang around the studio, went out on the road with me. And, as musicians will, they found each other, got together." He felt a "warm, proprietary pride" in their success.[93] Current Daredevils member Nick Sibley thought Carson "was Springfield's last connection to the real music world," describing how "he'd come into the studio and play songs he'd written the night before . . . Then three months later you'd hear them as hits on country radio by Merle Haggard."[94] Sibley thought "it was kind of like being around Elvis, in a smaller way."[95] Hanging out with Carson allowed Sibley to study lyrics, chords, and melodies of a great songwriter, and he played guitar on Carson's demos.

Some of Carson's advice to Sibley about songwriting echoes the advice Carson received from Siman when their relationship began. Carson told Sibley to keep it simple and develop an idea. Then there was his political advice: "He told me things like, 'Women buy most of the records, so never talk bad about a woman in a song. You can always put a man down, but not a woman. . . . When a woman gets sad, she cries. When a man gets sad, he drinks. Never have the man [in the song] crying or the woman drinking.'" Sibley thought that everything Carson told him seemed to "fly in the face" of the songs he liked from the Beatles and Bob Dylan.[96]

Sibley was very influenced by Siman, who he met in 1973 when he presented half a dozen songs to Siman for input. "There was only one song on there that he thought had possibilities," recalls Sibley. "In reality, they all sucked really bad." But he continued to write songs, thanks to the support of former Granny's Bathwater bassist and studio engineer Hugh Walpole, who was in the office with Siman. Walpole liked Sibley's arrangements and shared some of his own songs with him. Walpole was the first person Sibley had ever met who had made a record. The biggest favor Sibley received from Siman was his career in the jingle business. He was sitting in Siman's office in the spring of 1973 when Forrest Lipscomb, a local agricultural products magnate and Siman's friend, called to ask Siman if he would produce a dog food jingle. Siman gave Sibley the job. He wrote a series of jingles and sold them to Lipscomb for $150. Sibley was now in the jingle business, and he claims it's all he's done ever since.[97]

Siman's Top Talent Studio was the first of several professional recording enterprises established in Springfield. Many musicians who worked in the '70s music scene came to know Top Talent, well before and long after Joe Higgins and his backers bought the business from Siman in 1971 and changed the name to Century Custom Studio (and later, American Artists). Higgins engineered the first Daredevils demo during the winter of 1971-72.[98] Pat Shikany's Dungeon Studios at 212 W. McDaniel also produced demo recordings for the Daredevils, as well as for Ronnie Self, Red Foley, and Brewer & Shipley.

Although Springfield was historically a country music center, pop music had a strong presence in the city's culture. Siman and Carson didn't worry about genre labels. They took an early interest in vocalist Benny Mahan, whose rock n' roll band the Ravens became a favorite in the early 1960s. Mahan established and fronted many bands over the years and occasionally toured with Granny's Bathwater. He was a multi-instrumentalist, but fans mostly loved his powerful vocals. Siman and Carson helped him score several record deals, including one with a label called Pompeii Records. The label was having some success with singles by Ike & Tina Turner, including Carson's "You Got What You Wanted" and "Cussin' Cryin' & Carryin' On."

Siman also released several recordings of Mahan under his Scratch Records label, including "She Knows How" and "What You Never Had," both written and produced by Carson. The Box Tops had originally recorded "She Knows How" on their debut album and issued it as the B-side to Carson's "Neon Rainbow." Pompeii picked up the record and released it in 1969. The single failed to chart, and the deal with Pompeii was short-lived. In typical Siman fashion, he didn't give up and got Mahan another deal, this time with Monument Records. In 1970, Monument released a single of Mahan's with two more Carson tunes, "Laurel Canyon" and "Sandman." Although commercial success evaded Mahan, he became a much loved and respected member of the Springfield music community, performing with many bands, most recently Howie and the Hillcats. After Mahan's death in 2009, local musicians had volumes of Benny Mahan stories to tell and retell.

Success for Siman and Carson was all over the genre map. When disc jockey Ronald Johnson wanted to start writing hit pop songs, he managed to get a five-year contract with the Welk Group for the nucleus of a song called "Rocky." He went to Siman for advice about the contract before signing. Siman told Johnson that the five-year Welk contract was not a good deal and said, "You should let me publish that and [then] you can write your own contract."[99] Meanwhile, Siman's son Scott was screening material for his father and heard something special in the song. It was rare to find a gem, and "Rocky" easily stood out from the pack because of its tragic lyric with an upbeat melody. Siman took Johnson to Nashville and introduced him to many of his friends in the music business. Johnson was overwhelmed at Siman's kindness: "I never dreamed I would be getting compliments from Chet Atkins and Kris Kristofferson and Phil Everly. Holy cow! It was something to meet him! Brenda Lee, Willie Nelson, I got to meet these people! And they all loved Siman . . . He was highly respected, and rightfully so. He was an honorable, wonderful man."[100]

Siman set up a publishing company with the American Society of Composers, Authors and Publishers (ASCAP) for Johnson and named it Strawberry Hill. He pitched "Rocky" to Nashville producer Bob Montgomery, who had been close friends with Buddy Holly and had performed with him as Buddy and Bobby. After writing the classic country song "Misty Blue" (1966), Montgomery had moved on to being a successful publisher and producer. In 1975, Montgomery produced a version of "Rocky" with pop artist Austin Roberts. It became a top-ten pop record, and in 1976, country artist Dickey Lee's cover version of the song hit number one on the *Billboard* country charts. "Rocky" was also a huge international hit, with two versions in the top ten at the same time in Germany.[101] Although it would be Lee's only number-one record, Johnson said Siman changed his life: "I had nothing going on, and after that there was always something going on. I mean, my first trip to New York, Si Siman flew me up there to get my gold record."[102]

David Kershenbaum, a multiple Grammy-winning and Oscar-nominated record producer, Springfield native, and Siman family friend, was another one of the young performers who hung out in Siman's office. Siman thought Kershenbaum was an incredible talent, and he offered him a publishing contract on a song-by-song basis. Siman released several songs on Skipper Records for Kershenbaum's band, David and the Boys Next Door, including "Land O Love" and "If I Was King," cowritten by Carson.

Kershenbaum learned his early lessons in Springfield and, after recording an album for producer Mike Curb that included many songs written by Carson, eventually left to achieve international success. He later acknowledged Siman's influence and said he "had been real good to me; he took me to Nashville and introduced me around and he gave me some of Wayne's songs."[103] Kershenbaum went on to win three Grammy awards, establish his own group of companies, supervise music on many films, and produce hit records for artists such as Tracy Chapman ("Fast Car"), Joe Jackson ("Steppin' Out"), and Duran Duran ("Hungry Like the Wolf"). "Steppin' Out" was nominated for Record of the Year at the 25th Grammy Awards, going up against Willie Nelson's version of "Always on My Mind." Neither took the top prize, losing out to Toto's "Rosanna."

The Springfield music scene's greatest public relations musician was the irrepressibly funny and often quoted Lou Whitney, who was also an admirer of Siman. Academy Award- and Golden Globe-winning Springfield drummer and former Carson band member Tom Whitlock said Whitney was "one of the most fun humans ever."[104] Although he started in real estate, music was Whitney's first love. He spent his life learning about local bands, musicians, and the music business, and he was a tireless promoter of the Si Siman's influence on Springfield music community.

In a 2021 interview, Whitney spoke about the lessons he learned from Siman: "[Si] got into the publishing business and provided a home for people who were creative enough to come up with a song; he also offered them criticism and help . . . I'd sit there and listen to him; it'd go in one ear, out the other, then back in, but everything that the guy told me turned out to be spot-on."[105] Whitney said that "without the foresight of Siman and Ralph Foster . . . [Springfield] wouldn't have any more music than Duluth."[106] Whitney played bass in recording sessions and hot local bands, including the Symptoms, the Morells, and the Skeletons. By encouraging local musicians, just as Siman had done, he was a major influence on Springfield music. In the 1990s, rock artists came to Whitney hoping to capture the magic of the Ozarks at his studio at 329 South Avenue. Among Whitney's recording projects were Syd Straw's *War and Peace* and Wilco's *Being There*.

The musicians who consulted Siman respected his opinions; they didn't feel that he was just out to sign artists to his publishing company. Future Nashville Songwriters Hall of Fame member Tim Nichols was playing in a Springfield band during the 1980s when he began to dream about being a songwriter. As was customary in Springfield, Nichols took a few songs to Siman for feedback: "He would listen to these songs that weren't very good . . . I didn't know it at the time, but I know it now."[107] Siman told Nichols he might have trouble breaking into the industry from the Ozarks and advised him to move to Nashville and cited a favorite phrase: "If you're going to hunt tigers, you have to go where the tigers are."[108]

Siman's advice may seem ironic considering his lifetime commitment to promoting the Ozarks music industry from his office in Springfield, but he

David Kershenbaum. *Courtesy of Ralph Foster Museum.*

knew better than anyone the difficulties of maintaining a professional presence in Nashville while commuting. Nichols took Siman's advice: "Him saying that was all the motivation I needed to move to Nashville."[109] He headed out for Music City in 1980. His song, "Live Like You Were Dying," cowritten with Craig Wiseman, became a smash hit for Tim McGraw, a management client of Scott Foster Siman. "It was a full circle moment," said Scott. "My dad's belief in Tim Nichols [led] to one of the greatest country records of all time, one that I got to market and promote, and it is the last song in country music to spend ten weeks at the top of the airplay charts."[110] In 2004, McGraw won the Best Male Country Vocal Performance Grammy for "Live Like You Were Dying," and Nichols and Wiseman won the Grammy for Best Country Song.

As the end of '80s approached, Siman was ready to wind down his active music publishing career. He had proven that the Ozarks was a place to mine hit songs, and that he didn't have to choose between the quality of life he wanted in Springfield and being a music publisher. Carson signed with Screen Gems

Si Siman in his Springfield office showing his Grammy and CMA awards. *Courtesy of Siman Family Papers, private collection of Scott Foster Siman and Jayne Siman Chowning.*

Music in Nashville, but the deal never produced any big hits. His widow, Wyndi Harp Head (Carson), recalls Carson saying that "he just didn't have a Si Siman at Screen Gems."[111] Siman and Carson remained lifelong friends, but Siman was no longer tasked with the day-to-day stewardship of Carson's career.

Siman asked his son Scott to explore options for selling his publishing catalog that included more than two thousand songs. "It was a really difficult decision," recalls Scott, "but my dad wanted to spend more time hunting, fishing, and golfing, and less time with the day-to-day details of music publishing."

Scott considered acquiring the catalog himself: "We put a group together to buy the songs, but they got cold feet about the proposition, so we focused on finding other buyers."[112] German-owned Budde Music was keenly interested in the catalog because it wanted to expand its presence in the United States. Siman and Carson, who had a share of publishing ownership, closed the deal with Budde in December 1987. Siman said it took "years to build and months to sell. Those copyrights had almost become my kids to me. Every song in that catalog went in there because of my judgment."[113] His biggest regret was that the new owners had no idea how many good songs were there. He also grieved over letting go of the Earl Barton, Rose Bridge, and Strawberry Hill companies: "Putting those three companies to sleep—that really hurt me. It's terrible in a way. I guess you'd say it's a changing of the guard."[114] *Billboard* reported the sale of the catalog for an undisclosed price.

As if to demonstrate the rejuvenating influence of Si Siman, the Pet Shop Boys released a cover of Carson's "Always on My Mind" in 1988—a perfect example of how a great song can be successfully interpreted in different styles. The band had recorded a dance version of the song after doing a 1987 television performance of it in the UK to honor the tenth anniversary of Elvis's death. The Pet Shop Boys released the song as a single, and they soon had a worldwide smash hit on their hands when it peaked at number one in the UK, Canada, Finland, Poland, Spain, Sweden, Switzerland, and West Germany, as well as in the United States. Siman wasn't sure he liked the dance version. Carson and others warned him not to listen because he wouldn't like what he heard: "They changed some of the melody, they changed a couple of words and they added all these synthesizers and things," but when Siman finally listened to the record he thought it was great: "I don't think you can hurt a good song, and this is living proof."[115] The song became a million-seller when it appeared on dance compilation albums across Europe. In November 2004, the *Daily Telegraph* placed the version at number two in a list of the fifty best cover songs of all time. In October 2014, a public poll compiled by the BBC saw the song voted the all-time best cover song.[116] It was a fitting end to a brilliant publishing career.

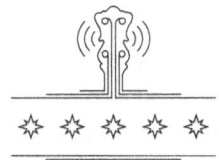

CONCLUSION

When Si Siman was diagnosed with Non-Hodgkin's lymphoma in 1989, he went into a deep depression, but in typical Siman style, he soon resumed having a positive attitude: "I decided [that] I don't have to let my emotions get so involved. I don't have to let misery become an option."[1] He played golf, worked with charity organizations, became partners in a movie production company called Ozark Pictures Corporation, and fed his mind while his body did what it was going to do.[2] Siman vowed to do chemotherapy as long as he could still enjoy some quality of life between treatments, but he struggled to keep his energy up and faced further problems with heart issues caused by the chemo.

Nevertheless, his sense of humor was still in place. His daughter Jayne recalled that when her father's cardiologist told him not to eat certain things, he sought another opinion from his oncologist, who told him he could eat anything he wanted, "so, he went with the cancer doctor's recommendation!"[3] Other cancer patients at the clinic he went to started requesting their chemo treatment on days that Siman would also be there because he was so entertaining. When a doctor once asked him if he was stressed, Siman responded, "You've got more nerve than an upstairs burglar to ask that question. I got more stress than Dolly's brassiere straps!"[4] Siman was full of corny jokes, but it was just the kind of humor that works well in the sadly absurd life situation that is familiar to cancer patients.

Siman had no cause or time for regrets. He had pursued his two great loves outside his family—baseball and entertainment—over many decades. He had booked big bands such as Glenn Miller in the 1930s, worked with KWTO's

Korn's-a-Krackin' during the golden age of radio in the 1940s, produced the first continuous live network country music television show in the 1950s, and one of the first in color in 1961. He influenced the careers of major country artists and published some of the most successful songs in music history. Siman had spent his life promoting a winning combination of positive thinking, capitalism, duty, hard work, self-improvement, and commitment to family, religion, and public service. He was grateful for his good fortune.

Siman was a spiritual man who said he wouldn't believe in reincarnation "until George Washington came back as a bridge," but that if he ever did reincarnate, he wanted to be "born in the Ozarks again. It's a great place to live. It's been so good to me, and I hope I've been good to it."[5] After almost five years battling cancer, Siman died on December 16, 1994, at Rosi Acres, with his family and his beloved mutt terrier, Jim Dandy, beside him.[6]

A standing-room-only crowd came to a celebration of Si Siman's life the following Monday at the family's 500-seat church, St. Paul Methodist. The memorial's program quoted Siman: "I recently purchased a cemetery lot, but I'd rather optimistically think of it as a heaven-bound launching pad!" Porter Wagoner was among the celebrities and friends in the crowd. Mel Tillis sang "Peace in the Valley," and church organist Dorothy Weaver played Siman's favorite Christmas hymn, "Joy to the World." Reverend Wilber Denny told a couple of jokes that Siman would have loved. The pallbearers were Siman's longtime friends and colleagues Wayne Carson, Dr. F. T. H'Doubler, Jack Lipscomb, John Mahaffey, Johnny Morris, and Jim Shirk. Among the flowers and cards sent to the memorial was a final farewell from Chet Atkins: "So long, old friend." In 2015 Carson followed Siman in passing. His wife Wyndi said that "when Si passed away a part of Wayne did too."[7] Siman's biggest supporter and partner in all of his projects was his wife Rosie, who died on November 12, 2017. They are buried side by side at Hazelwood Cemetery in Springfield.

In telling Si Siman's life story, *Broadcasting the Ozarks* fills a major gap in country music history. Siman worked at the cusp of the two biggest influences on twentieth-century American culture: radio and television. In the late 1940s, no one predicted that Springfield would or could surpass other cities' successes in entertainment and challenge Nashville, Tennessee, as the country music capital of the United States, but the creative vision and hard work of Si Siman, Ralph Foster, Lester E. Cox, John Mahaffey, and their crew made it happen. Considering Nashville's head start and the challenges of building an entertainment industry in a small city in the Ozarks, their accomplishments are even more impressive in hindsight.

Rosie and Si Siman at Rosi Acres. *Courtesy of Siman Family Papers, private collection of Scott Foster Siman and Jayne Siman Chowning.*

Wayne Carson photo autographed for Jayne Siman Chowning and Randle Chowning. *Courtesy of Siman Family Papers, private collection of Scott Foster Siman and Jayne Siman Chowning.*

Despite the lack of attention they have received from the chroniclers of country music history, Si Siman and the *Ozark Jubilee* impacted the trajectory of country music in ways surpassed by only a few people and institutions. After becoming a charter member of the CMA in 1958, Siman also worked to strengthen and expand the country music business. As a result, the genre spread from its rural-centric origins into cities and suburbs and became a favorite of much of mainstream United States and the world.

CONCLUSION

Siman's legacy permanently enriched music history at home in the Ozarks. Springfield was an especially exciting place to be during the 1970s to the 1990s, as local and regional songwriters who worked with Siman achieved commercial and critical success, bringing home Grammys, Oscars, and other awards from the highest echelons of the American entertainment industry. At the time of his death, Branson, Missouri, was rekindling some of the music-making magic of the Ozarks in the 1950s, attracting country music superstars to its crowded Highway 76 strip and grabbing headlines from New York to Los Angeles. Ultimately, Branson would prove no more successful in replacing Nashville as the center of the country music universe than Springfield had been four decades earlier—they had no Si Siman around to make it a closer fight than it should have been. The vision of a crossroads of country music in the Ozarks remains little more than a wistful dream, but it is a dream that would never have taken form in the first place without the imagination and tenacity of Si Siman.

APPENDIX
SI SIMAN PUBLISHING DISCOGRAPHY

Song Title	Artist	Highest Chart Position US or International	Year
1950s			
Trademark	Carl Smith	#2	1953
Company's Comin'	Porter Wagoner	#7	1954
Eat, Drink and Be Merry	Porter Wagoner	#3	1955
Make Believe	Red Foley w/ Kitty Wells	#6	1955
What Would You Do (If Jesus Came to Your House)?	Porter Wagoner	#8	1955
One Step at a Time[1]	Brenda Lee	#15	1957
1960s			
Somebody Like Me	Eddy Arnold	#1	1966
Do It Again a Little Bit Slower	Jon and Robin	#18	1967
The Letter	The Box Tops	#1	1967
Neon Rainbow	The Box Tops	#17	1967
Nine Pound Steel	Joe Siman	#19	1967
Who's Julie[2]	Mel Tillis	#10	1968
Keep On	Bruce Channel	#12	1969
Tulsa	Waylon Jennings	#16	1969
The Letter	The Arbors	#20	1969
Soul Deep	The Box Tops	#2	1969
I'm Gonna Do All I Can	Ike and Tina Turner	#25	1969

Song Title	Artist	Highest Chart Position US or International	Year
1970s			
The Letter	Joe Cocker	#5	1970
Something's Wrong in California	Waylon Jennings	#19	1970
Mary's Vineyard	Claude King	#17	1970
No Love at All	Lynn Anderson	#15	1970
No Love at All	B. J. Thomas	#5	1971
Don't Hang No Halos on Me	Connie Eaton	#56	1971
Tulsa	Billy Joe Royal	#81	1971
Always on My Mind	Elvis Presley	#3	1972
I See the Want to in Your Eyes	Conway Twitty	#1	1974
Drinkin' Thing	Gary Stewart	#10	1974
She's Got Everything I Need	Eddy Arnold	#24	1974
She's Actin' Single, I'm Drinkin' Doubles	Gary Stewart	#1	1975
Rocky	Austin Roberts	#1	1975
Rocky[3]	Dickey Lee	#1	1975
Cover Me	Sammi Smith	#33	1975
Rocky	Frank Farian	#1	1976
Rocky	Don Mercedes	#1	1976
Oh, Sweet Temptation	Gary Stewart	#23	1976
Barstool Mountain	Wayne Carson	#82	1976
Slide Off Your Satin Sheets	Johnny Paycheck	#7	1977
Ten Years of This	Gary Stewart	#16	1977
Bugle Ann	Wayne Carson	#99	1977

Whiskey Trip	Gary Stewart	#5	1978
Barstool Mountain	Moe Bandy	#9	1979
That's the Only Way to Say Good Morning	Ray Price	#18	1979
Liberated Woman	John Wesley Ryles	#14	1979
You Were Always on My Mind[4]	John Wesley Ryles	#20	1979
The Letter	Sammi Smith	#27	1979

1980s

The Clown	Conway Twitty	#1	1981
Always on My Mind	Willie Nelson	#1	1982
Always on My Mind	Pet Shop Boys	#1	1987

1 Brenda Lee's first charted hit single.
2 Mel Tillis's first top-ten chart single.
3 Dickey Lee's sole number-one single.
4 Different title for "Always on My Mind."

Other artists who recorded songs published by Siman include: Alabama, Chet Atkins, B. B. King, the Beach Boys, Gary U.S. Bonds, Michael Bublé, Glen Campbell, Clarence Carter, Eva Cassidy, Petula Clark, Roy Clark, Classics IV, Commander Cody and His Lost Planet Airmen, Floyd Cramer, Bobby Darin, Dave Edmunds, Fantasia, Dallas Frazier, Gin Blossoms, Vern Gosdin, Al Green, Dale Hawkins, Al Hirt, Homer and Jethro, Julio Iglesias, Rodney Lay, Lewie and the Seven Days, Trini Lopez, Benny Mahan, Melanie, the Mindbenders, the Morells, Ann Murray, Sandy Posey, Ronnie Prophet, Lou Rawls, the Royal Guardsman, Merrilee Rush, Sam the Sham and the Pharaohs, Ronnie Self, Joe Stampley, the Stylistics, the Tams, Johnny Tillotson, Ike and Tina Turner, Tracey Ullman, Leroy Van Dyke, Vanilla Fudge, Dionne Warwick, Gene Watson, and Faron Young.

NOTES

INTRODUCTION

1. As of 2022, there were 149 members in the Country Music Hall of Fame. Of these, thirty-four are listed as music business professionals, rather than performers, and four died before the *Jubilee* era. Of the remaining 111 performers—comedians, singers, and musicians—thirty-one were too young or not yet working at a level professional enough to perform on *Ozark Jubilee*. Of the remaining eighty, fifty performed on the *Ozark Jubilee* (1955-1960). A short list includes Roy Acuff, Eddy Arnold, Chet Atkins, Gene Autry, the Browns, the Carter Family, Johnny Cash, Patsy Cline, Red Foley, Lefty Frizzell, Sonny James, George Jones, Brenda Lee, Buck Owens, Minnie Pearl, Webb Pierce, Ray Price, Jim Reeves, Tex Ritter, Marty Robbins, Jean Shepard, Hank Thompson, Ernest Tubb, Conway Twitty, Porter Wagoner, Kitty Wells, Bob Wills, and Faron Young. "List of Country Music Hall of Fame Inductees," Wikipedia, accessed March 15, 2023, https://en.Wikipedia.org/wiki/List_of_Country_Music_Hall_of_Fame_inductees. Five *Jubilee* performers are in the Rock and Roll Hall of Fame: Bob Wills, Chet Atkins, Johnny Cash, Brenda Lee, and Johnny Gimble. A complete list of *Jubilee* performers is available at https://en.wikipedia.org/wiki/List_of_personalities_who_appeared_on_Ozark_Jubilee. An excellent history of the *Ozark Jubilee*, written by *Jubilee* director Bryan Bisney's son John, is also available on Wikipedia: https://en.Wikipedia.org/wiki/Ozark_Jubilee.
2. Diane Pecknold, *The Selling Sound: The Rise of the Country Music Industry* (Durham, NC: Duke University Press, 2007), 66.
3. Springfield became the "Birthplace of Route 66" because of a telegram sent from Springfield's Colonial Hotel on April 30, 1926. Cy Avery, the chairman of the Oklahoma Department of Highways, was writing to confirm the numbering of the highway after a long, national dispute over what the number would be. See Susan Croce Kelly, *Father of Route 66: The Story of Cy Avery* (Norman: University of Oklahoma Press, 2014), 189-92.
4. Dickson Terry, "Hillbilly Music Center," *St. Louis Post Dispatch*, February 5, 1956, 1.
5. Bill C. Malone and Tracey E. W. Laird, *Country Music USA* (Austin: University of Texas Press, 2018), 315.

CHAPTER 1

1. Siman, interview by John Rumble, September 19, 1989, Country Music Foundation Oral History Project, Frist Library and Archive, Country Music Hall of Fame and Museum, Nashville, Tennessee.
2. Newspaper articles, family history, and census reports of 1900, 1910, and 1920 are inconsistent regarding James Siman's birth date, marital status, number of children, and parents' names. The birth date that appears on James Siman's death certificate, obituary, and tombstone is April 10, 1844. The US Federal Census Records of 1900 and 1910 indicate that he was born in 1852 but emigrated to the United States in 1849. The US Federal Census Record of 1920 indicates he was born in 1848. A 1912 article in the *Springfield Republican* states that he was born in 1847 and came to the United States when he was nineteen months old. See "New Baby's Dad is 65 Years Old; Father of 19," *Springfield Republican*, August 20, 1912, 8. I have not been able to confirm any information about Siman's parents, his origins in Ireland, or his life in Louisville, Kentucky.
3. "Pioneer Smith Expires at 84," *Springfield Leader*, October 30, 1928, 6. The first Kentucky Derby was held on May 17, 1875, a year before James Siman moved to Springfield, Missouri.
4. One of Clementine's grandsons, Jerry Siman (son of Ely Siman Sr.'s brother James Jr.), remembers several conversations about his grandfather's two wives: "I was very concerned about having two mothers and my BIG question to my dad was that when you needed help and called out 'MOM' who answered or came to see what you needed? My dad laughed and said, 'Oh Jerry, that was so simple. One was called "Mom" and the other called "Ma."' Their world of peaceful family life apparently ended when a neighbor complained to the sheriff about 'That guy having two wives.' One day, when my dad was in first or second grade, he was taken home . . . the sheriff was there and so was his dad and mom and ma and the rest of the whole family. The sheriff demanded that my grandfather make a choice . . . separate the wives and their children, keep one and send the other away. It is my understanding that the choice was made based upon the fact that the children of one were now all grown-ups (or very nearly so). My dad told me that it was a devastating, calamitous event for the whole family." Jerry Siman, personal communication, August 22, 2012.
5. Greene County, Missouri, records show a marriage license for James and Clementine dated March 2, 1910, although a *Springfield Republican* newspaper article claims they married in 1892. Sarah Siman later showed up at the house of Clementine's son James Jr. and was not permitted to enter because she was the "other woman." Jerry Siman, personal communication.

6. Si Siman's daughter Jayne Siman Chowning counts fourteen children by Clementine (two did not survive). Sarah Siman evidently had five children. Jayne Siman Chowning, personal communication, March 14, 2021.
7. "Pioneer Smith Expires at 84."
8. Later in life, Charles changed the spelling of his last name from "Siman" to "Simon" so he would never be associated with his father. Charles Simon became a successful businessman as owner of the Simon Coffee Company, in association with Quinn Coffee Company, in Springfield. He was not the only offspring of James Siman who changed his name. Jayne Siman Chowning, personal communication, March 14, 2021.
9. James Siman's death certificate lists "apoplexy" as the official cause of death, which seems a likely result following a kick in the head. Missouri Digital Heritage, Missouri Death Certificates, 1910–1972, https://www.sos.mo.gov/images/archives/deathcerts/1928/1928_00034420.PDF.
10. Camp Pike was later named Camp Robinson.
11. The doctor was accurate in his diagnosis of the two girls. Maxine suffered from depression for much of her life. In 1945, twenty-five-year-old Virginia apparently planned to kill her six-year-old daughter Julie and then kill herself, but at the last minute she decided to let Julie live and died by suicide. Julie moved in with Ely and Lillian Siman after the tragic event. Jayne Siman Chowning, personal communication, March 14, 2021.
12. Ely Siman Sr. later worked at Dillon Brothers, Springfield Flying Service, and the local Lily Tulip paper-cup manufacturing plant, where he was maintenance manager. Obituary, *Springfield Daily News*, May 5, 1969, 16; Jayne Siman Chowning, personal communication, March 14, 2021.
13. Ely Sr. "passed away at the exact time on a Sunday morning that he would have been greeting everyone for church." Jayne Siman Chowning, personal communication, May 3, 2022.
14. Si Siman, interview by Lana Grosshart, Americana Network, April 21, 1994, Siman Family Papers, private collection of Scott Foster Siman and Jayne Siman Chowning.
15. "Br'er Fox Baseball Team to Close Long Season Here This Afternoon," *Springfield News-Leader*, October 28, 1934, A-11.
16. Contract of the Br'er Fox Theatre League, Siman Family Papers, private collection of Scott Foster Siman and Jayne Siman Chowning.
17. "Br'er Fox Baseball Team to Close."
18. Rusty D. Aton, *Baseball in Springfield* (Charleston, SC: Arcadia Publishing, 2005), 32–38.

19. Jim Sandoval, "Charley Barrett," Society for American Baseball Research, accessed May 1, 2022, https://sabr.org/bioproj/person/charley-barrett/.
20. Branch Rickey left the Browns in 1917 to briefly work for the St. Louis Cardinals before serving as a major in the US Army during World War I. After the war, he returned to the Cardinals in time to start the 1919 season. Mark Stang, *Cardinals Connection: 100 Years of St. Louis Cardinals Images* (Wilmington, OH: Orange Frazer Press, 2002), 20; Murray Polner, *Branch Rickey: A Biography* (New York: Athenaeum, 1982), 75–81.
21. Sandoval, "Charley Barrett."
22. Aton, *Baseball in Springfield*, 66.
23. Aton, *Baseball in Springfield*, 49.
24. Aton, *Baseball in Springfield*, 49.
25. Aton, *Baseball in Springfield*, 54.
26. E. E. Siman, "'Cards' Talent Scout Chased Down Some of the Big Names in Baseball," *AHOY! For Navy and Marine Corps Personnel of Charleston Navy Yard*, April 17, 1943, 2.
27. Siman, interview by Lana Grosshart.
28. The terms "batboy" and "mascot" were interchangeable in this era. "Batboy," Wikipedia, accessed August 3, 2023, https://en.wikipedia.org/wiki/Batboy.
29. Ely Siman Sr., "Minute Book," Br'er Fox Baseball Club, 1935 season, Siman Family Papers, private collection of Scott Foster Siman and Jayne Siman Chowning.
30. Jack Hamlin, personal communication, November 9, 2021.
31. Siman, interview by Lana Grosshart.
32. W. J. McGoogan, "Barrett Played Strong Role in Building Great Cardinals Systems," *St. Louis Post Dispatch*, July 6, 1939, 14.
33. Barrett to Siman, April 24, 1937. Barrett's letters to Siman have not been edited for grammar or spelling. Unless otherwise indicated, all cited letters are from the Siman Family Papers, private collection of Scott Foster Siman and Jayne Siman Chowning.
34. Si Siman to Lillian and Ely Siman Sr., June 5, 1937.
35. Siman, June 5, 1937.
36. Siman, interview by John Rumble, September 19, 1989.
37. Barrett to Siman, July 27, 1937; Barrett to Siman, November 9, 1937.
38. Barrett to Siman, December 26, 1937.
39. Barrett to Siman, September 28, 1937.
40. Barrett to Siman, December 26, 1937.
41. Barrett to Siman, January 3, 1938.
42. Siman to Lillian and Ely Siman Sr., June 1, 1938; "Mickey Owen," Wikipedia, last modified June 11, 2023, https://en.Wikipedia.org/wiki/Mickey_Owen.

43. After a very successful professional baseball career, Owen returned to Springfield. He served multiple terms as sheriff of Greene County and established a top-notch baseball school just outside of Springfield in Miller, Missouri. He and Siman remained lifelong friends. Jayne Siman Chowning, personal communication, March 14, 2021.
44. Siman, interview by Lana Grosshart.
45. Siman to Lillian and Ely Siman Sr., June 7, 1938.
46. US Inflation Calendar, accessed August 1, 2023, https://www.usinflationcalculator.com/.
47. Siman to Lillian and Ely Siman Sr., June 8, 1938.
48. Barrett to Siman, August 28, 1938.
49. Barrett to Siman, November 28, 1938.
50. Barrett to Siman, January 23, 1939.
51. Barrett to Siman, May 26, 1939.
52. John Snow, "Ear to the Ground Department," *Springfield Leader and Press*, July 9, 1939, A-11.
53. "Charley Barrett, Card Scout, Dies; Funeral on Friday," *St. Louis Star and Times*, July 5, 1939, 18.
54. Walsingham later became vice president of the St. Louis Browns and an executive with the American League's Baltimore Orioles. "William Walsingham Jr.," Wikipedia, accessed August 3, 2003, https://en.wikipedia.org/wiki/William_Walsingham_Jr.
55. Siman, interview by Lana Grosshart.
56. Fetzner to Siman, July 18, 1939.
57. Siman to Rickey, July 12, 1939.
58. Siman, interview by Lana Grosshart.
59. Siman, interview by Lana Grosshart.
60. "Tales of the Town," *Springfield Leader and Press*, June 21, 1940, 9. During most of Siman's life, morning, evening, and Sunday editions of the Springfield newspapers were published by the same company (other than trade publications). The titles assigned to each printing were *Springfield Daily News* (morning), *Springfield Leader and Press* (evening), and *Sunday News and Leader* (Sunday). In 1987, the papers were combined and renamed the *Springfield News-Leader*.
61. Siman, interview by Lana Grosshart.
62. Siman may have gotten films and equipment for his theater events through the Br'er Fox League's association with Fox Theatres.
63. Siman, interview by Lana Grosshart.
64. The road is now called Lone Pine Street, and Galloway is now part of southeast Springfield.

65. Now called Central High School, one of five high schools in Springfield.
66. Siman, interview by Lana Grosshart.
67. Siman, interview by Lana Grosshart.
68. At that time the Shriners permanently took over the concessions as a tool for the organization, and it remains one of their largest sources of income. Siman, interview by Lana Grosshart.
69. The "air cooled" system was two parallel metal vents extending the full length of the high, domed ceiling; these still exist in the main Shrine Mosque auditorium. The dancers were cooled by twelve-foot fans placed at each end of the vents and blowing behind blocks of dry ice. Bobby Pinegar, official tour guide for Abou Ben Adhem Shriners in Springfield, Missouri, personal communication, April 25, 2022.
70. Jarman Shoes, advertisement, *Springfield Daily News*, October 24, 1936, 14.
71. "Notes about Ellington," *Springfield Leader and Press*, October 25, 1936, D3.
72. Hickman sold Half-a-Hill in 1939 and died in 1941. Thomas Peters, "Memories of Half-a-Hill's First 20 Years," Ozarks Alive, accessed August 3, 2023, https://www.ozarksalive.com/stories/memories-of-half-a-hills-first-20-years.
73. Ella Fitzgerald, advertisement, *Springfield Leader and Press*, November 12, 1939, B11.
74. Chick Webb died on June 16, 1939, but his band continued to tour with Fitzgerald. "Chick Webb," Wikipedia, accessed August 3, 2023, https://en.wikipedia.org/wiki/Chick_Webb.
75. Now Missouri State University in Springfield.
76. "Tales of the Town," *Springfield Leader and Press*, December 8, 1939, 10.
77. Allen Oliver, "Springfield Slants," *Springfield Leader and Press*, November 20, 1939, 4.
78. The population of Springfield in 1940 was 61,238—small compared to Kansas City and St. Louis. "Missouri City Population 1900–1990," Missouri Census Data Center, accessed August 1, 2023, https://mcdc.missouri.edu/population-estimates/historical/cities1900-1990.pdf.
79. During Tommy Dorsey's time in Springfield, he reunited with two of his former band members who lived in the area: arranger and pianist Paul Mitchell and saxophonist John Langsford. Both were now playing with the renowned Marshfield native Joe Haymes in his swing/jazz group. Haymes was a regular at Half-a-Hill, and Mitchell became a staff arranger and pianist for KGBX/KWTO radio in Springfield. Mitchell also later played in the *Ozark Jubilee* band. Wayne Glenn, *The Ozarks' Greatest Hits: A Photo History of Music in the Ozarks* (Nixa, MO: Wayne Glenn, 2005), 162.
80. Allen Oliver, "Springfield Slants," *Springfield Leader and Press*, January 30, 1940, 4.

81. Oliver, "Springfield Slants."
82. Siman, interview by Lana Grosshart.
83. "Miller and Sigma Nu's," *Springfield Leader and Press*, July 8, 1941, 7.
84. "Band Leader Shaw 'Joins' Police Force as Honorary Chief," *Springfield News and Leader*, October 23, 1941, 3.
85. "Promotional Prodigy Obtains Mosque Wrestling Franchise," The Benchwarmer (Perry Smith), *Springfield Leader and Press*, June 1, 1941, 13.
86. The Benchwarmer, "Promotional Prodigy." Siman also had a refreshment concession at Fassnight Park. When he went into the navy in 1942, his father took it over and ran it until 1945. "Another Stand Asked at Park," *Springfield Leader and Press*, March 6, 1945, 12.
87. Siman, interview by Lana Grosshart.
88. The Benchwarmer, "Promotional Prodigy."
89. "Shultz Conquers Dusette in Two Straight Falls," *Springfield Daily News*, December 10, 1941, 11.
90. Siman, interview by Lana Grosshart.
91. A native of Elkton in Hickory County, Missouri, Rand became a chorus girl in Kansas City when she was thirteen. She danced and acted her way to California, where she appeared in silent films. Cecil B. DeMille changed her name from Helen Beck to Sally Rand after the Rand McNally atlas. "Sally Rand," Wikipedia, accessed August 3, 2023, https://en.wikipedia.org/wiki/Sally_Rand.
92. "Sally Rand," Wikipedia.
93. "Sees Sally Rand as Proof We're All Going to Dickens," *Springfield Leader and Press*, June 15, 1941, B7.
94. Stars Over America, advertisement, *Springfield News-Leader*, September 4, 1941, 8.
95. Siman, interview by Lana Grosshart.
96. Siman, interview by Lana Grosshart.
97. "New Manager Turns Mosque to Playhouse," *Springfield Leader and Press*, September 11, 1941, 1.
98. "Fair Attendance Sets New Record, 175,000 Visitors," *Springfield Leader and Press*, September 14, 1941, 1.
99. Officials estimated that two thousand men in Greene County would register by closing time at nine. Missouri registration totals were approximately 280,000—and nationwide 9,000,000—on that day. "Father and Son," *Springfield Leader and Press*, February 14, 1942, 10.
100. "Father and Son," 10.
101. Siman, interview by Lana Grosshart.

102. Siman to Ely Siman Sr., August 3, 1942.
103. Siman, interview by Lana Grosshart.
104. Siman to Ely and Lillian Siman, May 17, 1943.
105. "Schuylkill," *Naval History and Heritage Command*, accessed May 1, 2022, https://www.history.navy.mil/research/histories/ship-histories/danfs/s/schuylkill.html.
106. Siman, interview by John Rumble, September 19, 1989.
107. Siman, interview by Lana Grosshart.
108. "USS *Liscome Bay*," Wikipedia, accessed August 2, 2023, https://en.wikipedia.org/wiki/USS_Liscome_Bay.
109. Siman, interview by Lana Grosshart.
110. Siman, interview by Lana Grosshart.
111. Wendy Arevalo, "The V-12 Officer Training Program December 1942–June 1946," Naval History and Heritage Command, accessed August 2, 2023, https://www.history.navy.mil/browse-by-topic/wars-conflicts-and-operations/world-war-ii/1942/manning-the-us-navy/v-12-program.html.
112. Siman, interview by John Rumble, September 19, 1989.
113. "Berea College," Berea College, accessed August 2, 2023, https://www.berea.edu/.
114. "A Budget for the Boys," *Springfield Leader and Press*, April 30, 1944, B2.
115. Siman, interview by Lana Grosshart.
116. Siman, interview by Lana Grosshart.

CHAPTER 2

1. John K. Hulston, *Lester E. Cox 1895-1968: He Found Needs and Filled Them* (Cassville, MO: John K. Hulston, 1992), 133.
2. "The Spotlight," *KWTO Dial*, June 1949, 8. The *KWTO Dial* was a monthly subscriber newsletter for KWTO listeners published from August 1941 to December 1951. The *Dial* featured the daily radio schedule and promotional articles about radio performers and station events. The full series can be viewed via Missouri State University's digital collections at https://cdm17307.contentdm.oclc.org/digital/collection/KWTO.
3. "The Spotlight," June 1949.
4. Hulston, *Lester E. Cox*, 132-33.
5. Hulston, *Lester E. Cox*, 21-29.
6. "Find a Need—And Fill It," *Springfield News and Leader*, February 12, 1950, D2.
7. Hulston, *Lester E. Cox*, 133
8. US Inflation Calculator, accessed August 1, 2023, https://www.usdinflation.com/amount/35/1925.

9. Mary A. Bufwack and Robert K. Oermann, *Finding Her Voice: Women in Country Music, 1800–2000* (Nashville: The Country Music Foundation Press and Vanderbilt University Press, 2003), 68.
10. "'Hill Billies' Air Popuarlity [sic]," *The Billboard*, July 22, 1933, 13.
11. Bufwack and Oermann, *Finding Her Voice*, 68.
12. NBC established the first radio networks in the United States in 1926, and in 1927 it formed two networks called the Red and the Blue. The Red Network was the larger of the two in terms of coverage and budget. NBC sold the Blue Network in 1942 as a requirement of the FCC restrictions against conflict of interest. The Blue Network became the American Broadcasting Company (ABC) until 1945. The Red Network continued as the NBC Radio Network. KWTO was affiliated with the smaller Blue Network after January 16, 1944, when KGBX/KWTO separated as required by new FCC regulations. "NBC Radio Network," Wikipedia, accessed August 3, 2023, https://en.wikipedia.org/wiki/NBC_Radio_Network.
13. Glenn, *Ozarks' Greatest Hits*, 177.
14. "Ozarks' Greatest Lover is Slim Pickens Wilson," *Springfield Leader and Press*, April 11, 1937, 21.
15. "'If a Kid Is Smart He's Not Left-Handed?' Oh, Yeah?" *Springfield Leader and Press*, March 6, 1938, 23.
16. Boots was actually Grace Eloise Tartsch, and Bobby was Mary Genevie Brayfield. "Boots Faye," *Hillbilly-Music Dawt Com*, accessed February 23, 2023, http://www.hillbilly-music.com/artists/story/index.php?id=14759.
17. Jean Kappell, Editor's Column, *KWTO Dial*, October 1950, 13.
18. Siman's work duties at KWTO are not all discussed chronologically, since he did them at various times and often concurrently.
19. The hour-long Saturday morning KWTO broadcasts had several location-specific names during its history, such as *Breakfast at Keller's* (after Russell Keller's downtown restaurant), *Breakfast at Heer's* (after Springfield's signature department store), and *Breakfast at the Heritage* (for the Heritage Cafeteria). The unscripted, live-audience-participation programs featured interviews, contests, and conversation. A typical sequence began with an organist playing the show's theme music over an announcer encouraging everyone to sing the theme song printed in the program: "We're having breakfast at the Heritage! / Each Saturday you'll find it's all the rage! / It's lots of fun, no matter what your age! / For ev'ry Saturday we sing and laugh and play!" After the verse, the audience (mostly women) hummed the tune as George Earle gave a hearty welcome. The audience returned his greeting, and Earle proceeded with the program. The eldest woman in the audience would receive an orchid corsage from one of the show's sponsors and a kiss from George Earle. Anyone celebrating an anniversary or birthday

received flowers or gifts. Other awards might go to guests expressing the most appealing wish, wearing the most unusual hat, traveling from the farthest distance, or having the most distinguished look. *Breakfast in Hollywood* programs and artifacts, Siman Family Papers, private collection of Scott Foster Siman and Jayne Siman Chowning.

20. "'Breakfast in Hollywood,' Far Beyond Expectations," *Springfield News and Leader*, March 20, 1946, 7.
21. "Electrical Transcription," Wikipedia, accessed March 6, 2023, https://en.Wikipedia.org/wiki/Electrical_transcription.
22. The Assemblies of God established its national office in Springfield, Missouri, in 1915. The Pentecostal organization was founded in Hot Springs, Arkansas, in 1914 and moved to Springfield the following year. "The Assemblies of God," Assemblies of God, accessed August 3, 2023, https://ag.org/About/About-the-AG.
23. Don Richardson, press release for KWTO/RadiOzark, November 1954, Siman Family Papers, private collection of Scott Foster Siman and Jayne Siman Chowning.
24. The Articles of Partnership, dated February 28, 1944, established RadiOzark (for a period of five years) as an advertising business that would produce advertisements, radio transcriptions, continuity, and recordings for sale or lease to radio stations or advertisers. It would also serve as a booking agency, a production company, publisher of the *KWTO Dial*, and in any other capacity related to "assembling and writing of all materials used in radio broadcasts or amusements or theatre, stage or other forms of amusement." The partnership agreement was between Cox's wife Mildred (20 percent), his daughters Cathryn and Virginia (15 percent each), Foster's wife Harriett (33.8 percent), and Johnson's wife June (16.2 percent). Lester E. Cox Papers, 1917–1968, No. 3596, Personal Correspondence, State Historical Society of Missouri.
25. The Matthews Brothers Quartet evolved into the Jordanaires, who backed up many country artists during the 1960s and '70s, including Patsy Cline and Elvis Presley. "The Jordanaires," Wikipedia, accessed August 3, 2023, https://en.wikipedia.org/wiki/The_Jordanaires.
26. Figures in this section are from the sales charts of the *Tennessee Ernie Ford* transcription, Siman Family Papers, private collection of Scott Foster Siman and Jayne Siman Chowning. A sales chart for Smiley Burnette is identical to Ford's. The charts indicate that a radio station in a city the size of Springfield (about 76,000 in 1950) would pay $9 per episode for a show with 1–130 episodes, $8.75 for a show with 131–195 episodes, and $8.50 for 196 episodes and over. The price increased $3 to $5 with population increments of 50,000. The *Tennessee Ernie Ford Show* had 260 episodes, meaning a radio station

in New York City (with a population of nearly eight million in 1950) would pay $10,400 for the full run, while a station the size of Springfield would pay $2,200. The net rate was not subject to agency commission.
27. Siman, interview by Lana Grosshart.
28. Siman, interview by John Rumble, September 19, 1989.
29. "Ford-RadiOzark Deal," *KWTO Dial*, February 1949, 7.
30. "Ford-RadiOzark Deal," 7.
31. "Ford-Dearborn Crew," *KWTO Dial*, March 1949, 19.
32. Siman, interview by John Rumble, September 19, 1989.
33. Siman, interview by John Rumble, September 19, 1989.
34. Siman, interview by John Rumble, September 19, 1989.
35. Siman, interview by John Rumble, September 19, 1989.
36. Sherlu Walpole, "Music Man Si Siman," *Springfield!*, June 1986, 26–29, 56.
37. Ford was one of several country music stars who fell in love with the Ozarks after coming to Springfield to perform. He bought property in Branson and became a cattle rancher in the 1970s while also recording up to three albums a year, making radio and television commercials, and traveling for personal appearances throughout the country. He was inducted into the Country Music Hall of Fame in 1990. "Tennessee Ernie Ford," Wikipedia, accessed August 3, 2023, https://en.wikipedia.org/wiki/Tennessee_Ernie_Ford.
38. "Smiley Burnette," Wikipedia, accessed August 3, 2023, https://en.wikipedia.org/wiki/Smiley_Burnette.
39. "Smiley Burnette," Wikipedia.
40. Autry and Burnette had stopped doing movies together by 1951 but they reunited for *Whirlwind*. Holly George-Warren, *Public Cowboy No. 1: The Life and Times of Gene Autry* (New York: Oxford University Press, 2007), 266–67.
41. Siman, interview by John Rumble, September 19, 1989.
42. In 1952, RadiOzark purchased a half interest in Burnette's BMI-affiliated Rancho Music for $35,000. The catalog contained over three hundred songs. Burnette set up a home base in Springfield, where he made regular appearances on the *Ozark Jubilee* and *Jubilee USA*. Siman and Mahaffey considered a series of TV films with Burnette and produced a game show pilot for ABC called *Pig in a Poke* in 1957, but the network was uninterested. Other creative ventures failed to develop. During the 1960s, Burnette played the role of railway engineer Charley Pratt on the CBS television shows *Petticoat Junction* and *Green Acres*, both productions of Missourian Paul Henning, creator of *The Beverly Hillbillies*. All three shows played a significant role in drawing attention to the Ozarks as a travel destination and added value to the Ozarks hillbilly motif.
43. Siman to Ralph Foster, Lester E. Cox, and C. A. Johnson, May 1, 1952.

44. Don Cusic, *Discovering Country Music* (Westport, CT: Praeger, 2008), 26.
45. Cusic, *Discovering Country Music*, 28.
46. The KWKH *Louisiana Hayride* began on April 3, 1948. "Louisiana Hayride," Wikipedia, accessed August 3, 2023, https://en.wikipedia.org/wiki/Louisiana_Hayride.
47. Robert K. Oermann, *America's Music: The Roots of Country* (Atlanta: Turner Publishing), 42.
48. "Trio Takes Trip Seeking Secrets on Barn Dances," *The Dial*, February 1943, 1.
49. "'Barn Dance' Has Sponsor," *KWTO Dial*, April 1945, 1.
50. "Bulletin!," *The Dial*, April 1945, 1.
51. "*Korn's-a-Krackin'* to Mutual Net!," *KWTO Dial*, January 1946, 1.
52. "Show Moves on May 4th," *KWTO Dial*, April 1946, 1.
53. "*Korn's-a-Krackin'* Goes on Road!," *KWTO Dial*, June 1946, 1.
54. Siman held many positions during his time at KWTO, but the *Dial* is not always a helpful source for confirming which positions he held or when he held them. My sense is that he did anything Foster or the station needed, regardless of a formal position.
55. "*Korn's-a-Krackin'* Ready to Return," *KWTO Dial*, August 1946, 8.
56. Jim Owen is now in the Greater Ozarks Hall of Fame for his contribution to nature tourism in the Ozarks. He claimed to be the "King of the White River Floaters" from 1933 to 1958. He was fondly named the "King of the Hillbillies." "Fishing Sees Changes as Dramatic as Landscape's," *Springfield News-Leader*, September 25, 1990, 9-E.
57. Melvin Belew, "Our Ozark Vacation," *The Courier-Gazette*, August 28, 1948, 6.
58. "Begin Search for Queen of Ozarks," *KWTO Dial*, May 1946, 1.
59. "Begin Search for Queen of Ozarks," 8.
60. Siman, interview by Lana Grosshart.
61. Unless otherwise cited, all information and quotations in the following section are drawn from Siman's lengthy letters to Rosanne "Rosie" Sprague during his residency at Simmonds and Simmonds. Siman Family Papers, private collection of Scott Foster Siman and Jayne Siman Chowning.
62. "The Passing Parade in Pictures," *KWTO Dial*, May 1947, 5.
63. RadiOzark was a KWTO-related corporation originally established as a booking agency, a production company, publisher of the *KWTO Dial*, and other projects. After the organization moved across the street from KWTO into a first-floor office at the Shrine Mosque in 1948, it had several other industries within its purview besides the transcription business, such as producing radio commercials for Bromo-Quinine, Orange Crush, Dr. LeGear, Big Smith clothing, or

whatever client needed spots. It also promoted, produced, and sold books such as Lou Black's training booklet for square dancing fans titled *Square Dancing Ozark Style*. When KWTO radio performers Chuck Bowers and Bill Wimberly's Country Rhythm Boys signed with Mercury Records, RadiOzark produced their first record.

64. "Variety Acts Ready Now for Personals," *KWTO Dial*, June 1947, 8.
65. "Variety Acts Ready," 8.
66. All Star Colored Revue, advertisement, *Springfield Daily News*, March 8, 1947, 2.
67. KWTO, advertisement, *Springfield Leader and Press*, May 10, 1947, 11.
68. Siman, interview by Lana Grosshart.
69. "A Very Merry Christmas from the *Korn's-a-Krackin'* Gang!," *KWTO Dial*, December 1948, back cover.
70. Siman, interview by Lana Grosshart.
71. Chet Atkins and Michael Cochran, *Chet Atkins: Me and My Guitars* (Milwaukee, WI: Hal Leonard, 2003), 19–31.
72. Chet Atkins, with Bill Neely, *Country Gentleman* (New York: Ballantine Books, 1974), 122.
73. Atkins and Cochran, *Chet Atkins*, 32.
74. Siman, interview by Lana Grosshart.
75. Atkins and Cochran, *Chet Atkins*, 32.
76. "Speedy" and "Junior" were nicknames for Slim Wilson's nephew, guitarist Herschel Haworth Jr. Wayne Glenn, personal communication, August 22, 2021.
77. Atkins and Cochran, *Chet Atkins*, 31–32.
78. Atkins and Cochran, *Chet Atkins*, 32.
79. Les Paul was born Lester Polsfuss to parents of German descent in Waukesha, Wisconsin. "Les Paul." Wikipedia. Accessed August 3, 2023. https://en.wikipedia.org/wiki/Les_Paul.
80. His mentor and former band member Sunny Joe Wolverton brought Rhubarb Red to Springfield to play in a duo called the Ozark Apple Knockers at the new Springfield radio station, KGBX, in 1933, before KWTO went on the air. Wolverton was the lead guitarist, and Rhubarb Red played the role of his hillbilly sidekick. Paul remembered playing "La Rosita" on KGBX the day they arrived in Springfield: "It was on KGBX because KWTO wasn't ready to go yet." When KWTO signed on in December 1933, the duo started playing on both stations: "We'd go in at 4 a.m. and bang on those old carbon mics to activate them and then do the early morning broadcast. After that, we'd be around all day doing various broadcasts, or traveling to various shows we played all over the state." Foster

sent them out to play in Carthage, St. Joseph, Centralia, and Joplin, Missouri, as well as distant cities in Illinois. Wolverton and Paul became acquainted with a KGBX family band called Dad Wilson's Boys and hunted arrowheads on their farm. Paul loved living in the Ozarks: "I look back on those days and realize they were some of the best times of my life. We were popular, I was making money, I was learning guitar from one of the best, I was romancing my first girlfriend, and Joe and his wife treated me like a member of their family . . . It was a wonderful carefree time." However, Wolverton soon led him to another radio job at WBBM in Chicago, and they played at the Chicago World's Fair in the summer of 1934. Les Paul and Michael Cochran, *Les Paul: In His Own Words* (Hunt Valley, MD: Gemstone Publishing, 2005), 60, 63.

81. Paul and Cochran, *Les Paul*, 221.
82. Atkins and Cochran, *Chet Atkins*, 126.
83. Paul and Cochran, *Les Paul*, 221.
84. Siman, interview by John Rumble, September 19, 1989.
85. Atkins and Cochran, *Chet Atkins*, 33.
86. Siman, interview by Lana Grosshart.
87. Atkins and Cochran, *Chet Atkins*, 41.
88. "Roy Lanham," Wikipedia, accessed March 7, 2023, https://en.Wikipedia.org/wiki/Roy_Lanham.
89. "The Whippoorwills," *KWTO Dial*, June 1949, 6.
90. The Whippoorwills continued their association with Siman after leaving KWTO, and in 1951 they played on RadiOzark transcriptions of the *Smiley Burnette Show* Siman recorded in California. Roy Lanham returned to Springfield for a few performances on the *Ozark Jubilee* in the late 1950s. He joined the Sons of the Pioneers from 1961 to 1986 and became known as the group's second, and last, guitarist. "Roy Lanham," Wikipedia.
91. Atkins and Cochran, *Chet Atkins*, 41.
92. "The Carter Family," *KWTO Dial*, October 1949, 7.
93. Atkins, *Country Gentleman*, 143–44.
94. Atkins and Cochran, *Chet Atkins*, 42.
95. "The Carter Family," *KWTO Dial*, November 1949, 16.
96. "The Spotlight," *KWTO Dial*, January 1950, 5.
97. Mark Zwonitzer, with Charles Hirshberg, *Will You Miss Me When I'm Gone: The Carter Family and Their Legacy in American Music* (New York: Simon and Schuster, 2002), 281.
98. Atkins and Cochran, *Chet Atkins*, 55.

99. The 1950 RadiOzark transcription series of the Carter Sisters, Mother Maybelle, and Chet Atkins is available on Bruce A. McGuire's YouTube channel: https://www.youtube.com/@NashBruce/search?query=radiozark%20carter. A fascinating, special program from 1950 created to sell the show to sponsors is available at: https://www.youtube.com/watch?v=zoXl4QIXkEE.
100. Zwonitzer, *Will You Miss Me*, 278.
101. Siman, interview by John Rumble, September 19, 1989.
102. Zwonitzer, *Will You Miss Me*, 278.
103. Atkins and Cochran, *Chet Atkins*, 55.
104. "KWTO Staff Changes," *KWTO Dial*, June 1950, 3.
105. "The Spotlight," *KWTO Dial*, September 1950, 18.
106. Atkins and Cochran, *Chet Atkins*, 172.

CHAPTER 3

1. Hulston, *Lester E. Cox 1895–1968*, 152.
2. Tracey E. W. Laird, "Country Music and Television," in *The Oxford Handbook of Country Music*, ed. Travis D. Stimeling (Oxford: Oxford University Press, 2021), 251.
3. In 1946, only 1 percent of homes in America had TV sets and there were eighteen television stations. By 1952, 52.9 percent of American homes had televisions, and the number of stations had grown to 225. "Postwar American Television," Early Television Museum, accessed March 8, 2023, https://www.earlytelevision.org/us_tv_sets.html.
4. Siman, interview by Lana Grosshart.
5. Steve Eng, *A Satisfied Mind: The Country Music Life of Porter Wagoner* (Nashville: Rutledge Hill Press, 1992), 72, 74.
6. Eng, *A Satisfied Mind*, 74.
7. Siman, interview by John Rumble, September 19, 1989.
8. Eng, *A Satisfied Mind*, 77.
9. Glenn, *Ozarks' Greatest Hits*, 162.
10. The Super Chief was famous as the "train of the stars" because it served many celebrity passengers traveling between Chicago and Los Angeles. "Super Chief," Wikipedia, accessed August 4, 2023, https://en.wikipedia.org/wiki/Super_Chief.
11. A group of radio industry leaders had founded BMI in 1939 because they were unhappy with licensing fees and prejudicial policies of the dominant licensing

company, the American Society of Composers, Authors and Publishers (ASCAP). Pecknold, *The Selling Sound*, 56.
12. Siman, interview by John Rumble, Country Music Foundation Oral History Project, Frist Library and Archive of the Country Music Hall of Fame and Museum, September 24, 1991.
13. Siman, interview by John Rumble, September 24, 1991.
14. The name "Earl Barton" came from Siman and Mahaffey's respective middle names. Siman, interview by Lana Grosshart.
15. Si Siman, Letter to *Springfield News and Leader*, July 2, 1978, B2.
16. Siman, interview by Lana Grosshart.
17. "Talking Things Over," *Springfield Leader and Press*, December 20, 1953, 28.
18. The Philharmonics—Eldridge Moss, Homer Boyd, George Culp, James Logan, and Chick Rice—would also become regulars on the local *Jubilee* TV show and the ABC network *Ozark Jubilee* after its debut in 1955. Glenn, *Ozarks' Greatest Hits*, 290, 385.
19. Soon after the *Ozark Jubilee* began on network television in 1955, Ford would have two monster hits: "The Ballad of Davy Crockett" and "Sixteen Tons." The latter became the "fastest selling single in the history of the record industry, selling more than a million copies in the first three weeks of release. It reached No. 1 on *Billboard*'s Hot 100 on November 26, 1955 and stayed there for seven weeks." Ron Sylvester, "Ernie Ford Dies at Age 72," *Springfield News and Leader*, October 18, 1991, C1.
20. "Red Foley," Wikipedia, accessed March 21, 2023, https://en.wikipedia.org/wiki/Red_Foley.
21. Rita Spears-Stewart, *Troubles, Faith, and Peace in the Valley: The Red Foley Story* (Baltimore: Publish America, 2011), 90.
22. The *Opry* did not want Foley's personal image to represent them. Foley resigned as emcee of the Prince Albert Show on the *Grand Ole Opry* in 1953 and carried on with a heavy schedule of personal appearances. When R. J. Reynolds discontinued its sponsorship of the Prince Albert Show on NBC in 1957, it "marked the last of the radio network's live musical shows, making it one good candidate for the last gasp of the golden age of radio." Craig Havighurst, *Air Castle of the South: WSM and the Making of Music City* (Urbana: University of Illinois Press, 2007), 200.
23. Eng, *A Satisfied Mind*, 85.
24. Siman, interview by John Rumble, Country Music Foundation Oral History Project, Frist Library and Archive of the Country Music Hall of Fame and Museum, September 23, 1991.
25. Siman, interview by John Rumble, September 23, 1991.

26. Siman, interview by John Rumble, September 23, 1991.
27. Glenn, *Ozarks' Greatest Hits*, 330.
28. "[Letter of intent] to be followed by contract for . . . services as Star of the ABC-TV show to be known as the 'OZARK JUBILEE.' This contract is to be entered into within three months from this date (December 20, 1954) on the following terms and conditions: Sustaining (Network) minimum $350 per show, Commercial (Network) minimum $750 per show. The above prices call for and are on the basis of a one-hour show per week." Siman to Red Foley, December 20, 1954.
29. An article in *Business Week* claimed that the *Ozark Jubilee* operated for its first nine months without a national sponsor: "During that period, ABC sold local spots at 15-min. breaks . . . [then] Whitehall Pharmaceutical Co. took a half hour. A few weeks ago, American Chicle Co., sponsoring Beeman's Pepsin Gum, bought a share of the half hour." "Hillbilly TV Show Hits the Big Time," *Business Week*, March 10, 1956, 31.
30. *Cash Box*'s weekly news column usually highlighted the latest developments at four country music shows: the *Grand Ole Opry*, the *Louisiana Hayride*, the *Big D Jamboree*, and the *Ozark Jubilee*—the latter with the section header "From the Crossroads of Country Music." "The *Cash Box* Country Roundup," *Cash Box*, April 16, 1955, 33.
31. "Foley Signs with RadiOzark, TT for Personal Appearances," *The Billboard*, April 17, 1954, 16. Trade publications during the early 1950s often referred to country music as "hillbilly" or "folk music." By the mid-1950s, it was "country" or "country & western," and then "country" again.
32. Hank Thompson had to intervene to get Capitol producer Ken Nelson to sign Shepard because "producers didn't believe in female singers" back then. Bufwack and Oermann, *Finding Her Voice*, 158.
33. Jean Shepard, *Down Through the Years* (Nashville, TN: Don Wise Productions, 2014), 79.
34. Ferlin Husky, interview with John W. Rumble, Country Music Foundation Oral History Project, July 18, 2001.
35. Shepard and Hawkins both joined the ABC-TV *Ozark Jubilee* from its first program on January 22, 1955. On November 21, 1955, Shepard joined the *Grand Ole Opry* at a time when there were only three other female *Opry* cast members: comic Minnie Pearl, pianist Del Wood, and the "Queen of Country Music," Kitty Wells. Shepard and Hawkins eventually moved to Nashville and married on November 26, 1960. Shepard was the "only early-1950s country music woman who made it on her own" after her husband died in a plane crash in 1963. Bufwack and Oermann, *Finding Her Voice*, 160.

36. Grady Martin became a Nashville A-Team session musician after his time at the *Ozark Jubilee* and played on many country albums of the 1960s, including the memorable guitar solos on Marty Robbins's recording of "El Paso" (1959). Martin was elected to the Country Music Hall of Fame in 2015. "Grady Martin," Wikipedia, accessed August 4, 2023, https://en.wikipedia.org/wiki/Grady_Martin.
37. "Jewell Leased by Top Talent," *Springfield Leader and Press*, June 16, 1954, 17; "Top Talent Leases Springfield House," *The Billboard*, July 3, 1954, 1.
38. "Ozark Jubilee Airs Red Foley," *Cash Box*, October 23, 1954, 29.
39. On October 5, a separate ABC radio half hour segment began as a delayed broadcast on Tuesday nights from 10:30 to 11:00 with Porter Wagoner and others substituting for Foley as host. Bill Sachs, "Folk and Talent and Tunes: ABC Adds More 'Ozark Jubilee,'" *The Billboard*, October 1, 1954, 36.
40. Siman, interview by John Rumble, September 23, 1991.
41. "RadiOzark Artists," *Cash Box*, November 20, 1954, 61.
42. "RadiOzark Artists," 61. Owen Bradley had gathered a large roster of country music artists during the 1940s and '50s. As a result, Decca was the major competitor of RCA Victor during that period.
43. Heno Head Jr., *America's Favorite Janitor: The Life Story of Country Songwriter Johnny Mullins* (Independence, MO: The International University Press, 1986), 194.
44. Head, *America's Favorite Janitor*, 100.
45. Mountain Grove, Missouri, native Don Warden also had a radio show in West Plains where he met Wagoner. He performed with the Porter Wagoner Trio at the *Ozark Jubilee* and made appearances throughout the region. He came with Wagoner to Nashville when he joined the *Grand Ole Opry*. Warden performed for fourteen years on the syndicated TV program called the *Porter Wagoner Show* before leaving to manage Dolly Parton in 1974. Warden is in the Steel Guitar Hall of Fame. "Don Warden," Wikipedia, accessed August 4, 2023, https://en.wikipedia.org/wiki/Don_Warden.
46. Eng, *A Satisfied Mind*, 95.
47. "Company's Comin'" was later recorded by many artists, including Jack Benny, Tennessee Ernie Ford, Danny Kaye, Mel Tillis, and Mickey Mouse. It was translated and recorded in French in 1970. Melinda Mullins, "Johnny Mullins," *OzarksWatch*, Spring 2017, 68. Johnny Mullins wrote many songs in his career, including "Blue Kentucky Girl" and "Success" for Loretta Lynn. His daughter Melinda Mullins now performs her father's songs in tribute shows throughout the Ozarks.

48. "Company's Comin'" was Earl Barton Music's first BMI award. Scott Foster Siman, personal communication, August 22, 2023.
49. Porter Wagoner, interview by Archie Campbell, 1983, *Yesteryear in Nashville*, posted September 11, 2018, https://www.youtube.com/watch?v=D_9rS7cysy0.
50. "RadiOzark Artists," *Cash Box*, November 20, 1954, 61.
51. Siman, interview by Lana Grosshart.
52. Siman, interview by John Rumble, Country Music Foundation Oral History Project, Frist Library and Archive of the Country Music Hall of Fame and Museum, September 21, 1989.
53. Siman, interview by Lana Grosshart.
54. ABC purchased the property in 1949. Tom Miller, "The 1901 Durland's Riding Academy 7 West 66th Street," Daytonian in Manhattan, February 13, 2014, https://daytoninmanhattan.blogspot.com/2014/02/the-1901-durlands-riding-academy-7-west.html.
55. Leonard H. Goldenson with Marvin J. Wolf, *Beating the Odds: The Untold Story Behind the Rise of ABC: The Stars, Struggles, and Egos that Transformed Network Television by the Man Who Made It Happen* (New York: Charles Scribner's Sons, 1991), 115.
56. Goldenson, *Beating the Odds*, 116.
57. "ABC Plans Radical Revamp of Program Line-Up for Fall," *The Billboard*, March 3, 1956, 3.
58. Networks bought time from their affiliated stations and resold the time to advertisers for a program's broadcast. The networks scheduled the program and promoted it to attract viewers. Fred Silverman, "An Analysis of ABC Television Network Programming" (master's thesis, The Ohio State University, 1959), 27.
59. Siman, interview by Lana Grosshart.
60. Siman, interview by John Rumble, September 19, 1989.
61. "Pact Signed for Jubilee on Network," *Springfield Leader and Press*, December 24, 1954, 3.
62. Siman, interview by Lana Grosshart.
63. Siman, interview by John Rumble, September 19, 1989.
64. Siman, interview by Lana Grosshart.
65. "Standing-Room Crowd Watches Jubilee Premiere," *Springfield Daily News*, May 1, 1955, 37. Reserved tickets for the show were sold out by mid-week. The Ozark Hillbilly Medallion honored prestigious visitors to Springfield by proclaiming them a "hillbilly of the Ozarks." Honorees included President Harry Truman, US Army generals Omar Bradley and Matthew Ridgway, US Representative Short, J. C. Penney, Johnny Olson, Ralph Story, and country disc jockey Nelson King.

66. Plaster's Master Market, advertisement, *Springfield Leader and Press*, April 28, 1955, 43.
67. Aunt Martha was Slim Wilson's sister and the matriarch of the "Goodwill Family" that included guitarist Speedy Haworth. She later opened another popular restaurant called Aunt Martha's Pancake House. "Death Claims 'Aunt Martha,'" *Springfield Leader and Press*, August 16, 1966, 7.
68. The Corn Crib, advertisement, *Union Labor Record*, April 28, 1955, 8-9.
69. "The Spectator," *Springfield Daily News*, April 24, 1955, 30.
70. "The Spectator," 30.
71. Siman, interview by John Rumble, Country Music Foundation Oral History Project, Frist Library and Archive of the Country Music Hall of Fame and Museum, September 21, 1991.
72. Randle Chowning, personal communication, May 24, 2022.
73. Phil Dessauer, "Springfield, Mo.-Radio City of Country Music," *Coronet*, April 1957, 154.
74. Dessauer, "Springfield, Mo.," 154.
75. Siman, interview by John Rumble, September 21, 1989.
76. Anthony Harkins, *Hillbilly: A Cultural History of an American Icon* (Oxford: Oxford University Press, 2004), 99.
77. Charles Mercer, "Gotham Learns of Springfield," *Springfield Leader and Press*, April 20, 1956, 3.
78. " 'Tain't Hillbilly, Neighbor! It's 'Country Music' That's Making a Splash on TV," *TV Guide*, August 27-September 2, 1955, 10.
79. Earl Wilson, "It Happened Last Night," *Pittsburgh Post-Gazette*, January 26, 1956, 29.
80. John Lester, "Radio and Television," *Gazette and Daily*, January 8, 1955, 15.
81. Dessauer, "Springfield, Mo.," 152.
82. Siman, interview by Lana Grosshart.
83. Commenting on his brief time in Springfield during the *Ozark Jubilee* days, Nelson reportedly said he didn't wash enough dishes to get dishpan hands. He was in Springfield long enough to meet one of his future wives, *Jubilee* yodeler Shirley Caddell. Sid Pierce, personal communication, March 14, 2023.
84. Thomas Peters, "The *Ozark Jubilee*," unpublished manuscript, 126.
85. Marijohn Wilkin, interview by Patricia Hall, Country Music Foundation Oral History Project, Frist Library and Archive of the Country Music Hall of Fame and Museum, 1975.
86. "Country Round Up," *Cash Box*, January 4, 1958, 45.
87. A short list of musicians who traveled from the *Hayride* to work at the *Jubilee* includes Gene Autry, Johnny Cash, Jim Reeves, Tex Ritter, Webb Pierce, and

Faron Young. Horace Logan with Bill Sloan, *Louisiana Hayride Years: Making Musical History in Country's Golden Age* (New York: St. Martin's Griffin, 1999), 263-68.

88. Tracey E. W. Laird, *Louisiana Hayride: Radio and Roots Music along the Red River* (Oxford: Oxford University Press, 2005), 6.
89. Billy Walker and *Hayride* member Slim Whitman were partly responsible for getting Elvis Presley booked for a performance at the *Hayride* on October 16, 1954. Joe Carr and Alan Munde, *Prairie Nights to Neon Lights: The Story of Country Music in West Texas* (Lubbock: Texas Tech University Press, 1995), 147.
90. Logan with Sloan, *Louisiana Hayride Years*, 28.
91. Wayne W. Daniel, "Music of the Postwar Era," *The Hayloft Gang: The Story of the National Barn Dance*, edited by Chad Berry (Champaign: University of Illinois Press, 2008), 73.
92. Carr and Munde, *Prairie Nights*, 145.
93. The *Big D Jamboree* was the only country music show in Dallas, and it became one of many important stopovers for artists looking for gigs and radio jobs on the country music trail. It began as the *Lone Star Barn Dance* in 1947 and became the *Big D Jamboree* in 1948. The station acquired national coverage when the CBS Radio Network picked it up in 1956. Country music record producer and music publisher Jim Beck was one of the movers and shakers in Dallas. He was responsible for getting Lefty Frizzell's first record contract in 1950 and opened a recording studio where he recorded the first hit for Marty Robbins, "I'll Go On Alone." Frizzell and Robbins both came to Springfield for television exposure during the 1950s, along with Johnny Cash, Patsy Cline, Wanda Jackson, Sonny James, Carl Perkins, Webb Pierce, and Ray Price. Carr and Munde, *Prairie Nights*, 146-47.
94. Billy Walker with Bob Tubert, interview (interviewer unidentified), January 7, 1993, Patrick Jackson private collection.
95. Nelson King and Marty Roberts, "Hillbilly Hit Parade," *The Union-Banner*, October 7, 1954, 5.
96. Patsy Cline's manager Randy Keith convinced Walker that Nashville was place he needed to be: "I never did really want to come to Tennessee. I was from Texas, you know, and that's our home, and Texas is a big state." Carr and Munde, *Prairie Nights*, 148.
97. Maxine Brown, *Looking Back to See: A Country Music Memoir* (Fayetteville: The University of Arkansas Press, 2005), 111.
98. Brown, *Looking Back*, 112.
99. "I Take the Chance," Wikipedia, accessed March 21, 2023, https://en.Wikipedia.org/wiki/I_Take_the_Chance.

100. Brown, *Looking Back*, 113.
101. Their biggest hit was "The Three Bells" in 1959. Jim Ed Brown continued on RCA as a solo act after the group disbanded in 1967 and recorded several hit records, including his first solo effort, "Pop a Top" (1967). The Browns were inducted into the Country Music Hall of Fame in 2015. "The Browns," Wikipedia, accessed August 4, 2023, https://en.wikipedia.org/wiki/The_Browns.
102. Brown, *Looking Back to See*, 111.
103. Brown, *Looking Back to See*, 116.
104. Brown, *Looking Back to See*, 117.
105. "The 'Big Time' Beckons," *East Oklahoma Tribune*, July 14, 1955, 12.
106. Peters, "The *Ozark Jubilee*," 124.
107. Wanda Jackson with Scott B. Bomar, *Every Night Is Saturday Night: A Country Girl's Journey to the Rock & Roll Hall of Fame* (Nashville: BMG, 2017), 104.
108. Jackson, *Every Night*, 107.
109. Jackson, *Every Night*, 101.
110. Jackson, *Every Night*, 102.
111. Jackson, *Every Night*, 108.
112. Jackson, *Every Night*, 114.
113. Later hits included the 1960 rockabilly song "Let's Have a Party" and two huge country hits in 1961: "Right or Wrong" and "In the Middle of a Heartache." "Wanda Jackson," Wikipedia, accessed August 4, 2023, https://en.wikipedia.org/wiki/Wanda_Jackson.
114. Brenda Lee with Robert K. Oermann and Julie Clay, *Little Miss Dynamite: The Life and Times of Brenda Lee* (New York: Hyperion, 2002), 26.
115. Rita Spears-Stewart, "The Ozark Jubilee Saga," *Springfield! Magazine*, September 1995, 45.
116. Si Siman, interviewer unidentified, Siman Family Papers, private collection of Scott Foster Siman and Jayne Siman Chowning.
117. Lee, *Little Miss Dynamite*, 29.
118. "Country Round Up," *Cash Box*, November 17, 1956, 42.
119. Si Siman, interviewer unidentified.
120. Lee, *Little Miss Dynamite*, 31.
121. Lee, *Little Miss Dynamite*, 34.
122. Siman, interview by John Rumble, September 24, 1991.
123. "Country Round Up," *Cash Box*, March 30, 1957, 51.
124. Lee, *Little Miss Dynamite*, 39.
125. Lee, *Little Miss Dynamite*, 40.

126. Crossroads contract with Brenda Lee, Siman Family Papers, private collection of Scott Foster Siman and Jayne Siman Chowning.
127. Lee, *Little Miss Dynamite*, 40.
128. Lee, *Little Miss Dynamite*, 40.
129. "Crossroads TV Sues Brenda Lee's Mother," *Springfield Daily News*, August 8, 1957, 6.
130. Eng, *A Satisfied Mind*, 118.
131. Lee, *Little Miss Dynamite*, 41.
132. Eng, *A Satisfied Mind*, 118.
133. Hugh Ashley began his music career as a performer on radio stations in the Ozarks with his father's band, the Ashley Melody Men. He was one of the original members of the early hillbilly radio group called the Beverly Hill Billies. Country Music Hall of Fame members Red Foley, Brenda Lee, Bill Monroe Jim Reeves, and Porter Wagoner recorded his songs. Chad Causey, "Hubert Carl (Hugh) Ashley (1915–2008)," *Encyclopedia of Arkansas*, accessed April 5, 2023, https://encyclopediaofarkansas.net/entries/hubert-carl-5257/.
134. Ron Sylvester, "Brenda Lee: Pure Talent," *Springfield News-Leader*, June 17, 1996, 5B.
135. Douglas Gomery, "Patsy Cline: A Television Star," *Sweet Dreams: The World of Patsy Cline* (Champaign: The University of Illinois Press, 2013), 121.
136. Siman, interview by Lana Grosshart.
137. "*Jubilee USA (Ozark Jubilee)*, December 12, 1959, segment 3," Ozark Jubilee, posted March 26, 2019, https://www.youtube.com/watch?v=WLdcp9YMy_8&t=156s.
138. Siman, interview by Lana Grosshart.
139. Bob Tubert, Doc Martin, Vic Willis, Speedy Haworth, Norma Jean, and Bentley Cummins, interview (interviewer unidentified), March 5, 1993, private Patrick Jackson private collection.
140. Bob Tubert et al, interview, March 5, 1993.
141. Don Richardson, diary, private collection of John Richardson.
142. Siman, interview by Lana Grosshart.
143. Holly George-Warren, *Public Cowboy No. 1: The Life and Times of Gene Autry* (Oxford: Oxford University Press, 2007), 43.
144. Glenn, *Ozarks' Greatest Hits*, 150.
145. George-Warren, *Public Cowboy No. 1*, 82–83. The college is now Missouri State University.
146. "Gene Autry," Wikipedia, accessed August 3, 2023, https://en.wikipedia.org/wiki/Gene_Autry.

147. Siman, interview by Lana Grosshart.
148. Foley and Ritter recalled their experience making the film during an episode of *Ozark Jubilee* (12:15-17:15). "*Ozark Jubilee*, September 24, 1955, segment 2," Ozark Jubilee, posted July 8, 2021, https://www.youtube.com/watch?v=V9q6UhPm2Ws.
149. His 1965 hit "Waltz Across Texas" is still considered a popular anthem in Texas dance hall music.
150. Bryan Bisney, Scheduling Notebook for *Ozark Jubilee*, Book 1, page 41, https://cdm17307.contentdm.oclc.org/digital/collection/Bisney/id/754/rec/2, Bryan T. E. Bisney Collection, Missouri State University Digital Collections.
151. Bryan Bisney, scheduling notebook for *Ozark Jubilee*, Book 2, page 49b, https://cdm17307.contentdm.oclc.org/digital/collection/Bisney/id/530/rec/3, and Book 2, page 39d, https://cdm17307.contentdm.oclc.org/digital/collection/Bisney/id/509/rec/3, Bryan T. E. Bisney Collection.
152. Leroy Van Dyke, personal communication, October 5, 2021.
153. Van Dyke, October 5, 2021.
154. Walker, interview, January 7, 1993.
155. Laird, *Louisiana Hayride,* 94.
156. Siman, interview by John Rumble, September 24, 1991
157. Walker, interview, January 7, 1993.
158. Logan, *Louisiana Hayride Years*, 5.
159. Walker, interview, January 7, 1993.
160. Walker, interview, January 7, 1993.
161. If *Jubilee* financial records exist to confirm Tubert's claim, they are not evident in archives I have examined. Tubert worked as *Jubilee* scriptwriter in 1957-58.
162. Walker, interview, January 7, 1993.
163. Walker, interview, January 7, 1993.
164. Siman, interview by John Rumble, September 21, 1991.
165. Siman, interview by John Rumble, September 21, 1991.
166. Siman, interview by John Rumble, September 24, 1991.
167. Siman, interview by John Rumble, September 21, 1989.
168. Don Richardson, "Winding Up a Big Year of Personal Appearances," undated press release for Top Talent, Inc., Siman Family Papers, private collection of Scott Foster Siman and Jayne Siman Chowning.
169. Terry, "Hillbilly Music Center."
170. Porter Wagoner, interview (interviewer unidentified), January 7, 1993, Patrick Jackson private collection.
171. Norma Jean, interview (interviewer unidentified), January 7, 1993, Patrick Jackson private collection.

172. Lee, *Little Miss Dynamite*, 27.
173. Siman, interview by John Rumble, September 24, 1991.
174. Shepard, *Down Through the Years*, 81.
175. Shepard, *Down Through the Years*, 82.
176. Brown, *Looking Back to See*, 112.
177. Siman, interview by John Rumble, September 24, 1991.
178. Siman, interview by John Rumble, September 24, 1991.
179. Richardson, diary.
180. Norma Jean, interview (interviewer unidentified), March 5, 1993, Patrick Jackson private collection.
181. Siman, interview by John Rumble, September 24, 1991.
182. Richardson, diary entry, April 1, 1960.
183. Richardson, diary entry, February 3, 1960.
184. Siman, interview by John Rumble, September 24, 1991.
185. Siman, interview by John Rumble, September 23, 1991.

CHAPTER 4

1. Siman, interview by John Rumble, September 21, 1989.
2. Kinescope was a common method of recording during the mid-1950s. It involved placing a television camera lens in front of a program being broadcast on a television monitor and recording the program on film. The technique is evident in early *Jubilee* shows and can be detected by rounded corners of the screen view. Sometimes a reflection from the monitor can also be seen. The *Jubilee* television crew made kinescopes to broadcast later when the normal live network schedule was preempted for some reason. "Kinescope," Wikipedia, accessed August 4, 2023, https://en.wikipedia.org/wiki/Kinescope.
3. Eng, *A Satisfied Mind*, 120.
4. Terry, "Hillbilly Music Center."
5. "'Ozark Jubilee' Hits ARB Top for May TV," *The Billboard*, June 11, 1955, 22.
6. "Celebrating 95 Years of Innovation," Nielsen, accessed August 4, 2023, https://sites.nielsen.com/timelines/our-history/.
7. Silverman, "An Analysis of ABC Television," 42.
8. "Ozark Jubilee," Wikipedia, accessed August 4, 2023, https://en.wikipedia.org/wiki/Ozark_Jubilee.
9. Crossroads Productions and ABC Television Network, advertisement, *The Billboard*, January 21, 1956, 15.
10. Silverman, "An Analysis of ABC Television," 202.
11. Goldenson, *Beating the Odds*, 137.

12. Silverman, "An Analysis of ABC Television," 162.
13. *Wyatt Earp* would be the longest-running, most successful of the group; it would lead an increasingly large herd of adult westerns that would attract viewers during the next five years. Silverman, "An Analysis of ABC Television," 170.
14. Craig Havighurst, *Air Castle of the South: WSM and the Making of Music City* (Urbana: University of Illinois Press, 2007), 159.
15. Havighurst, *Air Castle of the South*, 160.
16. "Ralston Purina Inks 'Opry' for Monthly TV-er," *The Billboard*, July 30, 1955, 67.
17. "WSM's Grand Ole Opry Makes Network TV Debut," *Cash Box*, November 12, 1955, 56.
18. Cusic, *Discovering Country Music*, 82.
19. Howard Turtle, "Ozarks Folk Tunes and Comedy Make Springfield a TV Center," *Kansas City Star*, January 29, 1956, C1.
20. "Country Musicians Fiddle Up Roaring Business," *Life*, November 1956, 137.
21. Cusic, *Discovering Country Music*, 72; Havighurst, *Air Castle of the South*, 183.
22. "Rural Music Rocks Too," *Springfield News and Leader*, April 29, 1956, A16.
23. Perkins also played the flip side, "Honey Don't," on the *Jubilee* that night. "Carl Perkins," Wikipedia, accessed August 4, 2023, https://en.Wikipedia.org/wiki/Carl_Perkins.
24. Dick Kleiner, "Hill Music on Way Out," *Springfield News and Leader*, April 29, 1956, B6.
25. "'Country Music Carnival' Sponsored by Country DJ Association to be Held in Springfield, Mo. June 14, 15 & 16," *Cash Box*, June 2, 1956, 35.
26. "'Country Music Carnival,'" 35.
27. Bill Sachs, "C & W Deejays Kick Off First Annual," *The Billboard*, June 23, 1956, 29, 40.
28. Pecknold, *The Selling Sound*, 84.
29. Pecknold, *The Selling Sound*, 81–85.
30. Pecknold, *The Selling Sound*, 137.
31. Portions of this section were published as "Si Siman and the *Ozark Jubilee*: Getting and Keeping the First Continuous Live Country Music Show on Network Television," in *The International Country Music Journal*, ed. Don Cusic (Nashville: Brackish Publishing, 2022), 115–50.
32. Siman brought Richardson to Springfield from Grand Rapids, Michigan, after receiving his creative query letter about the job. Richardson demonstrated his quirkiness with a clever salutation that began: "I always heard that if you wanted to get an answer and get it quick, you go direct to the horse's mouth. 'Dear

Horse's Mouth . . . .'" Siman loved Richardson's approach and hired him to write the George Morgan *Robin Hood Flour Show* radio transcriptions. Richardson later transitioned to television with Siman. After the end of the *Jubilee* in 1960, Richardson was instrumental in giving theme park Silver Dollar City its name and had a successful career in Branson as a publicist for the park.

33. Siman, interview by John Rumble, September 21, 1989.
34. Walker, interview, January 7, 1993.
35. A fascinating record of planning *Jubilee* shows is available in Bryan Bisney's three scheduling notebooks, digitized by Missouri State University for the Bryan T. E. Bisney Collection. Many thanks to Thomas A. Peters, Director of Library Services, for administering this valuable archive.
36. A cowcatcher is a frame on the front of a train locomotive designed to throw things or animals off the track. Siman's usage would indicate a tease of what was coming after a commercial break.
37. Digitized copies of correspondence pertaining to the *Ozark Jubilee* production are available in the Bryan T. E. Bisney Collection at Missouri State University.
38. Siman, interview by John Rumble, September 21, 1989.
39. Opened in 1944, the Grove Supper Club at 1326 N. Glenstone was one of Springfield's favorite steak houses, but it was also famous for their one of their early cooks, Wing Yin "David" Leong, who invented Springfield-style cashew chicken. Leong emigrated to the United States from China. He became a World War II hero and landed on Omaha Beach on D-Day. Unfortunately, he suffered from racist attacks in Springfield, including discrimination while working for Bill Grove and later the bombing of his own restaurant, Leong's Tea House. He died in 2020 at the age of 99. Steve Pokin, "The Life of David Leong: Recipe of Success," *Springfield News-Leader*, May 21, 2018, A1, A6, A7.
40. Siman, interview by Lana Grosshart.
41. A few scripts of the *Jubilee* are digitized for viewing in the Bryan T. E. Bisney Collection, Missouri State University Digital Collections.
42. Siman, interview by Lana Grosshart.
43. Siman, interview by Lana Grosshart.
44. Siman, interview by John Rumble, September 23, 1989.
45. Tex Ritter, quoted in Peters, "The *Ozark Jubilee*," 35.
46. Siman, interview by John Rumble, September 21, 1989.
47. Promotional flyers distributed by ABC television, Siman Family Papers, private collection of Scott Foster Siman and Jayne Siman Chowning.
48. Siman, interview by John Rumble, September 21, 1989.

49. Siman, interview by John Rumble, September 24, 1991.
50. "Fishing Sees Changes As Dramatic as Landscape's," *Springfield News-Leader*, September 25, 1990, 9E.
51. "Fishing Sees Changes," 9E.
52. Vernon D. Snell, "Hook, Line and Sinker," *The Daily Oklahoman*, October 5, 1958, 98.
53. Snell, "Hook, Line and Sinker," 98.
54. The younger Morris founded Bass Pro Shops and Cabela's. Morris's home office and store on South Campbell Street in Springfield is so large it has its own zip code. Bass Pro Shops is the number-one tourist attraction in the state of Missouri, and its Wonders of Wildlife Museum & Aquarium is the world's largest wildlife attraction. "Springfield, Missouri," Wikipedia, accessed August 4, 2023, https://en.wikipedia.org/wiki/Springfield,_Missouri.
55. Jayne Siman Chowning, personal communication, March 20, 2022.
56. Chowning, March 20, 2022.
57. Chowning, March 20, 2022.
58. Siman, interview by Lana Grosshart.
59. Sara Eskridge, *Rube Tube: CBS and Rural Comedy in the Sixties* (Columbia: University of Missouri Press, 2018), 5.
60. Eskridge, *Rube Tube*, 5.
61. "Jubilee Ends Its Hookup with ABC," *Springfield News-Leader*, August 17, 1957, 2.
62. "Jubilee Schedule Is Revised Again," *Springfield Daily News*, September 13, 1958, 1.
63. "Red Foley's 'Country Music Jubilee' Receives 200,000th Visitor," *Cash Box*, October 19, 1957, 53.
64. Siman, interview by John Rumble, September 21, 1989.
65. Paradoxically, other acts and performers—square dancers in gingham costumes and rube comics such as Pete Stamper, Lennie and Goo Goo, Uncle Cyp and Aunt Sap, Shug Fisher—seemed invulnerable to network manipulation.
66. Wanda Jackson, *Every Night*, 165.
67. Silverman, "An Analysis of ABC Television," 272.
68. Foley and his wife Sally insisted that incomes determined by the IRS were "fictitious, erroneous and arbitrary." "Red Foley Sues U.S. Over Taxes," *Springfield Leader and Press*, April 4, 1959, 1.
69. "Red Foley Sues U.S. Over Taxes," *Springfield Leader and Press*, April 4, 1959, 1.
70. "Foley Confident 'No Law Violated' After Tax Indictment Is Returned," *Springfield Daily News*, December 11, 1949, 1.
71. Foley was also not a businessman and couldn't handle money. Among his

foolish, losing investments were a "heated toilet-stool top" and an "electric mattress." Siman, interview by John Rumble, September 21, 1989.
72. Don Richardson, diary entry, February 4, 1960.
73. Richardson, diary entry, February 9, 1960.
74. Richardson, diary entry, February 19, 1960.
75. Richardson, diary entry, February 20, 1960.
76. Richardson, "I Remember Red," The Curbstone Critic, *Springfield Leader and Press*, September 23, 1968, 17.
77. Richardson, diary entry, April 20, 1960.
78. Siman, interview by John Rumble, September 21, 1989.
79. Siman, interview by John Rumble, September 21, 1989.
80. Silverman, "An Analysis of ABC Television," 362.
81. "The Death of TV's Jubilee," *Springfield News and Leader*, September 18, 1960, 41.
82. Siman, interview by Lana Grosshart.
83. "Jubilee Near End of Line?" *Springfield Leader and Press*, August 1, 1960, 13.
84. "The Death of TV's Jubilee," 41.
85. Richardson, diary, February 21, 1961. On April 24, 1961, Foley was acquitted of income tax evasion charges, but by then the damage was done. The IRS issued a refund of $79,555 to Foley in October for sums collected during the long process. "U.S. to Refund $79,555 to Red," *Springfield Leader and Press*, October 27, 1961, 1.
86. "New Jubilee Has 5 Stars," *Springfield News-Leader*, March 10, 1961, 22.
87. Siman, interview by Lana Grosshart.
88. "Firm Set Up as Producers of Color TV," *Springfield Leader and Press*, July 5, 1963, 9.
89. Siman, interview by John Rumble, September 23, 1991.
90. Top Talent performance contracts with Red Foley, Siman Family Papers, private collection of Scott Foster Siman and Jayne Siman Chowning.
91. Richardson, "I Remember Red," The Curbstone Critic, *Springfield Leader and Press*, September 23, 1968, 17.
92. Siman, interview by Lana Grosshart.
93. "Talking Things Over," *Springfield Leader and Press*, January 15, 1961, 24.
94. Ron Sylvester, "'Slim' Wilson's Guitar Took Him to TV Glory," *Springfield News Leader*, October 10, 1999, 8.
95. Si Siman, "Recalling Slim Wilson: One of the Good Guys," *Springfield News Leader*, July 21, 1990, 4A.
96. Tom Carlson, "The Woman Behind the Park," *Springfield News-Leader*, December 7, 2014, 6A.

97. In 1953, Lee Mace's "Ozark Opry" had already established a country variety show at Lake of the Ozarks in Osage Beach, about one hundred miles northeast of Springfield.
98. Bob Mabe's show, "The Baldknobbers," was the first to open in Branson in 1959. Lloyd Presley opened his show on Highway 76 in Branson in 1967 as "Presley's Country Jubilee." "Branson: A History of Great Entertainment," Branson Tourism Center, accessed August 5, 2023, https://www.bransontourismcenter.com/articles/bransonarticle30.
99. Brooks Blevins, *A History of the Ozarks*, Vol. 3: *The Ozarkers* (Champaign: University of Illinois Press, 2021), 198.
100. Linda Leicht, "*Ozark Jubilee* Founder Recognized," *Springfield Daily News and Leader*, February 20, 2009, 3C.
101. Siman, interview by Lana Grosshart.
102. Siman, interview by John Rumble, September 24, 1991.
103. Jayne Siman Chowning, interview by Thomas Peters, *Ozarks Voices*, November 15, 2016.
104. Siman, interview by Lana Grosshart.

CHAPTER 5

1. Siman, interview by Lana Grosshart.
2. As Siman's catalog expanded during the following years, he established several more companies and became affiliated with each of the performing societies. BMI licensed songs published by Earl Barton, Rose Bridge with Wayne Carson, and Table Rock Music with Ronnie Self. SESAC licensed songs published by Shady Dell for Ronnie Reno and Wayne Carson. ASCAP licensed songs from Strawberry Hill Music with Ronald Johnson (Jay Stevens/Woody P. Snow). Siman, interview by John Rumble, September 24, 1991.
3. Bruce Eder, "Ronnie Self Biography," *AllMusic*, accessed April 16, 2022, https://www.allmusic.com/artist/ronnie-self-mn0000333181/biography.
4. Siman, interview by Lana Grosshart.
5. Eder, "Ronnie Self."
6. Eder, "Ronnie Self."
7. Vicky Self, interview by Jayne Siman Chowning, December 11, 2021.
8. Mary Sue Price, "2 Musicians Die, but Tales Remain," *Springfield Leader and Press*, September 3, 1981, C1.
9. Price, "2 Musicians Die."
10. Scott Foster Siman, personal communication, March 15, 2022. The $10,000 song was "Home in My Hand," recorded by Dallas Frazier in 1967.

11. Hawkins was highly respected in the music industry for writing and recording the classic 1957 rockabilly song "Susie-Q," featuring guitarist James Burton. Hawkins also produced many hits of the era, including "Western Union" for the Five Americans in 1967. "Dale Hawkins," Wikipedia, accessed August 5, 2023, https://en.wikipedia.org/wiki/Dale_Hawkins.
12. Siman, interview by Lana Grosshart.
13. To avoid confusion about performance names, Shorty Head Thompson will be referred to as "Thompson," and Wayne Head Carson Thompson will be "Carson."
14. "Shorty Thompson: A Homecoming," *KWTO Dial*, September 1948, 3.
15. Like his father, Carson changed his last name for a better show business presentation, first from Head to Thompson and then to Carson. Jayne Siman Chowning, personal communication, May 24, 2022.
16. As Carson had a tendency to stretch or modify the truth in interviews for publication, dates and specific sequences of events sometimes vary.
17. Thompson was, by all accounts, not easy to deal with, and Carson had grown up in a household where everything came second to his father's career goals. Thompson notoriously sold Wayne and Gary's childhood dog, and every family trip centered around his own ambitions. Wyndi Harp Head (Carson), interview, December 31, 2001.
18. Roben Jones, *Memphis Boys: The Story of American Studios* (Jackson: University Press of Mississippi, 2010), 79.
19. Bill Tatum, "Songwriter Keeps on Making Good," *Springfield News and Leader*, May 8, 1976, 2.
20. "Wayne Carson Accompanist for Buddy Ebsen at Rodeo," *Daily Standard*, August 1, 1966, 1.
21. Tatum, "Songwriter Keeps on Making Good," 8.
22. Stan Hitchcock, personal communication, July 10, 2021.
23. The pitch sheet is a list of artists and what songs they might like to use on an upcoming studio project. It helps music publishers decide which songs to suggest to the artist for potential recordings.
24. Siman, interview by Lana Grosshart.
25. Michael Brothers, "Lyrics that Endure," *Springfield News and Leader*, March 16, 2006, 1C.
26. "Siman Elected Board President," *The Billboard*, March 30, 1968, 3.
27. Moman's American Sound studio produced more than a quarter of the Billboard Hot 100 hits of the 1960s and 1970s, including Elvis Presley's 1969 album *From Elvis in Memphis*. "American Sound Studio," Wikipedia, accessed August 4, 2023, https://en.wikipedia.org/wiki/American_Sound_Studio. Moman later moved to Nashville where he won a Grammy award

for writing and producing B. J. Thomas's recording of "(Hey Won't You Play) Another Somebody Done Somebody Wrong Song" in 1975. He also cowrote "Luckenbach, Texas (Back to the Basics of Love)" for Waylon Jennings.

28. Mark Marymont, "Carson Cultivates Inspiration," *Springfield News and Leader*, October 10, 1982, 9-G.
29. Jones, *Memphis Boys*, 79.
30. Jones, *Memphis Boys*, 79–80.
31. Wayne Carson, interview by Michael McCall, "Poets and Prophets: Salute to Legendary Songwriter Wayne Carson," Country Music Hall of Fame, December 3, 2011, https://countrymusichalloffame.org/plan-your-visit/exhibits-activities/public-programs/poets-and-prophets/wayne-carson/.
32. Siman, interview by Lana Grosshart. Springfield musician Bill Jones said his band Lewie and the 7 Days went to Memphis with Carson in February 1967 to record "The Letter," but Chips Moman had already produced it with the Box Tops. Bill Jones, personal communication, October 5, 2021.
33. "The Letter," Wikipedia, accessed August 4, 2023, https://en.wikipedia.org/wiki/The_Letter_(Box_Tops_song).
34. Many writers have a hit song that reaches #1 on both the pop and country charts in a single year, but it is nearly unheard of for a writer to have two different songs that top separate charts at the same time.
35. "Studio Turns-On to City's Sounds," *Springfield Leader and Press*, November 16, 1969, B6.
36. Many other artists covered "The Letter" through the years, including Bachman Turner Overdrive, the Beach Boys, the Classics IV, Joe Cocker, Marc Cohen, Bobby Darin, Al Green, Jack Jones, Brenda Lee, Trini Lopez, Barbara Mandrell, Bob Marley and the Wailers, Al Martino, the Mindbenders, Lou Rawls, Cliff Richard, Johnny Rivers, Leon Russell, Sammi Smith, Amii Stewart, the Tams, Vanilla Fudge, Dionne Warwick, and Don Williams.
37. Bob Tubert also worked on the *Junior Jubilee*. He eventually moved to Nashville permanently where he managed Earl Barton Music, Regent Music, and Vintage Music during the 1960s. He was a founding member of the Nashville Songwriters Association International and helped to establish the Belmont University music business program. He later discovered Grammy-winning singer Shelby Lynne and wrote material for the CMA awards shows, benefit shows for the National Association of Recording Arts and Sciences, and CMA cable specials. Robert K. Oermann, "Life Notes: Music Publisher, Producer Bob Tubert Dies at 90," *Music Row*, April 15, 2016, https://musicrow.com/2016/04/lifenotes-music-publisher-producer-bob-tubert-dies-at-90/.

38. Roben Jones, *Memphis Boys*, 105.
39. Anthony's daughter Michelle worked with Siman's son Scott at Sony Music in the 1990s where the younger Siman helped develop the Dixie Chicks (now the Chicks), Joe Diffie, and Patty Loveless, among others.
40. Denny Cordell produced many rock and roll hit recordings during the 1960s and '70s with artists such as the Moody Blues, Procol Harem, and Tom Petty.
41. Phil Mershon and Elizabeth Fritze, "The Axis of Delaney and Bonnie," *Perfect Sound Forever*, January 2004, https://www.furious.com/perfect/delaneyandbonnie.html.
42. "The Letter," Wikipedia.
43. Geoffrey Himes, "Gary Stewart," *The Encyclopedia of Country Music*, edited by Paul Kingsbury (Oxford: Oxford University Press, 1998), 507.
44. Bradley succeeded Chet Atkins as head of RCA Records in 1973 and is best known for his role in helping to create the 1970s Outlaw movement in country music. He was inducted in the Country Music Hall of Fame in 2019. "Jerry Bradley," Wikipedia, accessed August 5, 2023, https://en.wikipedia.org/wiki/Jerry_Bradley_(music_executive).
45. Carson, "Poets and Prophets."
46. Malone and Laird, *Country Music USA*, 480.
47. Carson, "Poets and Prophets."
48. "I See the Want to in Your Eyes," Wikipedia, accessed August 4, 2023, https://en.wikipedia.org/wiki/I_See_the_Want_To_in_Your_Eyes.
49. Carson, "Poets and Prophets."
50. Himes, "Gary Stewart," 508.
51. Thom Jurek, "Gary Stewart," in *All Music Guide to Country: The Definitive Guide to Country Music*, 2nd ed., edited Vladimir Bogdanov, Chris Woodstra, and Stephen Thomas Erlewine (Lanham, MD: Backbeat Books, 2003), 171.
52. Randy Lewis, "Gary Stewart, 58; Sang Country Tunes Hinting at His Own Demons," *Los Angeles Times*, January 4, 2004, https://www.latimes.com/archives/la-xpm-2004-jan-02-me-stewart2-story.html.
53. Robert Hilburn, "The Surprising Sage of 'Always on My Mind,'" *Los Angeles Times*, April 24, 1988, 3.
54. This sequence of events is summarized from an interview with Wayne Carson conducted by Bobby Bare on May 16, 1984. *Bobby Bare & Friends Songwriter Showcase*, Season 2, Show #19, Country Music Hall of Fame and Museum, Nashville, https://digi.countrymusichalloffame.org/digital/collection/movingimage/id/46/rec/1. Johnny Christopher was in the studio when Wayne was trying to come up with a bridge. He claims a bigger writing

involvement, but Carson's original song demo supports Carson's view that it was only the bridge that was modified. To Mark James's credit, he thought it was a great song that needed a very simple, straightforward bridge.

55. Peggy Soric, "Simon [sic] Says 'Oh, Gosh,'" *Springfield News and Leader*, July 17, 1983, 3G.
56. See Jones, *Memphis Boys*, 199–218.
57. Jones, *Memphis Boys*, 105.
58. "Country on Our Minds," *Springfield Leader and Press*, October 12, 1983, 10A.
59. Mark Marymont, "Carson, Siman Shocked as Song Is First Again," *Springfield Leader and Press*, October 11, 1983, 24.
60. Julie Thanki, "Hall of Famer's Top Hit Had Over 300 Versions," *The Tennessean*, July 21, 2015, A4.
61. Stephan Thomas Erlewine, "Always on My Mind" by Willie Nelson (song review), *AllMusic*, accessed December 21, 2021, https://www.allmusic.com/song/always-on-my-mind-mt0043413717.
62. Mark Marymont, "Wayne Carson, Songwriter," *Springfield Leader and Press*, March 18, 1984, G1.
63. Marymont, "Wayne Carson, Songwriter."
64. "Si Siman," interview by Ed Fillmer, Ed Fillmer Video Journalist (YouTube channel), posted November 5, 2017, https://www.youtube.com/watch?v=gVcvk2LEh5Q.
65. "Ozarks Voices: Woody P. Snow, January 16, 2015," interview with Ronald Johnson by Thomas Peters, Missouri State University Libraries, posted April 20, 2015, https://www.youtube.com/watch?v=0q_Tdmq5Vlc.
66. "Si Siman, interview by Ed Fillmer.
67. "Ozarks Voices: Woody P. Snow."
68. Siman to unidentified recipient, no date, Siman Family Papers, private collection of Scott Foster Siman and Jayne Siman Chowning.
69. Information about Si Siman's views on songwriting have been compiled from Siman, unpublished interview by Lana Grosshart.
70. Siman, interview by Lana Grosshart.
71. Jones, *Memphis Boys*, 230.
72. "Studio Turns-On to City's Sounds," *Springfield Leader and Press*, November 16, 1969, B6.
73. "Studio Turns-On to City's Sounds."
74. Lee's song "Jackie Blue" was the Ozark Mountain Daredevil's most resilient hit single. He received a BMI Million Performance award for the song, and it continues to be in rotation on pop/rock radio stations. "Jackie Blue," Wikipedia, accessed August 5, 2023, https://en.wikipedia.org/wiki/Jackie_Blue_(song).

75. Larry Lee, personal communication, January 1, 2022.
76. Lee, personal communication.
77. Original members of the band with Larry Lee were Springfield musicians well known by local Springfield music fans of the 1960s and 1970s: Romeo Bonifacio, Mike Bunge, Lewie Taylor, Bill Jones, and Hugh Walpole.
78. Bill Jones, personal communication, October 5, 2021.
79. Lee, personal communication.
80. Lee, personal communication.
81. Siman also booked Missouri's official ragtime piano player Gary Ellison on US State Department shows in Vietnam and Korea in the 1960s. Ellison was a young high school student when he became the square dance caller for the high school-aged square-dancing group that performed on the *Ozark Jubilee* television show during its last two years. Siman put him on summer tours with *Jubilee* entertainers, and Ellison remembers the excitement and fun of being on the road as a teenager, especially when they got to do a show on the fifty-yard line of the Cotton Bowl at the Texas State Fair in front of forty thousand people. Red Foley and Slim Wilson's band were among the *Jubilee* staff entertainers on the show with Ellison and his troupe. Siman later booked him in hotel night club gigs across the country. Ellison said "I played everywhere from Nebraska to the Rio Grande Valley and up to Boston" after returning from Vietnam and Korea. Gary Ellison, personal communication, November 22, 2021.
82. Jones, personal communication.
83. Jones, personal communication.
84. Ed Peaco, "Immerse Yourself in Re-Drawn Granny's Bathwater," *Springfield News-Leader*, October 16, 2019, A3.
85. John Dillon, personal communication, September 11, 2021.
86. Mike Bunge died in an automobile accident in 1976. Jones, personal communication.
87. Conversation with Curtis Hargis, personal communication, March 16, 2023.
88. Lee, personal communication.
89. "Billboard's Recommended LPs," *Billboard*, November 24, 1973, 52.
90. Randle Chowning, personal communication, May 24, 2022.
91. Lee, personal communication.
92. The Ozark Mountain Daredevils are currently enjoying a revival with enthusiastic fans and an aggressively creative manager, Dwight Glenn.
93. Jones, *Memphis Boys*, 230.
94. Gregory J. Holman, "Country Artist Wayne Carson Dies at 72," *Springfield News-Leader*, July 29, 2015, 5A.
95. Holman, "Country Artist."

96. Nick Sibley, personal communication, September 8, 2021.
97. Sibley, personal communication.
98. Daredevils founder Randle Chowning confirms that Higgins produced the group's first demo but is uncertain of the date when Higgins bought Top Talent. Randle Chowning, personal communication.
99. Ronald Johnson (Jay Stevens/Woody P. Snow), personal communication, October 6, 2021.
100. Johnson, personal communication.
101. One was by Frank Farian, who worked for the German sub-publisher with foreign rights to Siman's catalog. When Farian couldn't get interest in the song from others, he cut it himself. Another artist finally cut the song again, and both versions raced up the German charts. Farian produced numerous hits on many artists during the 1980s and early 1990s. He is now known as the founder and producer of the infamous group Milli Vanilli, who had to return a Grammy Award for Best New Artist in 1999 because they lip-synched their recordings. "Frank Farian," Wikipedia, accessed August 5, 2023, https://en.wikipedia.org/wiki/Frank_Farian.
102. "Ozarks Voices: Woody P. Snow."
103. Mark Marymont, "Kershenbaum Goes Where the Bands Are," *Springfield Leader and Press*, January 15, 1984, 8-G.
104. Steve Pokin, "A Passion for Music," *Springfield News-Leader*, October 12, 2014, 6A. Tom Whitlock was another huge Ozarks talent, best known for his multiple-award-winning song from the movie *Top Gun*, "Take My Breath Away." He passed away in February 2023. Harrison Keegan, "Oscar-winning Springfield Songwriter Tom Whitlock Dies," *Springfield News-Leader*, February 21, 2023, A1 A2.
105. Vance Powell, "Lou Whitney: Del Lords, Dave Alvin, Wilco," *Tape Op*, accessed December 30, 2021, https://tapeop.com/interviews/98/lou-whitney/.
106. Ron Sylvester, "Musicians Congregate on Record Center Wall," *Springfield News-Leader*, July 31, 1995, 5-B.
107. Michael Brothers, "A Songwriter's Journey to the Top," *Springfield News-Leader*, February 13, 2005," 3-C.
108. Brothers, "A Songwriter's Journey."
109. Brothers, "A Songwriter's Journey."
110. Scott Foster Siman, personal communication, December 30, 2021.
111. Wyndi Harp Head (Carson), interview, December 31, 2001.
112. Scott Foster Siman, personal communication, December 30, 2021.

113. Siman, interview by Lana Grosshart.
114. Mark Marymont, "Siman Sells Copyrights to Almost 2,000 Songs," *News-Leader*, December 4, 1987, D1.
115. Robert Hilburn, "The Surprising Saga of 'Always on My Mind,'" *Los Angeles Times*, April 24, 1988, 3.
116. Siman, interview by Lana Grosshart.

CONCLUSION

1. Siman, interview by Lana Grosshart.
2. In 1994, Ozark Pictures produced *A Place to Grow*, a movie starring country singer Gary Morris and actor Denver Pyle, with musical help from Woody P. Snow and Randle Chowning. Siman died before its debut. "*A Place to Grow*," Wikipedia, accessed August 5, 2023, https://en.wikipedia.org/wiki/A_Place_to_Grow.
3. Jayne Siman Chowning, personal communication, May 18, 2022.
4. Siman, interview by Lana Grosshart.
5. Siman, interview by Lana Grosshart.
6. Siman rescued the dog from a golf course. Jayne Siman Chowning called Dandy the "most obnoxious dog on the planet" because he had bad breath and ran away at every opportunity. The moment Siman died, the dog began to howl and continued periods of howling day and night for many months. The family vet said Dandy was very old and grieving. When Rosie decided to sell Rosi Acres, the vet said that Dandy would not survive the move and recommended the dog be euthanized.
7. Wyndi Harp Head (Carson), interview, December 31, 2001.

BIBLIOGRAPHY

"ABC Plans Radical Revamp of Program Line-Up for Fall." *Billboard*, March 3, 1956.

All Star Colored Revue. Advertisement. *Springfield Daily News*, March 8, 1947.

"American Sound Studio." Wikipedia. Accessed March 21, 2023. https://en.wikipedia.org/wiki/American_Sound_Studio.

"Another Stand Asked at Park." *Springfield Leader and Press*, March 6, 1945, 12.

Arevalo, Wendy. "The V-12 Officer Training Program December 1942–1946." Naval History and Heritage Command. Accessed August 2, 2023. https://www.history.navy.mil/browse-by-topic/wars-conflicts-and-operations/world-war-ii/1942/manning-the-us-navy/v-12-program.html.

"The Assemblies of God." Assemblies of God. Accessed August 3, 2023. https://ag.org/About/About-the-AG.

Atkins, Chet. *Country Gentleman*. New York: Ballantine Books, 1974.

Atkins, Chet, and Michael Cochran. *Chet Atkins: Me and My Guitars*. Milwaukee, WI: Hal Leonard, 2003.

Aton, Rusty D. *Baseball in Springfield*. Charleston, SC: Arcadia Publishing, 2005.

"Band Leader Shaw 'Joins' Police Force as Honorary Chief." *Springfield News and Leader*, October 23, 1941.

"'Barn Dance' Has Sponsor." *KWTO Dial*, April 1945.

"Batboy." Wikipedia. Accessed August 3, 2023. https://en.wikipedia.org/wiki/Batboy.

"Begin Search for Queen of Ozarks." *KWTO Dial*, May 1946.

Belew, Melvin. "Our Ozark Vacation." *Courier-Gazette*, August 28, 1948.

Berea College. "Berea College." Accessed August 2, 2023. https://www.berea.edu.

Berry, Chad, ed. *The Hayloft Gang: The Story of the National Barn Dance* Champaign: University of Illinois Press, 2008.

"The 'Big Time' Beckons." *East Oklahoma Tribune*, July 14, 1955.

"Billboard's Recommended LPs." *Billboard*, November 24, 1973.

Blevins, Brooks. *A History of the Ozarks*. Volume 3, *The Ozarkers*. Champaign: University of Illinois Press, 2021.

"Boots Faye." *Hillbilly-Music Dawt Com* (website). Accessed February 23, 2023. Hillbillymusic.com/artists/story/index.php?id=14759.

Branson Tourism Center. "Branson: A History of Great Entertainment." Accessed August 5, 2023. https://www.bransontourismcenter.com/articles/bransonarticle30.

"'Breakfast in Hollywood' Far Beyond Expectations." *Springfield Leader and Press*, March 20, 1946.
"Br'er Fox Baseball Team to Close Long Season Here This Afternoon." *Springfield News-Leader*, October 28, 1934.
Brothers, Michael. "Lyrics that Endure." *Springfield News and Leader*, March 16, 2006.
———. "A Songwriter's Journey to the Top." *Springfield News-Leader*, February 13, 2005.
Brown, Maxine. *Looking Back to See: A Country Music Memoir*. Fayetteville: The University of Arkansas Press, 2005.
"The Browns." Wikipedia. Accessed August 4, 2023. https://en.wikipedia.org/wiki/The_Browns.
Bryan T. E. Bisney Collection. Missouri State Digital Collections. https://cdm17307.contentdm.oclc.org/digital/collection/Bisney/search.
"A Budget for the Boys." *Springfield Leader and Press*, April 30, 1944.
Bufwack, Mary A., and Robert K. Oermann. *Finding Her Voice: Women in Country Music, 1800–2000*. Nashville: The Country Music Foundation Press and Vanderbilt University Press, 2003.
"Bulletin!" *KWTO Dial*, April 1945.
"Cap Folksters to Top Talent." *Billboard*, May 29, 1954.
"Carl Perkins." Wikipedia. Accessed August 4, 2023. https://en.wikipedia.org/wiki/Carl_Perkins.
Carlson, Tom. "The Woman Behind the Park." *Springfield News-Leader*, December 7, 2014.
Carr, Joe, and Alan Munde. *Prairie Nights to Neon Lights: The Story of Country Music in West Texas*. Lubbock: Texas Tech University Press, 1995.
Carson, Wayne. "Poets and Prophets: Salute to Legendary Songwriter Wayne Carson." Interview by Michael McCall. Country Music Hall of Fame, December 3, 2011. https://countrymusichalloffame.org/plan-your-visit/exhibits-activities/public-programs/poets-and-prophets/wayne-carson/.
"The Carter Family." *KWTO Dial*, October 1949.
"The Carter Family." *KWTO Dial*, November 1949.
"The *Cash Box* Country Roundup." *Cash Box*, April 16, 1955.
Causey, Chad. "Hubert Carl (Hugh) Ashley (1915–2008)." Encyclopedia of Arkansas (website). Accessed April 5, 2023. https://encyclopediaofarkansas.net/entries/hubert-carl-5257/.
"Celebrating 95 Years of Innovation." Nielsen. Accessed August 4, 2023. https://sites.nielsen.com/timelines/our-history/.
"Charley Barrett, Card Scout, Dies; Funeral on Friday." *St. Louis Star and Times*, July 5, 1939.

"Chick Webb." Wikipedia. Accessed August 3, 2023. https://en.wikipedia.org/wiki/Chick_Webb.

Chowning, Jayne Siman. Interview by Thomas Peters. *Ozarks Voices*, November 15, 2016.

The Corn Crib. Advertisement. *Union Labor Record*, April 28, 1955.

"'Country Music Carnival' Sponsored by Country DJ Association to be Held in Springfield, Mo. June 14, 15 & 16." *Cash Box*, June 2, 1956.

Country Music Foundation Oral History Project. Frist Library and Archive of the Country Music Hall of Fame and Museum.

"Country Musicians Fiddle Up Roaring Business." *Life*, November 19, 1956.

"Country on Our Minds." *Springfield Leader and Press*, October 12, 1983.

"Country Round Up." *Cash Box*, November 17, 1956.

"Country Round Up." *Cash Box*, March 30, 1957.

"Country Round Up." *Cash Box*, January 4, 1958.

Crossroads Productions and ABC Television Network. Advertisement. *The Billboard*, January 21, 1956, 21.

"Crossroads TV Sues Brenda Lee's Mother." *Springfield Daily News*, August 8, 1957.

Cusic, Don. *Discovering Country Music*. Westport, CT: Praeger, 2008.

"Dale Hawkins." Wikipedia. Accessed August 5, 2023. https://en.wikipedia.org/wiki/Dale_Hawkins.

Daniel, Wayne W. "Music of the Postwar Era." In *The Hayloft Gang: The Story of the National Barn Dance*, edited by Chad Berry, 74–100. Champaign: University of Illinois Press, 2008.

"Death Claims 'Aunt Martha.'" *Springfield Leader and Press*, August 16, 1966, 7.

"The Death of TV's Jubilee." *Springfield News and Leader*, September 18, 1960.

Dessauer, Phil. "Springfield, Mo.–Radio City of Country Music." *Coronet*, April 1957.

"Don Warden." Wikipedia. Accessed August 4, 2023. https://en.wikipedia.org/wiki/Don_Warden.

"Dub Albritten Quits Clients to Join Foley." *Billboard*, August 28, 1954.

Eder, Bruce. "Ronnie Self." *AllMusic*. Accessed April 16, 2022. https://www.allmusic.com/artist/ronnie-self-mn0000333181/biography.

"Electrical Transcription." Wikipedia. Accessed March 6, 2023. https://en.Wikipedia.org/wiki/Electrical_transcription.

Ella Fitzgerald. Advertisement. *Springfield Leader and Press*, November 12, 1939, B11.

Eng, Steve. *A Satisfied Mind: The Country Music Life of Porter Wagoner*. Nashville: Rutledge Hill Press, 1992.

Erlewine, Stephan Thomas. "Song Review of 'Always on My Mind,'" *AllMusic*. Accessed December 21, 2021. https://www.allmusic.com/song/always-on-my-mind-mt0043413717.

Eskridge, Sara. *Rube Tube: CBS and Rural Comedy in the Sixties*. Columbia: University of Missouri Press, 2018.
"Fair Attendance Sets New Record, 175,000 Visitors." *Springfield Leader and Press*, September 14, 1941.
"Father and Son." *Springfield Leader and Press*, February 14, 1942.
"Find a Need—And Fill It." *Springfield News and Leader*, February 12, 1950.
"Firm Set Up as Producers of Color TV." *Springfield Leader and Press*, July 5, 1963.
"Fishing Sees Changes as Dramatic as Landscape's." *Springfield News-Leader*, September 25, 1990.
"Foley Confident 'No Law Violated' After Tax Indictment Is Returned." *Springfield Daily News*, December 11, 1949.
"Foley Home Sold, He Forms New Firm." *Tennessean*, July 18, 1954.
"Foley Signs with RadiOzark, TT for Personal Appearances." *Billboard*, April 17, 1954.
"Ford-Dearborn Crew." *KWTO Dial*, March 1949.
"Ford-RadiOzark Deal." *KWTO Dial*, February 1949.
"Frank Farian." Wikipedia. Accessed August 5, 2023. https://en.wikipedia.org/wiki/Frank_Farian.
"Gene Autry." Wikipedia. Accessed March 15, 2023. https://en.wikipedia.org/wiki/Gene_Autry.
George-Warren, Holly. *Public Cowboy No. 1: The Life and Times of Gene Autry*. Oxford: Oxford University Press, 2007.
Glenn, Wayne. *The Ozarks' Greatest Hits: A Photo History of Music in the Ozarks*. Nixa, MO: Wayne Glenn, 2005.
———. Interview by Tom Peters. *Ozarks Voices*, February 27, 2014.
Goldenson, Leonard H., with Marvin J. Wolf. *Beating the Odds: The Untold Story Behind the Rise of ABC: The Stars, Struggles, and Egos That Transformed Network Television by the Man Who Made It Happen*. New York: Charles Scribner's Sons, 1991.
Gomery, Douglas. "Patsy Cline: A Television Star." *Sweet Dreams: The World of Patsy Cline*. Edited by Warren R. Hofstra. Champaign: University of Illinois Press, 2013.
"Grady Martin." Wikipedia. Accessed August 4, 2023. https://en.wikipedia.org/wiki/Grady_Martin.
Harkins, Anthony. *Hillbilly: A Cultural History of an American Icon*. Oxford: Oxford University Press, 2004.
Havighurst, Craig. *Air Castle of the South: WSM and the Making of Music City*. Champaign: University of Illinois Press, 2007.

Head, Heno, Jr. *America's Favorite Janitor: The Life Story of Country Songwriter Johnny Mullins*. Independence, MO: The International University Press, 1986.

Hilburn, Robert. "The Surprising Saga of 'Always on My Mind.'" *Los Angeles Times*, April 24, 1988.

"Hill Billies' Air Popularity." *Billboard*, July 22, 1933.

"Hillbilly TV Show Hits the Big Time." *Business Week*, March 10, 1956.

Himes, Geoffrey. "Gary Stewart." *Encyclopedia of Country Music*. Edited by Paul Kingsbury. Oxford: Oxford University Press, 1998.

Hoekstra, Dave. "Rockin' in the Country: Springfield City Limits." *Journal of Country Music* 23, no. 1 (2002): 38–42.

Holman, Gregory J. "Country Artist Wayne Carson Dies at 72." *Springfield News-Leader*, July 29, 2015.

Hulston, John K. *Lester E. Cox 1895–1968: He Found Needs and Filled Them*. Cassville, MO: John K. Hulston, 1992.

"I See the Want to in Your Eyes." Wikipedia. Accessed March 21, 2023. https://en.wikipedia.org/wiki/I_See_the_Want_To_in_Your_Eyes.

"I Take the Chance." Wikipedia. Accessed March 21, 2023. https://en.wikipedia.org/wiki/I_Take_the_Chance.

"'If a Kid Is Smart He's Not Left-Handed?' Oh, Yeah?" *Springfield Leader and Press*, March 6, 1938.

"Jackie Blue." Wikipedia. Accessed August 5, 2023. https://en.wikipedia.org/wiki/Jackie_Blue_(song).

Jackson, Wanda, with Scott B. Bomar. *Every Night Is Saturday Night: A Country Girl's Journey to the Rock & Roll Hall of Fame*. Nashville: BMG, 2017.

Jarman Shoes. Advertisement. *Springfield Daily News*, October 24, 1936.

"Jerry Bradley." Wikipedia. Accessed August 5, 2023. https://en.wikipedia.org/wiki/Jerry_Bradley_(music_executive).

"Jewell Leased by Top Talent." *Springfield Leader and Press*, June 16, 1954.

Johnson, Ronald. "Ozarks Voices: Woody P. Snow, January 16, 2015." Interview by Thomas Peters. Missouri State University Libraries, posted April 20, 2015. https://www.youtube.com/watch?v=0q_Tdmq5Vlc.

Jones, Roben. *Memphis Boys: The Story of American Studios*. Jackson: University Press of Mississippi, 2010.

"The Jordanaires." Wikipedia. Accessed August 3, 2023. https://en.wikipedia.org/wiki/The_Jordanaires.

"*Jubilee* Ends Its Hookup with ABC." *Springfield News-Leader*, August 17, 1957.

"*Jubilee* Near End of Line?" *Springfield Leader and Press*, August 1, 1960.

"*Jubilee* Schedule Is Revised Again." *Springfield Daily News*, September 23, 1958.

"*Jubilee* to Continue as Network TV Show." *Springfield News-Leader*, August 27, 1957.

Jurek, Thom. "Gary Stewart." In *All Music Guide to Country: The Definitive Guide to Country Music*, edited by Vladimir Bogdanov, Christ Woodstra, and Stephen Thomas Erlewine, 721–22. Lanham, MD: Backbeat Books, 2003.

Kappell, Jean. Editor's Column. *KWTO Dial*, October 1950.

Keegan, Harrison. "Oscar-winning Springfield Songwriter Tom Whitlock Dies." *Springfield News-Leader*, February 21, 2023, A1, A2.

Kelly, Susan Croce. *Father of Route 66: The Story of Cy Avery*. Norman: University of Oklahoma Press, 2014.

"Kinescope." Wikipedia. Accessed August 4, 2023. https://en.wikipedia.org/wiki/Kinescope.

King, Nelson, and Marty Roberts. "Hillbilly Hit Parade." *Union-Banner*, October 7, 1954.

Kleiner, Dick. "Hill Music on Way Out." *Springfield News and Leader*, April 29, 1956.

"*Korn's-a-Krackin'* Goes on Road!" *KWTO Dial*, June 1946.

"*Korn's-a-Krackin'* Ready to Return." *KWTO Dial*, August 1946.

"*Korn's-a-Krackin'* Set for Electric Theatre, July 11–12." *KWTO Dial*, July 1944.

"*Korn's-a-Krackin'* to Mutual Net!" *KWTO Dial*, January 1946.

Kosser, Michael. *How Nashville Became Music City, U.S.A.: 50 Years of Music Row*. Milwaukee, WI: Hal Leonard, 2006.

KWTO. Advertisement. *Springfield Leader and Press*, May 10, 1947.

"KWTO Staff Changes." *KWTO Dial*, June 1950.

Laird, Tracey E. W. "Country Music and Television." In *Oxford Handbook of Country Music*, edited by Travis D. Stimeling, 249–61. Oxford: Oxford University Press, 2021.

———. *Louisiana Hayride: Radio and Roots Music Along the Red River*. Oxford: Oxford University Press, 2005.

Ledbetter, Kathryn. "Si Siman and the *Ozark Jubilee*: Getting and Keeping the First Continuous Live Country Music Show on Network Television." In *The International Country Music Journal*, edited by Don Cusic, 115–50 (Nashville: Brackish Publishing, 2022).

Lee, Brenda, with Robert K. Oermann and Julie Clay. *Little Miss Dynamite: The Life and Times of Brenda Lee*. New York: Hyperion, 2002.

Leicht, Linda. "*Ozark Jubilee* Founder Recognized." *Springfield News and Leader*, February 20, 2009.

Lester, John. "Radio and Television." *Gazette and Daily*, January 8, 1955.

"The Letter." Wikipedia. Accessed March 21, 2023. https://en.wikipedia.org/wiki/The_Letter_(Box_Tops_song).

Lewis, Randy. "Gary Stewart, 58: Sang Country Tunes Hinting at His Own

Demons." *Los Angeles Times*, January 4, 2004. https://www.latimes.com/archives/la-xpm-2004-jan-02-me-stewart2-story.html.
"List of Country Music Hall of Fame Inductees." Wikipedia. Accessed March 15, 2023. https://en.Wikipedia.org/wiki/List_of_Country_Music_Hall_of_Fame_inductees.
"A List of Personalities Who Appeared on Ozark Jubilee." Wikipedia. Accessed March 15, 2023. https://en.wikipedia.org/wiki/List_of_personalities_who_appeared_on_Ozark_Jubilee.
Logan, Horace, with Bill Sloan. *Louisiana Hayride Years: Making Musical History in Country's Golden Age*. New York: St. Martin's Griffin, 1999.
"Louisiana Hayride." Wikipedia. Accessed August 3, 2023. https://en.wikipedia.org/wiki/Louisiana_Hayride.
Malone, Bill C., and Tracey E. W. Laird. *Country Music USA*. Austin: University of Texas Press, 2018.
Marymont, Mark. "Carson Cultivates Inspiration." *Springfield News and Leader*, October 10, 1982.
———. "Carson, Siman Shocked as Song Is First Again." *Springfield Leader and Press*, October 11, 1983.
———. "Kershenbaum Goes Where the Bands Are." *News-Leader*, January 15, 1984.
———. "Siman Sells Copyrights to Almost 2,000 Songs." *News-Leader*, December 4, 1987.
———. "Wayne Carson, Songwriter." *Springfield Leader and Press*, March 18, 1984.
McGoogan, W. J. "Barrett Played Strong Role in Building Great Cardinals Systems." *St. Louis Post Dispatch*, July 6, 1939.
Mercer, Charles. "Gotham Learns of Springfield." *Springfield Leader and Press*, April 20, 1956.
Mershon, Phil, and Elizabeth Fritze. "The Axis of Delaney and Bonnie." Perfect Sound Forever (website), January 2004, https://www.furious.com/perfect/delaneyandbonnie.html.
"Miller and Sigma Nu's." *Springfield Leader and Press*, July 8, 1941.
Miller, Tom. "The 1901 Durland's Riding Academy 7 West 66th Street." Daytonian in Manhattan, February 13, 2014. https://daytoninmanhattan.blogspot.com/2014/02/the-1901-durlands-riding-academy-7-west.html.
Mullins, Melinda. "Johnny Mullins." *OzarksWatch*, Spring 2017.
"NBC Radio Network." Wikipedia. Accessed August 3, 2023. https://en.wikipedia.org/wiki/NBC_Radio_Network.
"New Baby's Dad is 65 Years Old; Father of 19." *Springfield Republican*, August 20, 1912.
"New Jubilee Has 5 Stars." *Springfield News-Leader*, March 10, 1961.
"New Manager Turns Mosque to Playhouse." *Springfield Leader and Press*, September 11, 1941.

"Notes about Ellington." *Springfield Leader and Press*, October 25, 1936.

Oermann, Robert K. *America's Music: The Roots of Country*. Atlanta: Turner Publishing, 1996.

———. "Dillard Dies." *Music Row*. Accessed April 11, 2023. https://musicrow.com/2015/05/lifenotes-nashville-sound-pioneer-dottie-dillard-dies/.

———. "Music Publisher, Producer Bob Tubert Dies at 90." *Music Row*. Accessed April 5, 2023. https://musicrow.com/2016/04/lifenotes-music-publisher-producer-bob-tubert-dies-at-90/.

Oliver, Allen. "Springfield Slants." *Springfield Leader and Press*, November 20, 1939.

———. "Springfield Slants." *Springfield Leader and Press*, January 30, 1940.

"The Ozark Jubilee." *Springfield Leader and Press*, January 10, 1957.

"Ozark Jubilee." Wikipedia. Accessed August 4, 2023. https://en.Wikipedia.org/wiki/Ozark_Jubilee.

"Ozark Jubilee Airs Red Foley and Top Artists." *Cash Box*, October 23, 1954.

"Ozarks' Greatest Lover is Slim Pickens Wilson." *Springfield Leader and Press*, April 11, 1937, 21.

"Pact Signed for Jubilee on Network." *Springfield Leader and Press*, December 24, 1954.

"The Passing Parade in Pictures." *KWTO Dial*, May 1947.

Paul, Les, and Michael Cochran. *Les Paul: In His Own Words*. Hunt Valley, MD: Gemstone Publishing, 2005.

Peaco, Ed. "Immerse Yourself in Re-Drawn Granny's Bathwater," *Springfield News-Leader*, October 16, 2019.

Pecknold, Diane. *The Selling Sound: The Rise of the Country Music Industry*. Durham, NC: Duke University Press, 2007.

Peters, Thomas. "Memories of Half-a-Hill's First Twenty Years." *Ozarks Alive*. Accessed August 3, 2023. https://www.ozarksalive.com/stories/memories-of-half-a-hills-first-20-years.

———. "The *Ozark Jubilee*. Volume 2: The *Jubilee* Era and Beyond." Unpublished manuscript.

Peters, Thomas, Wayne Glenn, and John Bisney. "Remembering the *Ozark Jubilee*." Panel discussion, Missouri Cherry Blossom Festival, April 23, 2021. https://www.youtube.com/watch?v=iE5CEvFLsbs.

Phillips, Virgil. "KWTO Musical Chief Finds Hillbilly Style is Booming." *KWTO Dial*, November 1947.

"Pioneer Smith Expires at 84." *Springfield Leader*, October 30, 1928.

"*A Place to Grow*." Wikipedia. Accessed August 5, 2023. https://en.wikipedia.org/wiki/A_Place_to_Grow.

Plaster's Master Market. Advertisement. *Springfield Leader and Press*, April 28, 1955.

Pokin, Steve. "The Life of David Leong: Recipe of Success." *Springfield News-Leader*, May 21, 2018, A1, A6, A7.

———. "A Passion for Music." *Springfield News-Leader*, October 12, 2014.

Polner, Murray. *Branch Rickey*. New York: Athenaeum, 1982.

"Porter Wagoner Moves to WSM 'Opry.'" *Billboard*, February 23, 1957.

Powell, Vance. "Lou Whitney: Del Lords, Dave Alvin, Wilco." *Tape Op*, Accessed December 30, 2021. https://tapeop.com/interviews/98/lou-whitney/.

Price, Mary Sue. "2 Musicians Die, but Tales Remain." *Springfield Leader and Press*, September 3, 1981.

"Program Changes." *KWTO Dial*, March 1949.

"Promotional Prodigy Obtains Mosque Wrestling Franchise." The Benchwarmer (Perry Smith). *Springfield Leader and Press*, June 1, 1941.

"RadiOzark Artists." *Cash Box*, November 20, 1954.

"Ralston Purina Inks 'Opry' for Monthly TV-er." *Billboard*, July 30, 1955.

"Sally Rand." Wikipedia. Accessed August 3, 2023. https://en.wikipedia.org/wiki/Sally_Rand.

"RE, KWTO Buy Slice of Rancho." *Billboard*, November 22, 1952.

"Red Foley Sues U.S. Over Taxes." *Springfield Leader and Press*, April 4, 1959.

"Red Foley's 'Country Music Jubilee' Receives 200,000th Visitor." *Cash Box*, October 19, 1957.

"Resume Personal Appearances!" *KWTO Dial*, March 1944.

Richardson, Don. Diary. Private collection of John Richardson.

———. "I Remember Red." The Curbstone Critic. *Springfield Leader and Press*, September 23, 1968.

———. Press Release for KWTO/RadiOzark, November 1954. Siman Family Papers. Private collection of Scott Foster Siman and Jayne Siman Chowning.

———. "Winding Up a Big Year of Personal Appearances." Undated press release for Top Talent, Inc.

"Roy Lanham." Wikipedia. Accessed March 7, 2023. https://en.Wikipedia.org/wiki/Roy_Lanham.

Rumble, John. "Si Siman." In *Encyclopedia of Country Music*, edited by Paul Kingsbury, 484–85. Oxford: Oxford University Press, 1998.

"Rural Music Rocks Too." *Springfield News and Leader*, April 29, 1956.

Sachs, Bill. "C & W Deejays Kick Off First Annual." *Billboard*, June 23, 1956.

———. "Folk and Talent and Tunes: ABC Adds More 'Ozark Jubilee.'" *Billboard*, October 1, 1954.

"Sally Rand." Wikipedia. Accessed August 5, 2023. https://en.wikipedia.org/wiki/Sally_Rand.

Sandoval, Jim. "Charley Barrett." Society for American Baseball Research. Accessed May 1, 2022. https://sabr.org/bioproj/person/charley-barrett/.

"Schuylkill." Naval History and Heritage Command (website). Accessed May 1, 2022. https://www.history.navy.mil/research/histories/ship-histories/danfs/s/schuylkill.html.

"Sees Sally Rand as Proof We're All Going to Dickens." *Springfield Leader and Press*, June 15, 1941.

Shepard, Jean. *Down Through the Years*. Nashville, TN: Don Wise Productions, 2014.

"Shorty Thompson: A Homecoming." *KWTO Dial*, September 1948.

"Show Moves on May 4th to 9:00 P.M." *KWTO Dial*, April 1946.

"Shultz Conquers Dusette in Two Straight Falls." *Springfield Daily News*, December 10, 1941, 11.

"Si Siman." Interview by Ed Fillmer. Ed Fillmer Video Journalist (YouTube channel), posted November 5, 2017. https://www.youtube.com/watch?v=gVcvk2LEh5Q.

Silverman, Fred. "An Analysis of ABC Television Network Programming from February 1953 to October 1959." Master's thesis, The Ohio State University, 1959.

Siman, E. E. "'Cards' Talent Scout Chased Down Some of the Big Names in Baseball." *AHOY! For Navy and Marine Corps Personnel of Charleston Navy Yard*, April 17, 1943.

Siman Family Papers. Private collection of Scott Foster Siman and Jayne Siman Chowning.

Siman, Si. "Recalling Slim Wilson: One of the Good Guys." *Springfield News-Leader*, July 21, 1990.

Siman, Si. Unpublished interview by Lana Grosshart. Americana Network, April 21, 1994.

"Siman Elected Board President." *Billboard*, March 30, 1968.

"Smiley Burnette." Wikipedia. Accessed August 4, 2023. https://en.wikipedia.org/wiki/Smiley_Burnette.

Snell, Vernon D. "Hook, Line and Sinker." *Daily Oklahoman*, October 5, 1958.

Snow, John. "Ear to the Ground Department." *Springfield Leader and Press*, July 9, 1939.

Soric, Peggy. "Simon [sic] Says 'Oh, Gosh.'" *Springfield News and Leader*, July 17, 1983.

Spears-Stewart, Reta. "The *Ozark Jubilee* Saga." *Springfield! Magazine*, September 1995.

———. *Remembering the Ozark Jubilee*. Springfield, MO: Stewart, Dillbeck & White Productions, 1993.

———. *Troubles, Faith, and Peace in the Valley: The Red Foley Story*. Baltimore, MD: Publish America, 2011.

"The Spectator." *Springfield Daily News*, April 24, 1955.

"The Spotlight." *KWTO Dial*, June 1949.

"The Spotlight." *KWTO Dial*, July 1949.

"The Spotlight." *KWTO Dial*, January 1950.

"The Spotlight." *KWTO Dial*, September 1950.

"Springfield, Missouri." Wikipedia. Accessed February 5, 2022. https://en.wikipedia.org/wiki/Springfield,_Missouri.

"Standing-Room Crowd Watches Jubilee Premiere." *Springfield Daily News*, May 1, 1955.

Stang, Mark. *Cardinals Connection: 100 Years of St. Louis Cardinals Images*. Wilmington, OH: Orange Frazer Press, 2002.

Stars Over America. Advertisement. *Springfield News-Leader*, September 4, 1941.

"Studio Turns-On to City's Sounds." *Springfield Leader and Press*, November 16, 1969.

Sylvester, Ron. "Brenda Lee: Pure Talent." *Springfield News-Leader*, June 17, 1996.

———. "Ernie Ford Dies at Age 72." *Springfield News and Leader*, October 18, 1991.

———. "Musicians Congregate on Record Center Wall." *Springfield News-Leader*, July 31, 1995.

"'Tain't Hillbilly, Neighbor! It's 'Country Music' That's Making a Splash on TV." *TV Guide*, August 27–September 2, 1955.

"Tales of the Town." *Springfield Leader and Press*, December 8, 1939.

"Tales of the Town." *Springfield Leader and Press*, June 21, 1940.

"Talking Things Over." *Springfield Leader and Press*, December 20, 1953.

"Talking Things Over." *Springfield Leader and Press*, January 15, 1961.

Tatum, Bill. "Songwriter Keeps on Making Good." *Springfield News and Leader*, May 8, 1976.

"Tennessee Ernie Ford." Wikipedia. Accessed August 3, 2023. https://en.wikipedia.org/wiki/Tennessee_Ernie_Ford

Terry, Dickson. "Hillbilly Music Center." Everyday Magazine, *St. Louis Post Dispatch*, February 5, 1956.

Thanki, Julie. "Hall of Famer's Top Hit Had Over 300 Versions." *The Tennessean*, July 21, 2015.

"Tin Pan Alley in the Ozarks." *Broadcasting Telecasting*, January 3, 1955.

"Top Talent Leases Springfield House." *Billboard*, July 3, 1954.

"Trio Takes Trip Seeking Secrets on Barn Dances." *KWTO Dial*, February 1943.

Turtle, Howard, "Ozarks Folk Tunes and Comedy Make Springfield a TV Center." *Kansas City Star*, January 29, 1956.

"USS *Liscome Bay*." Wikipedia. Accessed August 2, 2023. https://en.wikipedia.org/wiki/USS_Liscome_Bay.

"US to Refund $79,555 to Red." *Springfield Leader and Press*, October 27, 1961, 1.

"Variety Acts Ready Now for Personals." *KWTO Dial*, June 1947.

"A Very Merry Christmas from the *Korn's-a-Krackin'* Gang!" *KWTO Dial*, December 1948, back cover.

"WSM's Grand Ole Opry Makes Network TV Debut." *Cash Box*, November 12, 1955.

Wagoner, Porter. Interview by Archie Campbell. *Yesteryear in Nashville*. Accessed March 20, 2023. https://www.youtube.com/watch?v=D_9rS7cysy0.

Walpole, Sherlu. "Music Man Si Siman." *Springfield!*, June 1986.

"Wanda Jackson." Wikipedia. Accessed August 4, 2023. https://en.wikipedia.org/wiki/Wanda_Jackson

Watson, Gaylon H. "A History of KWTO, Springfield, Missouri." Master's thesis, The University of Missouri, 1964.

"Wayne Carson Accompanist for Buddy Ebsen at Rodeo." *Daily Standard*, August 1, 1966.

"The Whippoorwills." *KWTO Dial*, June 1949.

Wilson, Earl. "It Happened Last Night." *Pittsburgh Post-Gazette*, January 26, 1956, 29.

Wolfe, Charles. "The Triumph of the Hills: Country Radio, 1920–50." *Country: The Music and the Musicians*. Edited by Paul Kingsbury. New York: Abbeville Press, 1988.

Zwonitzer, Mark, with Charles Hirshberg. *Will You Miss Me When I'm Gone: The Carter Family and Their Legacy in American Music*. New York: Simon & Schuster, 2002.

INDEX

A

ABC (American Broadcasting Company) radio network, 47, 74, 179n12

ABC (American Broadcasting Company) television network: advertising, 116, 187n29; *Ozark Jubilee*, 76, 77–78, 105, 107, 114, 119–21, 123, 189n58; summer replacement shows, 99–101. *See also* Crossroads Productions, Inc.; *Ozark Jubilee*; Siman, Si

Acuff, Roy, 125

All-Colored Jitterbug Contest, 51

All-Star Colored Revue (dance group), 51

Allbritten, Dub (artist manager), 91–92, 93, 130

Allen, Rex (*Five Star Jubilee* host), 103, 125

"Always on My Mind," 142–45, 159

Arnold, Eddy, 100, 101, 103, 113, 127, 135–36

Ashley, Hugh, 93, 193n133

Assemblies of God, 39–40, 180n22

Atkins, Chet: Carson, Wayne, influence on, 135–36, 145; Carter Sisters and Mother Maybelle, 56, 58–61, 203n44; CMDJA, 111; *Eddy Arnold Show*, 100; Foster, Ralph, 54; *Grand Ole Opry*, 59–60, 61; Homer and Jethro, 56; *Korn's-a-Krackin'*, 53, 55; KWTO radio, 53–55, 56–61; Paul, Les, 54–55; RadiOzark transcription, 60; RCA Victor, 54, 55–56, 104, 203n44; Siman, Si, relationship with, 54, 55–56, 59, 61, 162; Springfield, 54, 57, 59; *Today on the Farm*, 101

Atkins, Jimmy (half-brother of Chet), 54

Aunt Martha, 36, 190n67. *See* Goodwill Family

Austin Horn's Smooth Steppers (dance group), 51

Autry, Gene: alcohol abuse, 103; Burnette, Smiley, 44, 181n40; Long, Jimmy (songwriter in Springfield), 95; *Ozark Jubilee*, 82, 94, 95, 114. *See also Ozark Jubilee*; Siman, Si

B

barn-dance format: radio shows, 45–46, 82–83; television shows, 63–64, 96. *See also Big D Jamboree*; Branson; *Korn's-a-Krackin'*; *Ozark Jubilee*

Barrett, Charley (St. Louis Cardinals talent scout), 9, 10; death, 16; Siman, Si, working relationship with, 11–16

baseball: Little League, 7–10; Springfield Cardinals, 9–10; St. Louis Cardinals, 10, 11, 15, 174n20. *See also* Barrett, Charley; Rickey, Branch

Beckham, Bob (Nashville record producer), 135, 140, 145

Berea College, 30, 31, 127

Big D Jamboree (barn-dance radio program in Dallas), 187n30, 191n93

221

Bisney, Bryan (*Ozark Jubilee* director), 67, 89, 93–94, 99, 101, 113
Black, Lou, 46, 47, 51, 55, 64, 88, 90
Blackwood Brothers, 112
"Blue Feeling," 134
"Blue Suede Shoes," 110
BMI (Broadcast Music International), 66, 74, 128, 185n11, 189n48, 200n2
"Bop-a-Lena," 130
Box Tops, The (Memphis recording artists), 137–38
Bradley, Jerry (head of RCA Records in the '70s), 140, 203n44
Bradley, Owen (Nashville record producer), 135, 142, 188n42
Branson, 127–28, 165, 200n98
Brayfield, Buddy (Ozark Mountain Daredevils), 151
Breakfast in Hollywood (KWTO radio show), 39, 179n19
Br'er Fox baseball club, 7, 9
Brooks, Garth, 86
Browns, The, 84–86, 111, 112, 192n101
Bruns, George (musician), 42
Budde Music (German publishing company), 159
Bunge, Mike (Springfield musician), 149, 151, 205n77, 205n86
Burnette, Smiley: as character actor, 43, 181n40, 181n42; as instrument builder, 44; as performer in Springfield, 111, 181n42; Siman, Si, 44; as songwriter, 44, 181n42; transcriptions 43–45. *See also* RadiOzark; Siman, Si
Bybee, Millie and Sue (KWTO radio performers), 38

C

Carroll, Colleen (*Ozark Jubilee* performer), 86
Carson, Wayne: and Atkins, Chet, 135–36; awards, 138, 143–45; death, 162; family, 132–33; Lewie and the 7 Days, 149–50; Mahan, Benny, 154; Moman, Chips, 136–37; musicians in Springfield, influence on, 149–54; Ozark Mountain Daredevils, 153; record contracts, 133–34, 142; Sibley, Nick, 153–54; Siman, Si, relationship with, 133–45, 158, 162; song plugging, 135, 137; as songwriter, 134–45; as studio producer, 147–48; Turner, Ike and Tina, 154. *See also* Arnold, Eddy; Box Tops, The; Cocker, Joe; Jennings, Waylon; Nelson, Willie; Presley, Elvis; Siman, Si; Top Talent Recording Studio
Carter Sisters and Mother Maybelle, 56–61, 185n99. *See also* Atkins, Chet
Cash, Johnny, 111, 190n87, 191n93
Cash, Steve (Ozark Mountain Daredevils), 151, 152, 153
Channel, Bruce (singer), 138
Chowning, Jayne Siman (daughter): 70, 117, 118, 128
Chowning, Randle (son-in-law), 79, 151–52, 207n2
Christopher, Johnny (songwriter), 142, 144, 203n54
Citadel, The, 31
Clement, Frank (politician), 79
Cline, Patsy, 93–94, 96–97, 191n93. *See also* Crossroads Productions, Inc.; *Ozark Jubilee*; Siman, Si; Foley, Red

C

CMA (Country Music Association), 112–13, 119, 164. *See also* Crossroads Productions, Inc.; Siman, Si

CMDJA (Country Music Disc Jockeys Association), 108–9, 111–12, 119. *See also* Crossroads Productions, Inc.; Siman, Si

Cocker, Joe (singer), 139–40

Collins, Tommy (singer/songwriter), 70

"Company's Comin,' " 74, 78, 188n47, 189n48. *See also* Mullins, Johnny; Wagoner, Porter

Cox, Lester E. (Springfield businessman): Crossroads Productions, Inc., 67, 128; death, 128; Earl Barton Music, 66–67, 128; education, 34; Foley, Red, counseling of, 124; KGBX radio, 34; KWTO radio, 35; *Ozark Jubilee*, 76, 78, 79; partnerships, 33, 45, 128; television, early interest in, 63, 64; Top Talent, Inc., 128; youth, 33–35. *See also* ABC television; Crossroads Productions, Inc.; Foster, Ralph; *Ozark Jubilee*; Siman, Si

Crossroads Productions, Inc.: ABC, 76–77, 106, 119–21, 123–24; advertisers, 116–17; events, 78–79, 111–13; Foley, Red, 70, 124; investments, 67; Landers Theatre, 124; Lee, Brenda, 89–93; partners, 67, 128; programming, 101, 105, 107–8, 114, 116, 120; ratings, 106–107; salaries 96–98, 105; Tele-Color, 126. *See also* Cox, Lester E.; *Five Star Jubilee*; Foley, Red; *Ozark Jubilee*; ABC television; Siman, Si

"Cussin' Cryin' & Carryin' On," 154

D

David and the Boys Next Door, 155. *See* Kershenbaum, David

Dea, Roy (Nashville record producer), 140

Dean, Jimmy, 125

Decca Records, 72, 74, 86, 89, 111, 130, 133, 135, 188n42

Dickens, Little Jimmy, 59, 72

Dillon, John (Ozark Mountain Daredevils), 151–52, 153

Donnelly, Phil (politician), 78

Dorsey, Tommy, 22–23

"Drinkin' Thing," 140

Drury College, 31, 34

Drusky, Roy, 111

Duff, Arlie (singer/songwriter), 70

Duke University, 31

E

Earl Barton Music: 66–67, 82, 128, 186n14, 189n48. *See also* Carson, Wayne; Mahaffey, John; Mullins, Johnny; *Ozark Jubilee*; Wagoner, Porter; Siman, Si

"Eat, Drink, and Be Merry," 74–75

Eckert, Al (Springfield Cardinals executive), 9

Electric Theatre, 7, 46

Ellington, Duke, 22

Ellison, Gary (musician), 128, 205n81

"Every Day Livin' Days," 138

F

Farian, Frank (singer), 206n101

Fellers, Buster (musician), 65

Fisher, Shug (singer and character actor), 198n65

Fitzgerald, Ella, 22, 176n74
Five Star Jubilee, 95, 124–26
Flash and Whistler (comedy duo), 36, 52, 73. *See also* Wilson, Slim; Rutledge, Floyd "Goo Goo"
Flatt and Scruggs, 125
Foggy River Boys, 79
Foley, Red: alcoholism, 68, 102–3, 122, 124, 126; Atkins, Chet, 54; Carson, Wayne, 133; Cline, Patsy, 93; Crossroads Productions, Inc., 70, 77, 111–13, 187n28; death, 126–27; domestic problems, 68, 70; fans, 126; *Grand Ole Opry*, 186n22; IRS, 121, 198n68, 199n85; KWTO, 73–74; Lee, Brenda, 88–90, 102; Martin, Grady, 72; memorials, 126, 127; Minnie Pearl, 94; money, attitude toward, 121–22, 198n71; music trends, response to, 110; *Ozark Jubilee*, 68, 70, 113–16; "Ozark Jubilee Day," 78–79; Prince Albert Band, 72; RadiOzark, transcriptions of, 42, 70; Ritter, Tex, 95; "A Satisfied Mind," 78; Shepard, Jean, 102; Siman, Si, 42, 70, 102; Springfield, influence on, 71; Top Talent, Inc., 70, 126; Tubb, Ernest, 95; Wagoner, Porter, 101–2; Wilkin, Marijohn, 82. *See also* CMA; CMDJA; Crossroads Productions, Inc.; Foster, Ralph; Mullins, Johnny; *Ozark Jubilee*; Siman, Si; Top Talent, Inc.
Ford, Tennessee Ernie: hit records, 186n19; *Ozark Jubilee*, as potential host for, 68; Ozarks, love for, 181n37; RadiOzark transcriptions, 42–43; Siman, Jayne, 118

Foster, Fred (Nashville record producer), 142
Foster, Jerry (songwriter), 145
Foster, Ralph: ABC television, 76–79, 126; Assemblies of God transcriptions, 39–40; Atkins, Chet, 54, 59; Cox, Lester E., 35; Crossroads Productions, Inc., 67, 76–79, 128, 180n24; Earl Barton Music, 66–67; Foley, Red, 121; Hall, Jerry, 33–34; Jewell Theatre, 72; KGBX/KWTO, 32–38; *Korn's-a-Krackin'*, 45–49; KYTV, 67; *Ozark Jubilee*, 63–64, 123; RadiOzark, 40, 67; Siman, Si, relationship with, 19, 22, 31, 38, 39, 45, 49–51, 66, 128, 182n54; Skipper Records, 149; Top Talent, 72, 147, 149; youth, 33. *See also* Cox, Lester E.; Crossroads Productions, Inc.; Foley, Red; KGBX/KWTO radio; KWTO Artists Bureau; KWTO radio; *Ozark Jubilee*; RadiOzark; Siman, Si; Top Talent, Inc.
Fox, Carl (KYTV manager), 113
Fox Theatre, 7, 72
Frizzell, Lefty, 191n93

G

Gamble, Violet and Vesta (KWTO radio performers), 38
Gately, Jimmy (*Five Star Jubilee* host), 85, 127
Gillioz Theatre, 7
Goodwill Family, 36, 190n67. *See also* Haworth, Herschel "Junior" or "Speedy"; Wilson, Slim
Granda, Michael (Ozark Mountain Daredevils), 151, 152
Grand Ole Opry: Atkins, Chet, 54, 59, 60, 61; Carter Sisters and Mother

Maybelle, 59, 60; CMDJA, 108; Foley, Red, 42, 54, 68, 70, 72, 186n22; Foster, Ralph, influenced by, 46, 48; Husky, Ferlin, 72; Jackson, Wanda, 88; *Louisiana Hayride*, 82–83; Minnie Pearl, 94; Morgan, George, 41–42, 59; *Ozark Jubilee*, competition with, 3–4, 53, 107–8, 171n1, 187n30; Prince Albert Band, 72; Shepard, Jean, 72, 187n35; Tubb, Ernest, 95; Wagoner, Porter, 188n45; Walker, Billy, 83. *See also* barn-dance format; Crossroads Productions, Inc.; KWTO radio; *Ozark Jubilee*; Siman, Si

Granny's Bathwater (Springfield band), 151, 153, 154

Grove Supper Club (Springfield restaurant/nightclub), 114, 197n39

H

H'Doubler, Dr. F. T. ("Ginger"), 122, 162

Haden Family (KWTO performers), 36–38, 49

Haggard, Merle, 143

Half-a-Hill (dance hall), 20, 176n72

Hall, Durward (Springfield Chamber of Commerce), 79

Hall, Jerry, 33–34. *See also* Foster, Ralph; KGBX radio

Hamlin, Jack, 11

Haverlin, Carl (BMI president), 66

Hawkins, Dale (Louisiana record producer), 132, 138, 201n11

Hawkins, Hawkshaw, 72, 73, 187n35

Haworth, Herschel "Junior" or "Speedy": Atkins, Chet, performances on KWTO radio with, 54; Goodwill Family, early performances with, 36; *Ozark Jubilee*, performing on, 67; Wagoner, Porter, RCA Victor recordings at KWTO with, 65, 74. *See also* Goodwill Family; *Ozark Jubilee*; Tall Timber Trio; Wilson, Slim

Hayloft Frolics, 51

Haymes, Joe (jazz musician), 176n79

"Headin' for a Wedding," 65

"Heavy on My Mind," 138

Henning, Paul (television producer), 127, 181n42

Hensley, Harold (musician), 42

Herman, Woody, 23

Hickman, Walter (owner of Half-a-Hill), 20–22, 176n72

Hicks, Bobby Lloyd (Springfield musician), 150–51

"High on Life," 132

hillbilly radio: *Korn's-a-Krackin'*, 45–46; KWTO, 33, 35, 36, 59, 38. *See also* Foster, Ralph; *Korn's-a-Krackin'*; KGBX/KWTO radio

Hindle, Al (RCA record producer), 55

Hitchcock, Stan (singer/songwriter), 134, 139

"Home in My Hand," 131

Homer and Jethro, 54, 56, 59, 61

Horton, Johnny, 101, 111

"Hurry Up Summer," 135

Husky, Ferlin, 70, 71-72

I

"I Heard the Bluebirds Sing," 86

"I See the Want to in Your Eyes," 140

"I Take the Chance," 85

"If I Was King," 155

"If You Wanna Get to Heaven," 152

"I'm Sorry," 130, 146

"Instant Reaction," 138
Isaacs, Bud (Nashville musician), 72
"It's You, Always It's You," 134

J

"Jackie Blue," 152
Jackson, Tommy (singer), 72
Jackson, Wanda: awards, 88; *Big D Jamboree*, 191n93; *Ozark Jubilee*, 86–88, 120–21; "Queen of Rockabilly," 88, 110, 192n113; touring with Presley, Elvis, 88
James, Mark (songwriter), 142, 144
James, Sonny, 110–11, 191n93
Jennings, Waylon, 138, 143
Jewell Theatre, 72–73, 78–79, 100, 123–24
Johnson, C. Arthur (radio engineer), 33, 34, 180n24
Johnson, Ronald, 146, 154–55, 200n2
Jones, Bill (Springfield musician), 149–50, 202n32

K

"Keep On," 138
Kennon, Leslie (KWTO VP), 39, 46, 76
Kershenbaum, David (music business executive), 155–56
kinescope, 105, 195n2
Kintner, Robert E. (ABC-TV executive), 77
KGBX radio, 33–34, 35, 38
KGBX/KWTO radio, 36, 38, 179n12. *See also* Cox, Lester E.; Foster, Ralph
Knothole Gang, 9–10. *See also* baseball, Little League
Korn's-a-Krackin', 45–49, 51, 52–53
KWTO Artists Bureau, 51, 67
KWTO *Dial*, 178n2, 180n24, 182n63
KWTO radio: ABC radio network, 76, 179n12; Artists Bureau, 51; Atkins, Chet, 53–61; Browns, The, 85; Carson, Wayne, 134; coverage, 35; Foley, Red, 74; Goodwill Family, 36; Haden Family, 36; hillbilly music, 36; *Korn's-a-Krackin'*, 46–47, 52–53; Long, Jimmy, 95; *Ozark Jubilee*, 74; programming, 36–38; Siman, Si, 19, 38, 45, 47, 51; Thompson, Shorty and Sue, 132–33; Wagoner, Porter, 64–65, 74–75; Walker, Billy, 83; Wilson, Slim, 36, 74, 127. *See also* ABC radio; Carter Sisters and Mother Maybelle; Cox, Lester E.; Foster, Ralph; KWTO Artists Bureau; *Korn's-a-Krackin'*; RadiOzark; Siman, Si
KYTV television, 64, 67, 72, 76, 77, 100, 101. *See also* ABC television; Crossroads Productions, Inc., *Ozark Jubilee*; Siman, Si

L

"Land O Love," 155
Landers Theatre, 124–26
Langsford, John (big-band saxophonist), 176n79
Lanham, Roy (guitarist), 56, 61, 184n90
Lanson, Snooky (*Five Star Jubilee* host), 101, 125
"The Last Thing I Want," 86
"Laurel Canyon," 154
Lee, Brenda: Allbritten, Dub, manager, 91; "Always on My Mind," 142; Ashley, Hugh, and "One Step at a Time," 93; Black, Lou, manager, 90; CMDJA, 90, 111; Crossroads Productions, Inc., lawsuit against, 91–93; Decca Records, 89–90;

earnings, 91; Foley, Red, 88–89, 102; *Ozark Jubilee*, 88–90, 96; Self, Ronnie, 93, 130; Siman, Si, 89–90, 110; Springfield, life in, 90; trust fund, 91. *See also* Crossroads Productions, Inc.; *Ozark Jubilee*; Siman, Si

Lee, Dickey, 155

Lee, Larry (Ozark Mountain Daredevils), 149–50, 151–53, 204n74, 205n77

Leech, Mike (music arranger), 137

Leong, David (Springfield restauranteur), 197n39

"The Letter," 137–38, 139–40, 147

Lewie and the 7 Days (Springfield band), 149, 150, 202n32, 205n77

Liebert, Billy (accordionist), 42

Lipscomb, Forrest, 153–55

Lipscomb, Jack, 162

"Live Like You Were Dying," 157

Logan, Horace (*Louisiana Hayride* producer), 83, 84, 85, 98

Long, Jimmy (songwriter with Gene Autry), 95

Lord, Bobby, 87, 99, 101, 112

Louisiana Hayride (barn-dance radio show in Shreveport): beginning, 182n46; Logan, Horace, producer of, 83, 84; music hub, 108; *Ozark Jubilee*, attracted performers from, 82–84, 108, 190n87; Walker, Billy, 83, 97, 191n89. *See also* barn-dance format; *Grand Ole Opry*; *Ozark Jubilee*

Lounsbery, Dan (*Your Hit Parade* producer), 119

M

Mabe, Bob, 127, 200n98

Mahaffey, John: Crossroads Productions, Inc., 66, 67, 76, 128; Earl Barton Music, 66–67, 128; *Ozark Jubilee*, 76, 79, 113; radio station ownership, 128; RadiOzark, 40, 42, 128, 181n42; Top Talent, 147. *See also* Crossroads Productions, Inc.; *Ozark Jubilee*; Siman, Si

Mahan, Benny (Springfield performer), 150, 154

Mandrell, Barbara, 125

Martin, Doc (Springfield musician), 40

Martin, Grady (Nashville musician), 70, 72, 73, 140, 188n36

Matthews Brothers (gospel group), 40, 51, 180n25

McCrae, Gwen (R & B artist), 142

McGraw, Tim, 157

McMahon, Gene (Gillioz Theatre manager), 7

Miller, Andy (set designer), 67, 113, 127

Miller, Glenn, 23, 38

Minnie Pearl, 94, 125

Mitchell, Paul (pianist), 65, 67, 176n79

Moman, Chips (Nashville record producer): "Always on My Mind" (songwriter Wayne Carson) 142–43, 201n27, 202n32; "The Letter" (songwriter Wayne Carson), 136–38

Money, Bob (Springfield musician), 40

Montgomery, Bob (Nashville record producer), 155

Morgan, George, 41–42, 59

Morris, Gary, 207n2

Morris, John (Siman neighbor), 117

Morris, John, Jr. (Bass Pro Shop owner), 117, 162, 198n54

"Mr. Busdriver," 138

Mullins, Johnny (songwriter), 74, 188n47

Mullins, Melinda, 188n47
Musial, Stan, 79
Mutual Radio Network, 47, 52

N

NBC (National Broadcasting Company) radio, 35, 179n12, 186n22
NBC (National Broadcasting Company) television, 64, 76–77, 95, 101, 106–7, 124–25, 127
Nelson, Willie, 82, 143–45, 190n83
"Neon Rainbow," 138
Nichols, Penny (*Ozark Jubilee* performer), 40
Nichols, Tim (songwriter), 156–57
"Nobody," 138
Norma Jean, 94, 102, 103

O

"Oh Sweet Temptation," 142
"On a Rainy Day," 138
"One Step at a Time," 93
Owen, Jim (outdoors outfitter), 47, 117, 182n56
Owen, Mickey, 14, 175n43
Owens, Buck, 171n1
Ozark Empire District Fair, 24–26
Ozark Jubilee: ABC-TV, 76–78, 107, 119–21; advertising, 105, 113, 116–17, 187n29; Branson, influence on, 127–28; budget, 105, 107; competition, 76–77, 106–7; country music industry, 110, 111–13; daily routine, 113–17; *Five Star Jubilee*, 124–26; investors, 128; Jewell Theatre, 78; longevity, 121; mail, importance of, 78–80; management, 66–68; name changes, 120; "Ozark Jubilee Day," 78–79; package shows, 101; performers, managing, 82, 96–97, 98–99, 101–4; prejudices against, 119, 120–21; preparing for, 66–68, 70–71, 72–74, 78; press response, 79–80, 106, 108, 116; ratings, 106–7, 119; rehearsals, 113; rock and roll, 110; rockabilly, 88; salaries, 96–98; summer replacement shows, 100–101; themes, 114; women, 71–72, 85–86, 93–94, 187n35; writers, 114. *See also* Browns, The; Cline, Patsy; Crossroads Productions, Inc.; Foley, Red; Jackson, Wanda; Lee, Brenda; Norma Jean; Shepard, Jean; Siman, Si
Ozark Mountain Daredevils, 151–53, 154, 205n92, 206n98
Ozark Pictures Corporation, 161, 207n2

P

Paul, Les, 54–55, 183n79, 183n80
Pease, Dave (Springfield bassist), 151
Penn, Dan (Memphis record producer), 137. *See also* "The Letter"
Perkins, Carl, 110, 191n93, 196n23
Pet Shop Boys, 159. *See also* Carson, Wayne; Siman, Si
Philharmonics, 67, 186n18
Pierce, Webb, 74, 83, 103, 112, 130, 190n87, 191n93
Presley, Elvis, 83, 87–88, 143, 191n89
Presley, Lloyd (Branson country music show owner), 127, 200n98
Price, Ray, 125, 191n93
Pyle, Denver (actor), 207n2

R

RadiOzark: advertising, 42; Articles of Partnership, 180n24; artist booking, 51, 187n31; BMI, 66–67; book production, 182n63; Burnette, Smiley, and purchase of Rancho Music, 181n42; Carter Sisters and Mother Maybelle with Chet Atkins, 60–61, 185n99; *Dearborn Roundup*, 40–41; Foley, Red, 70, 72; KWTO, 51, 182n63; Landers Theatre, purchase of, 124; Matthews Brothers Quartet, 40; Morgan, George, and *Robin Hood Flour Show*, 41; record production, 182n63; *Smiley Burnette Show*, 43–45; *Tennessee Ernie Ford Show*, 42, 43; Thompson, Shorty and Sue, Saddle Rockin' Rhythm, 40, 133; transcriptions, 39–42. *See also* Assemblies of God; Burnette, Smiley; Mahaffey, John; *Ozark Jubilee*; Top Talent, Inc.; Siman, Si

Rae, Della (Moore), 135

Rains, Fred (*Ozark Jubilee* floor director), 99, 113

Rand, Sally (fan dancer), 24–26, 177n91

Reed, Jerry, 111

Rhodes, George (guitarist), 65

Rice, Bill (songwriter), 145

Richardson, Don: as *Ozark Jubilee* publicity director, 67, 90, 106; as *Ozark Jubilee* scriptwriter, 90, 99, 114; as RadiOzark writer, 40, 42; as Silver Dollar City publicity director, 127; Siman, Si, 196n32. *See also* Crossroads Productions, Inc.; Foley, Red; *Ozark Jubilee*; Silver Dollar City

Rickey, Branch (St. Louis Cardinals general manager), 16, 174n20; Springfield Cardinals, role in establishing, 9–10; White City Park, renovator of, 16–17

Ring, Bill (announcer and singer), 42, 47, 101, 113. *See also* Crossroads Productions, Inc.; KWTO radio; *Korn's-a-Krackin'*; *Ozark Jubilee*

Ritter, Tex, 95, 101, 116, 125, 190n87

"The Road Keeps Winding," 132

Rockabilly: Jackson, Wanda, 88, 121, 192n113; James, Sonny, 110; Lee, Brenda, 93, 110; Perkins, Carl, 110; Self, Ronnie, 93, 130–32; Siman, Si, opinions about, 110. *See also Ozark Jubilee*; Siman, Si

"Rocky," 154–55

Rose Bridge Music, 159, 200n2

Rose, Fred (Nashville songwriter and publisher), 59, 66

Rosi Acres (Siman home near Lake Springfield), 118, 162, 207n6

Rush, Merrilee (1960s pop singer), 138

Russell, Leon, 139

Rutledge, Floyd "Goo Goo" (comic), 36, 73, 198n65

Ryles, John Wesley, 142

S

"Sandman," 154

"A Satisfied Mind," 74, 78

Schaffer, Ann and Dora (KWTO performers), 38

Schultz, Dwight, 27

Self, Ronnie (songwriter), 93, 130–32, 146, 200n2

Selph, Jimmy (Nashville musician), 72
Sermons in Song (early RadiOzark transcription), 39–40
"Settin' the Woods on Fire," 65
Shady Dell Music, 200n2
Shaw, Artie, 23
"She Knows How," 154
"She's Actin' Single (I'm Drinkin' Doubles)," 141
Shepard, Jean: Foley, Red, 102, 126; Hawkins, Hawkshaw, 187n35; *Ozark Jubilee*, 70–73; "A Satisfied Mind," 78. *See also Ozark Jubilee*
Shikany, Pat (Springfield studio owner), 154
Shirk, Jim, 27, 162
Sholes, Steve (RCA record producer), 55–56, 65, 74–75, 85
Short, Dewey (politician), 79
Shrine Mosque (Springfield event venue), 20, 24, 176n68, 176n69, 182n63
Sibley, Nick (Springfield musician and studio owner), 153–54
Silver Dollar City, 111, 127, 196n32
Siman, Ely Earl, Sr. (father), 6, 8, 23, 24, 26
Siman, James (grandfather), 5–6
Siman, Lillian Saxton (mother), 6
Siman, Maxine and Julie (stepsisters), 4, 173n11
Siman, Rosanne "Rosie" Sprague (wife): death, 162; domestic life, 118; Foley, Red, 70; honeymoon, 52; Nashville, 118, 128–29; Siman, Si, letters from, 49–52
Siman, Sarah (wife of James), 5–6
Siman, Scott Foster (son), 118, 143, 155, 158–59

Siman, Si: as advertising salesman, 39; as artist manager, 132–43; as baseball scout driver, 11–16; as batboy, 9–11; as booking agent, 20–23, 90, 126; *Breakfast in Hollywood*, involvement in, 39; CMA, 112–13; CMDJA, 108–9, 111–12; courtship and marriage with Rosie, 49–52, 67, 70, 118, 128, 129, 162; Crossroads Productions, Inc., partnership in, 67, 105; as event organizer, 20, 24–26; family history, 5–7, 172n2, 172n4, 172n5, 173n8, 173n10; family life, 5–7, 23–24, 51–52, 117–18, 128; Foster, Ralph, relationship with, 19, 22, 38, 45, 50, 64, 66, 128; *Korn's-a-Krackin'*, involvement in, 46–49; KWTO radio, resignation from, 45; military career in WWII, 26–31; as movie theater entrepreneur, 18; as music publisher with Earl Barton Music and BMI, 66–67; as music publisher for Wayne Carson, 134–35, 137–39, 141–44, 153, 157–59; as music publisher for Ronald Johnson, 154–55; as music publisher for Johnny Mullins, 74–75; as music publisher for Ronnie Self, 130–32; as outdoorsman, 47, 49, 117; performers, attitudes about, 99, 103–4; promoter of big-band shows as teenager, 20–23; RadiOzark, involvement with, 39–45; as refreshment sales boy, 18–19; secondary education, 30–31; as song plugger, 134–36, 137, 139; songwriters, advice to, 145–47, 151–57; songwriters, influence on, 134, 144–45, 150–57; Springfield, influence on, 165; as television producer, 67, 76, 82, 113–17, 119, 125; Top Talent Studio, 154–55; as wrestling promoter, 24. *See also* Carson, Wayne; Crossroads Productions, Inc.; Earl Barton Music; Lee, Larry; Mullins, Johnny; *Ozark Jubilee*; RadiOzark; Sibley, Nick

Skinner, Jimmy, 112

Skipper Records, 149, 155

Slattery, Joe, 40–41, 102, 127

Smith, Carl (*Five Star Jubilee*), 97, 103, 107, 122, 125

"Somebody Like Me," 135–36, 138

"Someone Sometime," 135

Sosebee, Tommy (singer), 67

"Soul Deep," 138

Sour, Bob (BMI lyrics editor), 66

Springfield Cardinals, 9–10

St. Louis Cardinals, 10, 11, 15, 79, 174n20. *See also* Barrett, Charley; Rickey, Branch

Stewart, Gary, 140–42

Stone, Cliffie (artist manager), 42

Strawberry Hill Music, 155, 159, 200n2

"Sweet Nothin's," 130

T

Table Rock Music, 132, 200n2

Talent Round Up, 101

Tall Timber Trio (Tall Timber Boys), 36, 42, 53, 54, 100, 133. *See also* Tennis, Zed; Thompson, Shorty; Wilson, Slim

Tele-Color, 126

Television, 61, 63–64, 76–77, 185n3, 195n2. *See also* ABC television; Crossroads Productions, Inc.; NBC television; *Ozark Jubilee*; Siman, Si

"Ten Years of This," 142

Tennis, Zed (fiddler): Atkins, Chet, 53, 54, 55; *Ozark Jubilee*, 67; Tall Timber Boys, 36, 53, 54, 55; WLW in Cincinnati, 56. *See also Ozark Jubilee*; Wilson, Slim

"That Silver Haired Daddy of Mine," 95

"That's the Way a Man Is," 135

"There's No In-Between," 134

Thompson, George (Springfield auto dealer), 7

Thompson, George, Jr., 7, 10

Thompson, Hank, 171n1

Thompson, Shorty, 201n13; as father of Carson, Wayne, 133, 137, 201n17; KWTO radio, 36, 44, 55, 133; Shorty and Sue, 40. *See also* Atkins, Chet; Carson, Wayne; Siman, Si; Wilson, Slim

Thompson, Sue (wife of Shorty), 132–33

Tillis, Mel, 130, 140, 162

Top Talent Booking Agency, 67, 70, 72, 101, 111, 126, 128. *See also* Black, Lou; Foley, Red; Foster, Ralph; RadiOzark

Top Talent Recording Studio, 147, 148, 154

Torok, Mitchell, 82

"The Traveler," 133

Travis, Merle, 54, 55, 96

"Try Me," 138

Tubb, Ernest: 82, 95–96, 113, 115. *See also* Decca Records; *Ozark Jubilee*; Siman, Si

Tubert, Bob: Earl Barton Music, 139; *Ozark Jubilee*, 40, 92, 94, 98–99, 113, 114, 202n37. *See also* Earl Barton Music; *Ozark Jubilee*; Siman, Si

"Tulsa," 138
"Turn Around and Look Again," 135
Turner, Ike and Tina, 154
Twitty, Conway, 140

U

Uncle Cyp and Aunt Sap (comics), 198n65

V

Van Dyke, Leroy, 97, 99, 127

W

Wagoner, Porter: Foley, Red, 101–2; KWPM radio in West Plains, 64; KWTO radio, 64–65, 70, 74–75; *Ozark Jubilee*, 73, 78, 188n39. *See also* Mullins, Johnny; *Ozark Jubilee*; Warden, Don; Siman, Si
"Waitin' for the Gin to Hit Me," 132
Wakely, Jimmy (*Five Star Jubilee*), 125
Walker, Billy: Brown, Maxine, accusations of sexual harassment, 85–86; career path, 83, 191n96; *Louisiana Hayride*, 83, 191n89; *Ozark Jubilee*, 83, 97–99, 113. *See also Ozark Jubilee*; Siman, Si
Walker, Jerry Jeff, 145
Waller, Fats, 21
Warden, Don (musician), 74, 188n45
Weaver Brothers and Elviry (comedy musicians), 46, 73, 94
Wells, Kitty, 74, 171n1, 187n35
West, Speedy, 42
"What You Never Had," 154
Whippoorwills, 44, 56, 184n90
"Whiskey Trip," 142
White, Bob (musician), 40, 54, 65, 67, 127

White City Park (Springfield baseball park), 9–10
White, Dennis (KYTV engineer), 113
Whitlock, Tom (songwriter), 156, 206n104
Whitney, Lou (Springfield musician), 156
Wilkin, Marijohn (songwriter), 82
Willis Brothers, 67
Wills, Bob, 171n1
Wilson, George Earle (KWTO announcer), 39, 46, 179n19. *See also Breakfast in Hollywood*; KWTO radio; *Korn's-a-Krackin'*
Wilson, Slim: Atkins, Chet, 55; CMDJA convention, 111; Goodwill Family, 36; *Home Folks Reunion*, 68; KGBX/KWTO radio, 36; *Korn's-a-Krackin'*, 46; *Ozark Jubilee*, 73–74, 111, 113, 122; *Talent Varieties*, 100; Tall Timber Trio, 53, 54, 100, 127; *Today on the Farm*, 127. *See also* Crossroads Productions, Inc.; *Korn's-a-Krackin'*; *Ozark Jubilee*; Tall Timber Trio; Siman, Si
Winn, Susan Siman (daughter), 70, 117, 118

Y

"You Can't Have My Love," 86
"You Got What You Wanted," 154
Young, Faron, 103, 112, 125, 171n1
"Young Love," 110
Your Hit Parade, 101, 119
"Your Lovin' Eyes Are Blind," 138

www.ingramcontent.com/pod-product-compliance
Lightning Source LLC
Chambersburg PA
CBHW020236170426
43202CB00008B/104